THOSE LEFT BEHIND

Jack McCabe

MIKE,
IT WAS AN HONOR
SERVING IN THE SAME
UNIT IN VIETNAM.
WELCOME HOME !

VIETNAM
1970-1972

You smug-faced crowds with kindling eye

Who cheer when soldier lads march by,

Sneak home and pray you'll never know

The hell where youth and laughter go.

Siegfried Sassoon, *"Suicide in the Trenches"*

RED SMOKE

(RED SMOKE OF WAR)

It drifts, a silent eerie shadow

Over ground where men have battled

Marking the place where men have died

Who never heard their first born cry

Dropped from plane to mark the spot

Falls red smoke to tie the knot

Sealing the fate of those below

Soon to be in Heaven's abode

A country which did not care

Sent them to die, over there

Profit was cause enough to send

Soldiers to war which had no end

My question I now ask of thee

What have you done for World Peace?

David P. Schultz

Dedication

I dedicate this book to the families and friends of those lost in the Vietnam War. There are hundreds of thousands of mourners who still grieve the loss of those held dear. The families, friends and lovers of the 58,318 names inscribed on the Vietnam Memorial in Washington, DC. There are also an untold number of suicide and Agent Orange–related deaths, ultimately caused by that war. The exact count of these will never be known.

A good friend of mine, Larry Sossamon, lost a brother in Vietnam. Larry had already served in the army and completed his 365-day tour, returning home in March of 1969. His brother Ed was sent over in June of that same year. Ed served as an infantryman in the 101st Airborne Division. Ten months into his tour, a mine accidentally exploded, severely wounding him. He was medevacked to the closest field hospital but died from his wounds. His parents and brother were overcome with despair. So close to the end of his tour and now he was gone.

Ed's death affected Larry for the rest of his life. He struggled with the effects of PTSD from his tour, and the demise of his brother only made it worse. His parents were devastated. Larry attributes their early deaths in 1978 and 1979 to the worry, sadness, and overwhelming grief they could never get past.

This work tells the story of a small action in Vietnam, where nine men lost their lives. But every man who survived that incident bore the effects of that war for the rest of his life. They did not suffer alone. Everyone close to them suffered also.

Perhaps someday we will learn and not send our young people into harm's way for some politically motivated game waged by those who will never hear the firing of shot or shell.

Table of Contents

Preface

"How can the dead be truly dead when they still live in the souls of

those who are left behind?"

-Carson McCullers, *The Heart Is a Lonely Hunter*

The Phu Loi flight line was a bustle of activity. It was always that way, especially in the early morning hours. July 19, 1971 was a typical day at this helicopter base northwest of Saigon. It was 08:30. Several formations of helicopters had taken off on the way to pick up troops for a combat assault somewhere in Military Region III. Soon they would approach the pickup zone and load up their cargo of men who would begin their hunt for Charlie. Men on both sides would probably die out in the steaming jungle today. The writing was on the wall that the war would soon be over. It was just a matter of time until all the troops would be pulled out and sent home. For now, the war went on and the killing continued.

This was my home and had been for the last nine months. The almost constant hum of helicopters taking off and landing would continue throughout the day. The temperature was starting to climb as the sun rose and cut through the morning haze. There was something peaceful and comforting about the familiar sound of whirring rotors, smells of aviation gas and exhaust. Even the smell of the shit-burning details was almost unnoticed after all this time.

And then…the powerful impact of incoming rockets shattered the peace of the morning! Three exploded in rapid succession. This all-too-familiar noise stopped the bustling activities of virtually everyone on the base as we all hit the deck or ran for the nearest bunker. I was on the south side of the runway when I heard the loud *wump* of the exploding 122mm rockets. I threw myself face down in the dirt, heart-pounding, adrenaline pumping, waiting to see if more rounds were coming in. There was always an eerie silence after a mortar or rocket attack. Then the sirens started to wail, signaling an attack. *A little late, I am afraid*, I thought. I slowly got to my feet, dusted myself off, and looked for smoke from a burning helicopter after a direct hit. But there wasn't any—just the regular plumes of smoke from the shit burners here and there. I could see no sign of damage anywhere I looked. I breathed a sigh of relief and shook my head, thinking, *I hope they don't learn how to aim those damn things.*

As it turned out, the rockets impacted the northwest corner of the airfield, probably aimed at the Navy Seawolves, located there. Yes, the navy had gunships at Phu Loi. This morning they had already left on a mission. The rockets overshot the Seawolves area and struck the hooches of the MARS station personnel.

My friend Rick Page had finished his shift at the Phu Loi MARS station. The MARS acronym stood for Military Auxiliary Radio System, which was our only contact with the world outside of good old letter writing. Lonely soldiers would come to the MARS station to try and make a phone call home. Rick would get on the shortwave radio and contact ham radio operators in the States. They would patch in the call to the soldier's home. It was a great system, but it had a few flaws. Whenever either side finished talking, they had to say, "Over" to switch over from transmit to receive. Of course, that meant at least two radio operators were on the call, so you had to watch what you said.

Rick was my first hooch mate when I arrived in Vietnam. We quickly became friends. We often sat on a bunker in the evening, sharing a beer or two. When he transferred over to the MARS station, he was able to patch in two calls home for me. Each time my sister was the only one home. I reassured her that I was OK. No wounds.

Rick's hooch took the brunt of the attack, killing him instantly while he slept. Rick had a premonition that he was going to die in Vietnam. Now it was true. He was gone, but in that instant, I didn't know that.

I can't remember who told me, but one of the guys came up to me and said: "Hey, McCabe did you hear that a rocket hit Page's hooch?"

"No shit?" I replied. "Is he OK?"

The response was "He's dead."

Dead? Rick is dead? Just like that? Typical morning and he is dead?

I jumped in a three-quarter-ton truck and drove over. The thought of Rick being dead raced through my mind over and over. When I arrived, I saw several soldiers milling around the wreckage. "Where is Rick?" I yelled.

"Gone" was the response from a soldier I didn't know. "Medevac took him out along with another guy who was wounded."

Gone, just like that. A three-rocket harassing attack that could have hit anyone.

I stared at the wreckage of his hooch. Slowly my mind drifted away, and I once again heard the almost constant helicopter traffic. Another day, just like any other. Back to work.

We who served in war did not have the luxury of mourning our dead. Either there was no time, or the dead were just gone. Out in the field with infantry, artillery, engineers, and others, the dead were bagged, put on a helicopter, and whisked away never to be seen again. For the helicopter units, it was usually different. They were just not there anymore. Remains from a helicopter crash or shoot-down were, in many cases, recovered by another unit and transported to a graves registration collection point, mortuary, or field hospital. Their friends were left in a daze, maybe watching while an officer or noncommissioned officer cleaned out the personal effects of the dead in preparation for them to be sent home to the next of kin. They made sure to cull anything that might be deemed offensive to the family.

No one thought about the devastation the family back home experienced upon hearing of the death of a husband, wife, son, daughter, brother, sister, or friend. It never occurred to us. We dealt with the loss differently than those back home. Sometimes we cried, but usually, we just buried it and carried on. It was war, and more deaths would be coming.

Many years later, the enormity of the loss of our friends would be felt when we visited the Vietnam Memorial (the Wall) in Washington, DC. Now, we were able to grieve and understand how devastating the violent death of one so young could be. We were able to feel the loss so deeply it hurt. Finally, the tears were able to flow, and, for many, the healing began.

I first learned of another terrible Vietnam incident in 2016, the crash of Chinook #65-07999. What drew me into this story? Why did I feel compelled to write it? Why did I think it needed to be told? I imagine the answers can all be traced to Larry "Doc" Butcher, whom I met over the internet that year. I was interviewing Vietnam veterans for a book I was writing called *When We Came Home: How the Vietnam War Changed Those Who Served*. Larry agreed to be interviewed for the book, telling his own experiences in Vietnam and what happened when he came home.

In the course of this interview, he told me of an incident that happened in Vietnam on July 10, 1970. This was his twenty-first birthday, and the day Chinook #65-07999, *Love Craft*, was shot down. Larry had two friends on that helicopter, Carey Pratt and Harlen Metzger. Another member of his company was on board but from a different platoon, Denny Martin.

Larry told me about his meeting Carey's family many years after Carey's death. He sent me a photo his wife took of that day. The intensity of their looks captivated me. As I mentioned at the beginning, we never thought about the families and loved ones who were left behind. But here it was. A glimpse into a world I had never been a part of.

I saved the photo and kept looking at it every day. I was drawn to it. Every time I looked at it, I could imagine the loss. It brought back a lot of feelings long since buried.

I did several internet searches and found some details on the crash. Very basic. Then I found an outrageous story. The author never really identified who he was, just a name. The details of the story didn't match up with the reality of what happened, as I had read. But it had been fifty years, and maybe our memories were fading as fast as our remaining days.

This narrative stated that the flight engineer (Ross Bedient) had been with the 242nd for quite a while, but the crew chief (Rickey Wittner) and gunner (David Schultz) were relatively new guys. The fact was that Ross and David had been there since January and Rickey since February. David had just started to fly as a door gunner but was not new to the unit or Vietnam.

The story went on to say that a helicopter from the 242nd went to this same location every Friday at approximately the same time to refuel and supply a navy PBR (patrol boat). According to everyone I interviewed, this was simply not the case. The river boats would never refuel at the same place every week. They refueled when needed. Never on a specific day of the week. That would be suicide.

"Anyway," the article's author wrote, "a week before the rocket attack, the 242nd's new Major had wanted to kiss some brass ass and wanted to get a birthday gift for some higher up officer. He sent us into the Mushroom to steal a baby water buffalo. We got the thing on board and back to base, but obviously someone got highly pissed at having his water buff stolen. The next ship in was 999."

Really? Really? This all seemed pretty preposterous to me. So, this inferred that a farmer had his baby water buffalo stolen and just happened to have an RPG around to shoot down the next helicopter. Also, what major would want to impress the higher-ups with a baby water buffalo?

This seemed out of the realm of reality. I spent nineteen months in Vietnam and saw some crazy things but never anything close to this. So, with the impact of the photograph and the wild story about the shoot-down, I began to investigate.

I pulled army mortuary files to find out the names of the passengers and was lucky enough to find that in Denny Martin's record, all the names were there. The next step was to try and find relatives of those lost as well as any of the survivors who would talk to me.

I started talking to everyone I found. Almost everyone wanted to talk about it. They remembered their loved ones and spoke to me with fondness and sadness mixed. The survivors still deal with the nightmares, sorrow, and guilt of the events so long ago.

There were some surprises along the way. Larry Crozier was a member of the PBR crew that was being resupplied. He was under the Chinook when it was struck by the RPGs and was lucky enough to survive. One of the other sailors took photos purely by chance of the ship being hit by the first RPG and subsequent crash. It was a miracle that anyone survived.

Larry was awarded a Bronze Star with *V* for Valor for his actions that day. His citation states:

> For heroic achievement while serving with River Patrol
> Group Five Two engaged in armed conflict against the North
> Vietnamese and Viet Cong communist aggressors in the
> Republic of Vietnam. On 10 July 1970, Petty Officer
> CROZIER was an advisor assisting in resupplying four river
> patrol boats on the upper Saigon River. As the helicopter
> hovered to have a sling attached to its cargo hook, two
> rockets suddenly hit the aircraft's tail section. There was an
> immediate explosion, and the helicopter went out of control
> and ·crashed. Reacting immediately, he ran directly to the
> rear portion of the aircraft where eighteen injured men were

partially trapped. The enemy had now moved to a tree line about two hundred meters from the helicopter and were peppering the aircraft and the surrounding area with heavy automatic weapons fire. Petty Officer CROZIER, with complete disregard for his own personal safety, exposed himself to the enemy fire and intense heat of the burning helicopter to assist the injured men. He aided in smothering the flames, while still receiving heavy enemy fire. Petty Officer CROZIER made three trips from the burning wreckage to the riverbank to evacuate the men from the kill zone. Due to his efforts, men were safely evacuated from the area of the burning helicopter. Petty Officer CROZIER's professionalism, initiative and devotion to duty were in keeping with the highest traditions of the United States Naval Service.

The Combat Distinguishing Device is authorized.

Rickey Wittner, the crew chief on that fateful day, saw the story written about the water buffalo. His written response was this: *I must reply to this. When I first read this story, it made me sick to my stomach, just think this is an official document about the shooting down of a chopper in Viet Nam that cost many lives. The person that wrote it was not there, and where did he get his facts? Maybe there are a few "pilots" that only wanted a seasoned crew. Well, most of us that volunteered to fly did so because we wanted to do something. The chopper was one hundred seventy-five feet off the ground not fifty feet as he said. Yes, the door gunner was new, and he was at the wrong place at the wrong time. Even if I had been flying for years what difference would it have made, they shot RPGs at us, it was not a malfunction of the chopper. Ross was never able to be shipped out of country because he was in too bad of shape, and he died on the 13th of July 1970.*

Ed Whittle, the aircraft commander saw Rickey enter the burning helicopter, repeatedly rescuing who he could. Ed recommended him for the Medal of Honor. He certainly deserved it. But the army, in its infinite wisdom, downgraded it to the Soldiers Medal. The citation states:

> For Heroism not involving actual conflict with an armed enemy force: Specialist Wittner distinguished himself by exceptionally valorous actions while serving as crew chief on a helicopter resupplying river patrol boats southwest of Dau Tieng. While his aircraft was hovering, it was struck by heavy enemy fire injuring all passengers on board and trapping many in the flaming wreckage. Completely disregarding exploding ammunition and fuel, Specialist Wittner reportedly went into the burning aircraft to rescue the survivors. Acting with complete disregard for his own personal safety, on several occasions he extinguished fires on their clothing while severely burning both of his hands. Due to calm bravery in the face of grave danger and his repeated willingness to risk his own life for others, twelve of the passengers survived the conflagration. His personal heroism, disregard for his own safety, and concern for the life of his fellow man is in keeping with the highest traditions of the

military service and reflects great credit upon himself, his unit and the United States Army.

Denny Martin's personnel file also contained interesting information. When I first wrote for his file from the National Personnel Records Center, my request was refused. I was told that I needed to provide them his death certificate and a signature of his next of kin for them to release this information to me. I wrote them a letter back saying, *I don't have to provide this to you. This is a Freedom of Information Act Request. The person is deceased. If you refuse to send this information to me, please provide the name of a person of higher authority for me to appeal.* They then sent me the file without further delay.

In his file was a citation for the award of the Bronze Star with *V* for Valor. The citation states:

> For heroism in connection with military operations against a hostile force Specialist Four Martin distinguished himself by heroic actions on 10 July 1970, while serving with Company D, 2d Battalion, 14th Infantry in the Republic of Vietnam. On the date cited above, a supply helicopter was involved in a supply operation when it came under intense small arm and rocket propelled grenade fire from a large enemy force. The hostile fire caused the aircraft to crash and burst into flames. Suffering from severe burns, Specialist Four Martin crawled from the blazing inferno. With complete disregard for his own safety Specialist Four Martin exposed himself to continuing small-arms fire as he reentered the blazing aircraft

to help personnel to reach safety. On his final trip, Specialist Four Martin was trapped inside the wreckage and received fatal wounds. His valorous actions contributed immeasurably to saving the· lives of his fellow soldiers. The bravery and devotion to duty exhibited by Specialist Four Martin are in keeping with ·the highest traditions of the military service and reflect great credit upon himself, his unit, the 25th Infantry Division, and the United States Army.

When I forwarded this to Denny's widow, Sue, and his sister, Barbara, they were shocked. They had no idea he had sacrificed his life saving others. Up to this point they did not know exactly how he died or where. The army never told the family the circumstances surrounding his death.

The orders were dated October 11, 1970, long after Denny was buried. In most likelihood, the orders were never sent to his family. Barbara was a little pissed off finding this out. "All these years, I've thought that he just was killed instantly when the helicopter crashed, and now I see he performed those incredible acts of heroism. He could not have done that, and he could have ended up coming home."

She continued, "It's a whole bunch of mixed-up things, Positive and negative. I've read the email, and I was just really… It just kind of knocked me over. Gosh! It just feels like he just died again. And it's just a whole bunch of mixed feelings about it, just that he had the courage to go back in there. And they didn't say how many times he went back in and how many people he got out. And just that he would do that, and knowing that he was on his way to go see his wife that he would do that?" The soldiers I talked with who knew Denny were not surprised. That was the kind of man he was— a man of courage and conviction.

Sue also was surprised that she never knew this before. She pulled out all the papers that she had on Denny, and this citation was not there. She never received it, had never even heard of it. She never knew where he was in Vietnam when he died. She had just been told that he died, basically on impact. The explosion. The fire, and he died. He burned. So, now she was thinking, *Wait a minute. These are two different stories.*

She wrote to me, *Well, thank you, so much for letting me know that. I mean, it was a shock, but it's good to know. I mean, it just, sort of, like, "Oh, my gosh." It's, oh, what could have happened and didn't happen, and, you know, it's just tossing around ideas in your head. Feeling proud, but yet devastated.*

In March of 2019, Sue and Barbara were able to get together for the first time in almost fifty years. They spoke of Denny and the circumstances surrounding his death. Why was there no explanation about the circumstances surrounding his death and the crash? They were never told any of this.

Denny chose to save some of the other passengers and paid for it with his life. Others are alive today because of him.

One other surprise and seeming contradiction was the case of Bruce M. Thompson. According to the *Tropic Lightning News*, he was awarded a Soldiers Medal for heroism during the crash. His personnel file only shows the award of the Army Commendation

Medal with two oak leaf clusters and the *V* device for valor. The award with *V* was for the action on July 10, 1970. Was the award downgraded or upgraded and the orders never caught up with his records? We will probably never know.

The more I learned about the attack on the Chinook, the more I wanted to know. In many ways, I feel this event was a microcosm of the Vietnam War. It was much like the rocket attack that took the life of Rick Page. A small action within a much larger war. An action forgotten by everyone except those involved or those who loved them. Neither action made the papers except for maybe a notice of death in the local news. Just some more soldiers who lost their lives in one of many small actions that typified the war in Vietnam.

Just more tragic loss of young men and heartbreak for the surviving family members who would have to live lives wondering what could have been.

Those who knew the dead from the neighborhood or school may have been surprised. They may not even have known the individual was in the service. They may have attended the funeral or maybe forgot about them altogether. Perhaps his name came up in some discussion over a beer with friends. Perhaps they used his name as a battle cry when they protested the war. For the troops who served there and the loved ones at home, the story of this crash is, in many ways, the story of the Vietnam War.

As I researched this story, I was amazed to find out that the family members did not know the real story behind how their loved ones died that fateful day in July 1970. Information floating around on the internet isn't just vague but, in most cases, completely wrong!

The story presented here is the result of firsthand accounts and available records relating to this combat incident. The story didn't end when the Chinook was shot down. In some ways, that was when the story began. It is the story of the family and friends and how they dealt with the loss and how they were impacted by young lives cut tragically short.

It is hoped that the telling of this story will assuage the guilt felt by some of those involved. Could things have been done differently? Could the contact with the enemy been avoided? Why did some live and others die? It was war. It can't be second-guessed. Fate, I guess you would call it. In actuality, the enemy had all day to set up this ambush. People were going to die that day. It was their time. That could not be avoided, delayed, or denied. A series of events, seemingly random led up to this crash. Once the wheels were in motion there was no stopping it. Rick knew he would die in Vietnam. He knew it. If it hadn't been a rocket, it would have been an accident. He was destined to die there. If this ambush hadn't happened, then the Chinook would have crashed due to mechanical failure. It was time.

There were twenty souls on board Chinook #65-07999 (*Love Craft*) on that fateful day, July 10, 1970. No one who was involved or who witnessed the crash was immune to the lasting effects of it etched indelibly in their memory. The tragedy of this crash was that of the fifteen passengers five were on their way to R & R and three had finished their tour and were heading home. One of the crew was also going on R & R.

I wasn't able to find everyone involved in the crash. Of those I found some did not want to talk to me. They found it too unbearable to relive that horrible day. I completely understand their feelings and did not intrude on their quest for peace. I hope they will be able to find it over the years. I just pray that the families of the victims have found it.

The focus of this story, of course are the men involved and their families. I initially concentrate on the stories of seven men: Larry Butcher *(14th Infantry)*, Denny Martin *(14th Infantry)*, Harlen Metzger *(14th Infantry)*, Carey Pratt *(14th Infantry)*, Elroy Simmons *(13th Artillery)*, David Schultz *(242nd Assault Support Helicopter Co.)*, and Mike Vullo *(725th Maintenance Bn.)*. You will begin meeting them now; later, just as the service brought soldiers in and out of each other's lives, more will join the story.

Jack McCabe
1st Aviation Brigade
Vietnam, 1970-1972

It Always Begins with Those Left Behind

Donna slowly walked down the dusty street toward the Christian Youth Ranch. She was glad to be out of the trailer she called home. Living with her mother and younger brother was not easy. Donna and her mom were like oil and water.

She needed an excuse to get out of the house, and the only place she could go to get away from her mom without any kind of argument was the ranch. Donna spent a lot of time there; it was peaceful and fun hanging around with the local kids. It was where she met David. She and David loved each other and planned to get married when he was discharged from the army in 1971. But right now, he was thousands of miles away, serving in Vietnam.

Donna and David did not tell anyone of their plans to marry. Donna was still too young, and besides, her mother would not approve of the union. For now, they kept their plans secret, but she would be old enough when David came home. Then her mother's opinion wouldn't matter.

It was already hot, in the mid-eighties. But that was typical for Pharr, Texas, in July 1970, and on this day, the eleventh, it would be no different. The summer heat in Texas could be stifling.

Donna casually sauntered into the old white house that housed the ranch and saw the pastor, Wally Morillo. He was quietly talking to two or three of the kids who frequently hung out there. Their conversation was in hushed tones. It was unusual to see Wally standing still. He was always busy, working on a project of some sort. As Donna walked over and joined the group, she heard Wally quietly say to the kids he was with, "Oh, by the way, I heard David is missing in action."

Donna stopped dead in her tracks, a wide-eyed look of disbelief on her face, and said, "What do you mean, he is missing?"

Wally replied, "Well, the helicopter he was on was shot down behind enemy lines, and he's missing."

Missing? Missing? What does that mean? Are they trying to find him?

Donna was in shock. She had received a letter from him yesterday. How could he be missing? This was a nightmare! She turned and left in a daze, slowly walking out onto the hot, sunlit street. This couldn't be happening.

She had received a letter from him yesterday.

Chapter 1

A Life of Promise

There is a time for everything,

and a season for every activity under the heavens

-Ecclesiastes 3:1

The 1950s and early 1960s were good times in America, for most people anyway. The economy had recovered from the World War II years. Jobs were plentiful, incomes were on the rise, housing was affordable, and society, for the most part, was upwardly mobile. Traditionally, most households had a working father and a stay-at-home mother who raised the children. Couples married younger than they do now, and divorce was much less common.

Unfortunately, this was not the case in Vietnam. The French colonial rule of Indochina officially began in 1877. Indochina encompassed Vietnam and parts of Laos and Cambodia. Like most colonial empires, they exploited Indochina for their own financial benefit. The resources in Indochina were vast. Tea, rice, pepper, coffee, coal, zinc, and tin were available for the taking. Huge rubber plantations were formed to meet the demands of the blossoming automobile industry. The blooming economy did help some Vietnamese. The rich ones. It mostly enriched the French. Growing resentment of the French led to burgeoning Nationalist and Communist movements.

French influence and control changed with World War II. After a series of skirmishes and negotiations, all favoring Japan, Japan acted in a big way. Southern French Indochina was invaded by 140,000 Japanese troops on July 28, 1941. They achieved a great source of rice as well as other natural resources. By controlling it, they also stopped supplies from coming through its seaports and going on to China. Their main fear was an oil embargo, which would cripple their war machine. Indochina was used a s a springboard for the invasion of the oil-rich Dutch East Indies. For now, the French were out and the Japanese in. They claimed they were liberating Indochina from the French. Their cry was "Asia for Asians!" The reality was that they ruled brutally, and their policies brought economic disaster.

President Roosevelt and Prime Minister Churchill met in Newfoundland in 1941 and drafted the Atlantic Charter. This was their vision of the world after the end of the war. All nations were to be allowed to enjoy self-determination and independence. This was what the Vietnamese had always hoped for—independence from French rule.

A Communist-led coalition of various Nationalist groups was formed and called themselves the Viet Minh. They were well organized and led by a fifty-one-year-old Communist revolutionary named Ho Chi Minh. This peasant resistance battled the Japanese throughout World War II believing they would achieve independence when the war ended.

When the war ended the Viet Minh declared themselves the rightful leaders of an independent Vietnam. On September 2, 1945, four hundred thousand Vietnamese gathered in Hanoi to declare their independence. Ho Chi Minh addressed the crowd. His first words were "All men are created equal. The Creator has given us certain inviolable rights: the right to life, the right to be free and the right to achieve happiness. These immortal words were taken from the Declaration of Independence of the United States of America!"

Unfortunately, an independent Vietnam was not to be. At least not yet. President Truman decided to support the French in reclaiming their colony. So began a nine-year struggle that would culminate in a final decisive battle between the Viet Minh and the French at a little-known location called Dien Bien Phu. The battle began on March 13, 1954, and ended with the French surrendering on May 7.

Vietnam was divided with the Communists ruling the north. We supplied military advisors to South Vietnam. Our war had begun even though most Americans couldn't find Vietnam on a map. The men being drafted, of course, soon could.

Elroy Simmons

Jerry Simmons and Mildred Bell hailed from the small rural town of Tyronza, Arkansas. In the 1960s, the population was less than seven hundred. Jerry was a tenant farmer there. Life wasn't easy for sharecroppers in the South. Times might have been good in most of the country, but it wasn't there.

In the 1930s, Tyronza was the site where the Southern Tenant Farmers movement started what became a national outcry against the abusive discrimination by wealthy landowners toward the mostly African American sharecroppers. Although the movement secured better living conditions and wages, life was still hard, and wages barely at subsistence level. Jerry was a strong man and athletic. He was able to use his talents playing minor league baseball, a welcome escape from the hard life he lived.

Elroy was born in Tyronza on July 15, 1940. He was one of ten children born to Jerry and Mildred. Six boys and four girls. Large families like that are scarce these days. In the '40s and '50s it was not uncommon to have a brood as large as that. With his family growing, Jerry needed to find a way to make a better living.

By 1945, the war was over, and there were better employment opportunities in the St. Louis area. The Simmons's packed up their children and meager belongings for a new start and moved north. Jerry landed an excellent job at East St. Louis Casting Company, where he continued to work for the remainder of his life. Mildred always wanted to be a teacher, but when the family moved to East St. Louis, Jerry was doing so well that she settled in as a mother and housewife. Typical of the times, the husband worked, and the wife stayed home, running the household and raising the children.

Jerry and Mildred were staunch Baptists, strict parents. They raised their children with a strong religious faith. One of the other essential things to Jerry and Mildred was the children's education. They all took it to heart and did well in their studies, developing a strong desire to learn. Jerry was not an educated man, having only completed the eighth grade, but he was very intelligent. Despite his lack of formal education, he was able to teach his son, Dwight, geometry, among other things.

Elroy was nine years older than Dwight, but they were close. Elroy was a good role model, honest, reliable, athletic—someone Dwight always looked up to. Elroy played football and basketball and ran track while attending East St. Louis High School. Dwight followed in his footsteps, playing football and running in track.

Elroy was a good student. He liked to have a good time with his friends but did not get into trouble. Good clean fun. He soon caught the eye of Barbara Jean Morris. Barbara saw the serious side of Elroy and immediately found him to be a nice, polite young man. They began dating and soon were sweethearts.

Elroy graduated high school in 1959 and examined his future prospects. By this time, he and Barbara had a daughter, Sherry, who was born in 1958. He didn't want to go to college, and the draft was a distinct possibility. There were 96,153 men drafted in 1959. Despite the fact that there was no conflict going on, the peacetime draft continued. The Army seemed like a good way to be insured employment and an income at least for the next two years. Plus, he figured he would get it over with, so right after his high school graduation, he volunteered. Volunteering for the draft was a two-year commitment. There was no choice of a job or MOS. The Army would decide for Elroy. He went active on July 2, 1959.

He attended basic training at Fort Leonard Wood, Missouri, where he learned how to be a soldier in the heat, rain, and mud. His initial military experience was like many before and after him. Long lines, a battery of tests, shots, uniform issues, and his hair completely shaved off. Like all recruits at the time, he lived in temporary World War II wooden barracks. One platoon on the first floor and another on the second. The day usually began at 05:00 or sooner and ended long after sundown.

Meeting the drill instructors was always a shock no matter who you were or how tough you thought you were. The army drill instructors were hard on the recruits, but they had only eight weeks to turn them from civilians into soldiers. They always accomplished their tasks, and in two short months, the recruits had learned the necessary skills of soldiering.

Elroy graduated from basic training on September 2, 1959. He had a thirteen-day leave, and during this time, he and Barbara married. Following his leave, it was time to proceed to Fort Sill, Oklahoma, for a two-month training program to be an artillery crewman. Barbara stayed behind in East St. Louis with the baby while Elroy learned the nuances of firing, aiming, and maintenance of artillery pieces. The course completed; he came home to East St. Louis for a short leave before proceeding to his first assignment. That assignment was with the 35th Infantry Regiment in Hawaii. It was a good assignment, and Barbara was able to join him.

Barbara liked Hawaii, but it was expensive, even back then. Being on an army budget as a Private First Class did not make life any easier. To keep the budget balanced, Barbara found a job on base as a maid. She worked cleaning temporary houses for GIs relocating to Hawaii. This extra income took off some of the financial pressure.

Hawaii was a good experience for Elroy and Barbara. It gave them a chance to get to know one another. As she put it, "You either learned to live together, or you killed each other! There was no place to run. If you get mad at each other, you couldn't say, 'Well, I'm going home.' That just wasn't an option."

Like most men, when Elroy's term of service was complete, he decided to get out of the army. The draft had taken him to beautiful Hawaii, but he felt it was time to move on. He just couldn't see being able to pay all the bills on his meager army salary. Yes, the army offered security, but Elroy had had enough of army life.

He and Barbara came home to East St. Louis. Elroy had ninety days to reenter the army without losing rank if he chose to. He didn't see that happening. "I'm free of the army" was his feeling. But then the reality of job prospects and a family to support hit him. They had another baby on the way, and it was more difficult to find a good job than he thought it would be. There was always the army to fall back on. Maybe it could be a possible career. After much deliberation and discussion with Barbara, Elroy decided to reenlist. Hawaii had been a great place to be assigned, and perhaps he would be sent back. On August 7, 1961, two months after his discharge, Elroy returned to army life.

He didn't go back to Hawaii. His next assignment was Fort Riley, where he joined the 6th Artillery Regiment. He and Barbara settled into army life in Kansas. But sometimes there isn't a lot of stability in the army. He found this out in 1964 when he was sent on a tour of duty in Korea with the 80th Artillery. Barbara and the children couldn't accompany him there. The couple had three children then, and Barbara was pregnant with their fourth, and last, child, Michelle.

During Elroy's military career, he was sent to Fort Leonard Wood for drill instructor training and the Noncommissioned Officer Academy, and he graduated as a Sergeant. Back to Fort Riley training troops bound for Vietnam. In 1965 he was assigned to the 1st Battalion, 11th Artillery, which became part of the 9th Infantry Division. Vietnam was building up, and the division was ordered there in November 1966.

The main body of the 9th Division departed the United States by boat on December 12. The 1st Bn., 11th Artillery boarded the USNS *Maurice Rose* and left for the combat zone. Elroy's first tour in Vietnam had begun.

Dennis "Denny" Keith Martin

The Martin family was from Indiana. They lived in Indianapolis, where Dennis was born on the 4th of July 1946—in the words of James Cagney, a "a real Yankee Doodle dandy!" His sister, Barbara, was born four years later, in 1950. Their parents, Robert and Gladys Martin, enjoyed a good life in Indiana.

Robert took a job as the manager of a family-run dairy in Evansville in 1954 and moved his young family south. The owners of the dairy and the Martins quickly became close friends. In 1958 the Martins were blessed with another son, Scott. Growing up in Evansville was idyllic. The children had a lot of friends, and life was good. They've described their time in Evansville as the happiest time of their lives.

To his family and all who knew him, Dennis was known as Denny. He grew up an incredibly supportive and caring person. He loved children and become a camp counselor during the summer. He was always organizing fun things in the neighborhood, like art shows and magic shows. He was athletic and become an accomplished swimmer and diver.

Denny was also passionate about music. His favorite genre was folk, and topping the list were bands like the Kingston Trio. Denny didn't just listen to music; he was also a musician. When Denny was sixteen or seventeen, he wanted to get a guitar. Barbara, also musically talented, wanted them to get a banjo. Denny vetoed her and said, "No, we should get a guitar." And they did. Their musical talent didn't stop at the strings. Barbara also played the clarinet, and Denny played the trumpet. They would perform duets together, amusing their family and friends.

Things in Evansville slowly started to change. The dairy began losing money and struggled to keep the doors open. Even though the Martins were close to the owners, it wasn't possible to give Robert any raises, and his job appeared in jeopardy. He had to do some serious soul searching and review his options. Moving to find more lucrative work was one of them.

With the close of the Korean War in 1953, the country became enveloped in a nationwide recession, which hit Evansville particularly hard. Over the next ten years of peace, the city's reliance on industries with ties to defense contractors forced many closures. Eventually, new companies moved into the area, but at that moment, Robert had to make a decision.

Robert was offered a job in Cedar Rapids, Iowa with the Penick & Ford Company, a manufacturer of corn byproducts, primarily corn starch and corn syrup. He decided to take the job.

The sales of these products took off when the price of sugar went up. Robert had found a way to make a comfortable living and a good life for his family. The timing of the move was horrible for Denny, however. He was a senior in high school and leaving his friends at this vital time of his life was a tough pill to swallow. Like it or not, it had to be done. Denny finished his senior year, graduating from high school in Cedar Rapids.

Denny wasn't in Cedar Rapids that long. After he finished high school, he went to Iowa State University in Ames. New friendships were made, and life was good again. The unhappiness he felt leaving Evansville disappeared. Iowa State was a perfect fit for Denny. He found that college life was fun and rewarding. The classes challenged his mind.

While Denny was in college, his dad kept telling him that he should get into ROTC because if he was drafted he would become an officer like he had been. Denny's father and uncle LaRue both served in the navy during World War II. They were trained as pilots and commissioned as officers. LaRue was sent to the Pacific to fight the Japanese while Robert remained in the States as a flight instructor. While serving in this capacity in Atlantic City Robert met Gladys, his future wife.

LaRue met his end when he was killed in action on March 21, 1945. His body was never recovered.

Robert knew firsthand that the life of an officer was much better than the drudgery of the enlisted ranks. Under pressure from his father, Denny joined the ROTC. He hated it, so he dropped out. He had no interest in the military.

Denny met Sue Rundall while they were in college. She was at the University of Northern Iowa in Cedar Falls, less than two hours from where Denny was at Ames. Denny's roommate was dating a girl who lived in the same dorm as Susie, actually, right across the hall. They arranged for a blind date to introduce Susie and Denny. Susie's impression of Denny was that he was kind of quiet yet funny, a man with many varied interests, especially science. They hit it off and dated for the next two years.

Sue graduated with a teaching degree in June of '68, and they married in August of that year. They lived in Ames while Denny finished up the last quarter of his education, graduating in November 1968 with his bachelor's degree in chemical engineering.

The country was reeling from all the fighting in Vietnam stemming from the Tet Offensive earlier in 1968. Protests flared across college campuses, demanding that the US stop participating in the war. The draft was in full swing. Thousands of men were called up each month to serve in what would become America's quagmire in Vietnam. Fighting the Communists in Southeast Asia caused President Johnson to double the draft. The old policy of not drafting married men without children was scrapped. Now all married men without children were eligible. Soon even married men with children would also be conscripted.

The draft was foremost on the minds of Denny and Susie. They were married, but they knew that it might not help him avoid military service. In the fall of 1968, Denny and his friend, Tim Petersen, went down to Des Moines to take physicals for the navy. Denny passed his physical, but Tim did not due to a problem with his hearing. For some unknown reason, Denny never pursued the navy after that. Possibly he hoped he would get a deferment because he was married. But Vietnam was going at full tilt; the odds of avoiding military service were slim at best.

Denny got a good job right after college in Wilmington, Delaware, but life abruptly changed when he received his draft notice. There were 296,406 men drafted in 1968. Denny was one of them.

Harlen Walter Metzger

Harlen was born in Boonville, Indiana, on March 3, 1948, the son of Hendrix (Hank) Metzger and Mary Jane Seib. He was the oldest of five children. Hank was working for Maxon Construction in 1942 when he registered for the draft during World War II. He ultimately decided not to wait to be called up and joined the navy in September 1942. With his construction background, he was assigned to the Navy Seabees, Construction Bn. 45 and sent to Kodiak, Alaska. He was discharged from the navy in 1945 and returned home to Indiana. After working several jobs, he and his brother Gene founded Metzger Construction Co. They were in the asphalt business, an excellent field to be in with the economy expanding in the early 1950s.

Hank was a significant influence in Harlen's life. Hank had his kids call him by his first name instead of Dad. He said, if they got lost and called "Dad," he wouldn't know they were calling for him. If they yelled, "Hank!" he would know it was one of his kids.

Hank was a demanding father. He bristled when anyone disagreed with him. He only had a seventh-grade education but was very intelligent. Harlen's mother, for the most part, was subservient to his father. Harlen played football for a short time in high school, and his dad never once came to a game. Hank believed in one thing only, and that was working. About the age of twelve, with little choice, Harlen started working summers in the asphalt business. It was hot, hard, and demanding work. The heat of the sweltering Indiana summer was bad by itself; it was worse radiating off the asphalt.

Harlen graduated from Boonville High School in 1966. He applied and was accepted at Purdue University in the engineering program. His first year of college was a big success. He was on the dean's list. He took it seriously and excelled as a student. Purdue was a conservative school, and although there was a lot of fun to be had the students worked hard at their studies.

On a Sunday evening in the summer of 1968, Harlen was with his brother Mike, and Mike had been drinking. Mike had just broken up with his girlfriend, Carol, and was very upset. Harlen called Carol and told her about the state Mike was in and asked her to come over to Boonville and help him deal with him. Carol was with her friend Brenda Galloway at her house, and they were getting ready to go into Evansville, Indiana, for a dance at a community center. She said if Brenda could come and if the guys would meet them, Carol would talk with Mike.

Harlen agreed, and they met at a drive-up restaurant where they all got in Harlen's car and went for a ride, looking for a place to park and talk. They found a quiet place, and Mike and Carol were in the back seat talking while Harlen and Brenda were up front. Harlen and Brenda connected and were chatting away when Carol asked them what they were talking about. Harlen said, "We are talking about getting married."

Their first official "date" was on July 4, 1968. Harlen acted forward and overconfident, trying to push for second base, but Brenda quickly dispelled him of that idea. They were part of the crazy '60s generation of drugs and sex, but neither had much, or any, experience with either.

The summer of 1968 ended with Harlen heading back to Purdue University and Brenda beginning her freshman year at the University of Evansville. Starting college was always an exciting time. The thrill of getting away from home, on your own. New friends. Returning to school was exciting for Harlen too. He moved out of the dormitory and into an off-campus apartment with three other guys. With this freedom came drinking and partying. Brenda went up one weekend to visit him, and the party was completely out of control! Harlen was sure that the police were going to be called, and they wanted no part of that. They left the apartment in a hurry and checked into the student union.

After he came home for Christmas break in 1968, he never returned. Finally, he confessed to Brenda and his parents that he had been uninvited back to Purdue because of low grades. He had basically quit going to classes. This common malady was called the sophomore slump. But with Vietnam going strong, it wasn't a good time to lose your student deferment.

At the end of May 1969, Harlen and Brenda got engaged while sitting in Harlen's car in a parking lot. Excitedly, they went to a department store and picked out Brenda's ring then the couple went to his sister Mariann's eighth-grade graduation party and told all his relatives.

By the time Harlen received his draft notice in the early summer of 1969, he had gained a lot of weight. First, he had to pass the physical. Three days before he was to report for it, he drank and partied a lot. Was it intentional to fail the physical?

When he reported for the physical, his blood pressure was too high. Each day for three days, he had to return and have it rechecked. Finally, they deemed it normal, and he passed the physical. No surprise there. Almost everyone passed eventually. Harlen never expressed any negative comments regarding the war. He just knew he didn't want to go.

Carey Jay Pratt

Carey Jay and his twin sister, Cheri Kay, were born on August 27, 1948, in Marion, Indiana, to Thomas Richard (*called Dick*) and Glendora Pratt. Cheri Kay died less than a year after birth, on January 1, 1949. She died of neuroblastoma; a condition she had been born with.

The Pratts had eight children in all, four boys and four girls. The family struggled raising their large family and putting food on the table. They never went hungry but lacked extra money for those little luxuries in life. Financially, life changed for the Pratt family when both parents began working at the General Motors plant in nearby Kokomo.

Carey's maternal grandmother, Grace Lyons, lost her husband around the time Carey was born, and she moved in with the Pratt family. Her presence in the household worked out well as she watched the children while the parents worked. Carey and his grandmother formed a strong bond, almost a mother-son type of relationship during Carey's formative coming-of-age years. Grandma Lyons was a devout Christian and taught the children sound Christian values.

Carey was a busy, inquisitive, happy child. As he grew, he became an avid outdoorsman. His father and older brothers taught him to hunt and fish. He became a crack shot with a rifle, a skill that would be extremely important later, when he was in Vietnam.

Carey attended Kokomo High School, where he was an average student. He was a member of the choir and known as a superb baritone. He was a popular and fun-loving kid, especially among the girls, which may account for his average grades.

Carey graduated from Kokomo High School on July 15, 1966, and one day shortly after that, he happened to meet Theresa Hill, who was a sophomore. Carey had picked up a girl for lunch, and Theresa was with her. Theresa sat in the back seat, and Carey looked at her in the rearview mirror a little bit longer than he should have considered he had another girl in the car.

Cary had a part-time job driving for the Star company newspapers, dropping off the morning's deliveries. It just so happened that the house where he dropped off the papers was right next door to Theresa's house. He would stop, and they would talk. Eventually, their talks led to dating and romance.

Like his parents, Carey found work at the Delco Electronics plant in Kokomo. He started as an hourly employee cleaning offices and sweeping floors. It didn't take long for a promotion to a line job.

Theresa graduated from high school in 1968. By this time, they were engaged to be married. Theresa's brother was in the service and stationed in Korea but was coming home in July, so the couple decided to get married then. They tied the knot on July 20, 1968, after Theresa graduated from high school.

The couple was married in the First Baptist Church in Kokomo. It wasn't a large wedding but still a beautiful and formal affair. After the wedding, the couple drove down to Fort Lauderdale for their honeymoon. They checked in to a beautiful hotel, but there wasn't a pool, and they both loved to swim. So, they changed to a slightly smaller hotel that did have a pool. They had a wonderful time that week, not caring about the accommodations. All too quickly, the honeymoon was over, and it was time to head home to Indiana. They only had twenty dollars left when they arrived back home, causing Theresa to panic because she knew the rent was due soon. Fortunately, Carey received his check from Delco just in time, and they were able to get by.

Life was good for the newlyweds until Carey was scheduled for a physical examination by the draft board. Of course he passed, the army needed bodies, and he was one.

It was a beautiful day in September 1968 when Carey left their second-floor apartment to retrieve the mail. Theresa heard him say, "Oh no." It was a letter from Uncle Sam. Carey opened it as he walked up the steps to their apartment. It contained instructions for him to report for military service. He probably could have fought the draft board because of his feet, but he accepted his fate and coped as well as he could.

Carey was to report for basic training shortly after New Year's Day in January 1969. His imminent departure could have cast a pall over the Pratt family Christmas celebrations. But the children and grandchildren were pretty much oblivious to things like the draft and a war in a far-off place called Vietnam.

So, as was their custom, the family gathered at Carey's parents' house for the unwrapping of presents, and a big family dinner. Everyone knew it might be the last Christmas the entire family had together for a couple of years, so they made the best of it, and all had a great time.

After all the gifts were open, Carey's dad, Dick, asked everyone to gather in the front yard around the flagpole. It was a cold, snowy day, and everybody bundled up. Soon, the entire family gathered in the front yard, shivering, stomping their feet, and joking around to stay warm. As they surrounded the flagpole, Dick fastened a brand-new American flag to the lanyard. Stepping back, he asked Butch—as the family called Carey—to slowly raise the stars and stripes.

As the flag neared the shiny brass eagle at the top, it began whipping in the chilly morning breeze. Carey's mom and grandma were quietly crying; soon so were others. Tears streamed down his dad's cheeks. Carey had never seen his dad cry until that moment. In a voice choked with emotion, Dick vowed, "We will not lower this flag until Butch is safely home."

On January 21, Carey left Kokomo on a bus that would take him to basic training at Fort Knox, Kentucky.

Michael "Mike" Phillip Vullo

November temperatures in Los Angeles were typical in 1948. Mid-seventies to low eighties. But on the 15th, they began to drop. But as the sun rose on the fifteenth of that month, it was a chilly forty-seven degrees. It was on this unusual day that Michael Phillip Vullo was brought into the world.

Mike, as he was called, was the oldest of four children born to Charles and Cherie Vullo. His parents were an interesting combination. Charles was a proud, full-blooded Sicilian with jet black hair and blue eyes. Cherie was Scandinavian, blond hair and green eyes. Cherie's genes were the stronger as all of their children had blond hair and blue or green eyes.

Mike, his brother, Mark, and his sisters Pam and Sharon enjoyed a good life in the 1950s. The Southern California weather was pretty close to idyllic, the economy was strong, and the country was at peace. But there were problems in the Vullo household. Charles and Cherie divorced in the 1960s when Mike was in high school. The family was torn apart. Mike moved in with his grandparents, Pam moved in with their mom, and Mark and Sharon stayed with their dad and his new wife, another Sicilian this time.

Known to be a fun guy at Alhambra High School, Mike was pleasant and friendly. He liked to have a good time but never to excess. He would hang out on the corner, enjoying a cigarette and joking around with his buddies, but they weren't troublemakers like you see depicted in some movies. Mike was a clean guy who was well-liked by everyone around him.

Mike was close to his cousin Gary and a friend of Gary's. They were about a year and a half younger than Mike, but the age difference didn't matter. In fact it helped them all once Mike turned sixteen and obtained his driver's license. His grandfather, who was always proud of him, helped him buy a Ford Mustang. Everything only got better after that. The three buddies would cruise in the Mustang to Hermosa Beach, Redondo Beach, the mountains, anywhere they wanted to go. They even drove to the Rose Bowl Parade in Pasadena one year after an all-night party at Mike's grandparents' house in Alhambra. True to Mike's good heart, there was no damage, and everything put away and clean before they left.

While in high school, among his standard courses, Mike took an electronics course. It wasn't his cup of tea, and he didn't do well in it. Was it the subject matter, the teacher, or just a typical teenage lack of motivation? We will never know. But the tests were known to be extremely difficult, and Mike struggled to get a passing grade. After passing the course, he moved on to different studies. This is interesting because Mike ultimately was in electronics while in the army, where he did well. Different motivation.

Mike's sister Pam, who attended a different high school, had a girlfriend named Kathleen, nicknamed Kathi, and Mike started dating her, and they soon became a steady couple.

After high school, he began working and enrolled in night school at East LA Junior College. He and Kathi continued to date, but ominously, the headlines and TV news were full of reports of pitched battles and high casualty counts in Vietnam. In March 1969, the draft caught up with Mike, and he received his notice. Life would have to be on hold for now.

The idea of going to Canada or somehow dodging the draft never occurred to him. He was only the second generation in the United States, and he felt it was his duty to serve his country. With military service hanging over them and the Vietnam War raging, Mike and Kathi decided to get married.

Larry Butcher

Grand Opening!

F. W. Woolworth Co. opened a new store in Modesto, California, in 1949. The five-and-dime giant was expanding greatly after the end of World War II. The country was getting back on its feet after the war. Jobs were plentiful, and opportunities were endless. Another great event happened in Modesto in 1949—Larry Butcher was brought screaming and kicking into the world on July 10.

Larry was the younger of two children born to Albert Jr. and Virginia Butcher. Larry's father was an only child. His grandfather, Albert Floyd Butcher Sr., worked in the Alameda shipyards as a young man. He narrowly escaped death one morning when an explosion shook the plant. He had just walked off the ferry that took workers back and forth to the yards when something blew. He was not seriously injured but was bleeding from his nose and ears. A few minutes earlier and Larry would never have been.

Albert Sr. started a business building trenchers, ditch diggers for irrigation pipes. When Larry's father was old enough, he went to work with his dad in the business. They built diggers in four sizes to accommodate all standard irrigation pipe widths. They went by the name of Butcher Ironworks, also known as Floyd Butcher Trenching.

When World War II broke out, Albert, like so many other young men, was drafted into the army. He reported for basic training but never finished it and was given a less-than-honorable discharge. The circumstances of his service were never discussed in the Butcher household.

Larry's parents were strict Seventh-day Adventists. Larry and his older sister, Cheryl, had to toe the line. They were not allowed to play with their toys or ride their bicycles from Friday sundown to Saturday sundown. During this time, they attended church services, took nature walks, and read. They anxiously waited for sundown on Saturday so they could resume their childhood games.

Larry worked with his grandfather and dad in the family business from the tender age of thirteen. He learned to do it all, welding, cutting, and blacksmithing and operated all the equipment, including the bulldozers and trenchers. One day when he was thirteen, his grandfather took him to Oakdale, where he loaded a bulldozer on a flatbed truck. Grandpa then gave Larry the choice of driving the pickup to Waterford, which was about twenty miles away, or the semi with the bulldozer. Larry chose the semi and drove it sitting at the front edge of the seat so he could reach the pedals. His grandfather instructed him that if he were stopped by the police not to say a word; he would do the talking. As it turned out, the drive was uneventful except how pissed off his mother was when she learned her son drove a semi twenty miles at the age of thirteen!

It didn't take long for Larry to realize that he didn't want to live his life working in that business. It was hard, dirty work. Trenching was done in the winter when the canals were empty.

There was no heat in the machines. He froze all day.

In 1966 Vietnam military action was on the rise, dominating the news. There was a concern that, eventually, Larry would be drafted and have to serve. His father and grandfather were 100 percent anti-military. They did not want Larry to get drafted, and they told him about different ways to get out of it. His grandfather wanted Larry to get his girlfriend pregnant and apply for a deferment based on that. The spoke with him about other ways to avoid the draft like bedwetting, but none were an option for Larry.

Larry was seventeen years old and a junior in high school when his grandfather bought him a brand-new 250CC Suzuki X-6 Hustler motorcycle. He told Larry to leave the country to avoid being drafted and sent to Vietnam. He explained to him that if he went into the service, he would die there. Despite still being in high school, Larry followed his grandfather's plan.

On a Monday morning, his mother dropped him and his sister off at school. The first bell rang; Larry waited, making sure his sister went to her first class; then he left the campus, walked to his grandfather's business to collect his bike, and immediately left Modesto for Mexico. His mother and sister had no clue about this plan.

He spent the first night in Mexicali, Mexico. All night there was loud music playing popular songs of the day like "(I Can't Get No) Satisfaction," in Spanish. He never forgot that night. Early the next morning, he left for Sonoyta and arrived about noon. He was stopped at a border checkpoint a few miles south of Sonoyta and was not allowed to continue.

He rode back up to Lukeville, Arizona, filling the bike with gas. He sat quietly on his motorcycle for a while, thinking, *"Is this the way I want to live my life?"* He decided, no, it wasn't. He found a telephone booth and called his mother, telling her where he was and why and that he was coming back home.

That night he stayed in El Centro, California, and rode back to Modesto the next day. He took the motorcycle back to his grandfather and told him he could have it back because he did not keep his part of the deal. His grandfather said, "Keep it and enjoy it for now. If you register and are drafted, you will die in Vietnam."

Larry graduated from high school in June 1967. He was dating Rita Marsh, a classmate since fifth grade. Their relationship strengthened, and a year later, in the summer of 1968, they married.

The couple enjoyed married life for less than a year before Larry received his draft notice in April 1969. Married life would be on hold for the next two years.

David Paul Schultz

David was born to Donald Schultz and Ofelia Cadena on October 3, 1951, in Madison, Wisconsin, but he grew up in Texas. That was where he would call home. While in Texas, the marriage of Donald and Ofelia fell apart. When the divorce was final, Donald moved back to the Midwest, and Ofelia and David remained in Texas.

Divorce is never easy for a child. It can take a toll on their future attitude and spirit no matter whether they are young children or adolescents when it happens.

It certainly affected David when his parents separated. As he grew, David kept the details of his home life pretty much to himself. He wasn't a complainer or a liar. He just kept his feelings on this buried.

Ofelia married Truman Oliver in May 1960. David, just nine years old, did not seem to get along with his stepfather. The conflict worsened as time went on, but David rose above it and didn't fall prey to bitterness and anger. As he grew, he found other activities to absorb his time. Healthy, productive things. Things that got him out of the house and kept him occupied. He didn't dwell on the past, or on the present, for that matter.

David was a lanky kid, easy going and friendly, without a mean bone in his body. In school, he fit in well and seemed to get along with everyone. No enemies. Despite his family difficulties, he had a smile about everything, never seeming sad or angry.

Late in junior high school, David joined the Civil Air Patrol (CAP). There was a composite squadron in Harlingen that took in cadets from the area. Harlingen didn't have a lot to offer kids, and they were lucky this squadron was there. This CAP unit owned a Piper Cub and a Cherokee Piper 140. If the cadets helped clean and maintain the airplanes, change tires or wipe them down once in a while, they would get rides one or two Saturdays a month. It was great for the cadets. They would take them up flying up for fifteen, twenty, thirty minutes at a time. The CAP was very active in those days. Sometimes the CAP pilots would pick up cadets and fly them up to Amarillo Air Force Base for a weeklong encampment. The cadets would go to air force classes and other military activities. It was a big, exciting time for David and the kids in Harlingen.

When David was in high school, the recruiters visited, trying to get students to join the air force or army ROTC programs. They explained that if you finished the program and went into the military, you would start basic as an E2 enlisted rank, one step higher than buck private. The thought of entering the service as an E2 appealed to David, so he dropped out of the CAP and joined the air force ROTC. It was a surprise to everyone who knew him. He was the last guy they would ever think would be in the military. He was just too gentle, too naïve, too accepting.

But David had other interests besides the CAP and the ROTC. He was religious and became involved in the Christian Youth Ranch in Pharr. At the time, the ranch consisted of an old white house on a couple of acres of vacant land. Reverend Wally Morillo founded the ranch in September 1967. Morillo had attended Bible College classes while working nights as an airline mechanic. He graduated from Florida Bible College in 1966, and later that year, Wally felt a calling into ministry. The decision made, he left his airline job in January 1967. He and his wife, Jane, moved to the Rio Grande Valley. In September 1967, they started the Christian Youth Ranch, where they ministered to neighborhood kids.

It was a big thing for teenagers in the area. They would have a weekly church service, but it was also a social gathering place. The ranch was a place to get away from their parents and hang out with friends in a safe setting.

There was no public transportation between the two towns. So, the church would send a van to Harlingen, which was about thirty miles away, picking kids up and bringing them to the ranch. The van would also take them home at the end of the day.

David, who didn't have a car, hitchhiked. He took his time at the ranch seriously. He did a lot of work while there, helping to fix things, paint, repair fences, and dig ditches. All without pay, of course, but that was David.

David quit school in his senior year of high school in 1969. On April 1, he joined the army. He was only seventeen years old, so his mother had to sign for him. His entry was delayed, training wouldn't begin until July. His active-duty time would be up in July 1971; then he would have to serve four years in the reserves. David was patriotic, but he also wanted to get away from his stepfather. The army offered the perfect solution.

Donna met David in early April. The day that they met, Donna was just wandering around the ranch. She couldn't even remember what she was thinking or doing. She was just wandering around, looking for friends. She spent a lot of time there. That was the one place she could go to get away from her mom without having to offer long explanations. Donna did not get along with her mother. Her mother was toxic and controlling. The ranch was her escape and she took full advantage of the freedom it offered.

That day David and Donna were walking toward each other, not intentionally; then, as they passed each other, they both stopped and took a step back. They both felt a strong attraction and connection the moment their eyes set on each other. She couldn't even tell you what it was about David that attracted her. Donna didn't have a specific type of boy who appealed to her, but David immediately caught her eye. She wouldn't call it love at first sight because she was too young to know what love was. But there was something!

From that moment on, they were inseparable. David and Donna hung out at the ranch every second they could; that was their social life and their dating life. Eventually, Donna's mother gave her permission to bring him over to their house. She wanted to meet him, and they were allowed to sit on the couch in the living room but no other place in the house, no privacy. They just talked. Talked about the future, talked about the things that they liked. He told her of his desire to be a missionary in Mexico when he got out of the army.

While waiting for basic training to begin, David continued to help out at the ranch. He would often drive the church van to Harlingen to pick up kids and bring them over. Hitchhiking to Pharr to get the van became a daily ritual. Once he picked up the van, Donna would join him, and they would spend a few hours alone in the van. Then they would hang out at the ranch. Even though their attraction was powerful, David was always the perfect gentleman.

After David and Donna's romance began to bloom, he began to regret his decision to go into the army. He wanted to try to get out of his enlistment contract but wasn't able to. He told Donna that he wouldn't have enlisted if he had met her before. Now he wanted to stay home and start a life with her.

As David's entry into the army approached, he spent as much time as he could at the ranch with Donna. He helped with construction projects and driving the van, which gave the couple time to be together.

Finally, the time came, and David quietly left Harlingen on June 30 for Fort Bliss and basic training. Their romance would have to be put on hold for now, limited to letters and an occasional leave.

Chapter 2

Vietnam Looms Closer

He who sweats more in training

bleeds less in war.

-Spartan Warrior Creed

Even though World War II was over, the draft continued with a significant upswing during the Korean War period, from 1950 to 1954. All males were required to register for the draft within months after turning eighteen. The draft continued during peace and war until it was finally terminated in 1973. During peacetime, it created a minor disruption of a young man's life for two years; however, during the Vietnam era, it could mean the difference between life and death.

Between 1964 and 1973, 1,728,344 men were drafted; of these, 648,500 served in Vietnam and accounted for approximately 31 percent of combat deaths.

In 1965, 230,991 men were drafted into the armed services. There were 1,863 deaths classified as war-related casualties. Things heated up in 1966 when 382,010 men were drafted, and there were 6,143 war-related deaths and 30,093 wounded. In 1967, when Elroy Simmons served his first tour, 228,263 men were drafted, and there were 11,153 war-related deaths, not to There were significant changes in the war in 1968. The Tet Offensive resulted in major fighting across the whole country. Americans back home anxiously watched the events in Vietnam unfurl on their TV sets. Worried parents and other loved ones searched the faces for their sons fighting there. Most were afraid that they may get an unwanted visit from military representatives telling them of sudden death, an unbearable loss that would cause grief for the rest of their lives.

In 1968, 296,406 men were drafted, and there were 16,592 deaths. An additional 92,820 troops were wounded. These figures were staggering to the American public, and protests against the war sprung up on college campuses and in cities throughout the land. Although the North Vietnamese and Viet Cong lost militarily, they appeared to have won a major propaganda victory. When the six o'clock news showed South Vietnamese General Loan execute a Viet Cong operative, the country was stunned. The year also saw Walter Cronkite's call to exit Vietnam because he thought the war was unwinnable. The US entered into peace talks with North Vietnam.

Still reeling from the increased fighting during 1968, the draft in 1969 continued full bore. In total, 283,586 men were selected. Many of these were sent to Vietnam where 11,616 of men and women died and 70,198 were wounded.

In 1970, Washington created plans to withdraw troops from Vietnam. Pressure was being placed on North Vietnam to finish negotiations at the Paris talks, but it seemed like there was little progress made. President Nixon decided on an incursion into Cambodia to destroy supply lines, the North Vietnamese headquarters, and the estimated 40,00 troops there. The offensive began with South Vietnamese troops crossing the border on April 29 and US troops on May 1. Large amounts of supplies were captured or destroyed, but the elusive North Vietnamese Army (NVA) managed to escape. On June 30, American troops were finally withdrawn back to South Vietnam. Things calmed down after this as the enemy tried to rebuild their supplies and replace their killed and wounded soldiers. Although enemy activity slowed, Americans were still dying.

In 1970, 162,746 men were drafted. There were 6,081 war-related deaths. That's 6,081 heartbroken families, including the families of the nine who died as a result of the shooting down of Chinook #65-07999 on July 10. There were 30,943 soldiers, sailors, marines, and airmen who were wounded that year. The war was far from over.

Basic training for recruits was the same if you were an enlistee or draftee. Transitioning from civilian to army life was always a shock for the newly inducted. The days were long and the nights short.

The first week was at the reception station. The group of civilians, the soon-to-be soldiers, were herded off the bus and put in some type of loose formation. Welcome to the United States Army.

It all began with haircuts. It wasn't actually a haircut. They were shorn like sheep. Bald as a babies, except with a little stubble. Next was ID cards, then batteries and batteries of tests. The tests would show your qualifications. For many, it didn't matter how well you scored. Infantry, artillery, and combat medics drew the most people.

Medical exams were given to weed out those with any underlying health problems. Shots followed. Needle anxiety would grip some, and down they would go, passed out cold.

The uniform issue was next. The new troops stood in endless lines and had nice crisp uniforms thrown at them. Usually they fit, but sometimes they didn't.

The recruits rode on a short bus ride from the reception station to their training companies. It was time to meet those warm and pleasant drill sergeants. These DIs, as they were called, were waiting for the recruits' arrival, pacing back and forth liked caged tigers. They greeted them with screams, scaring the hell out of everyone as the boys clutched their duffel bags full of all their belongings, which always seemed to weigh a thousand pounds (at least it felt like it).

Now their training began in earnest.

Endless close-order drill and formations. Then came the obstacle course, first aid, and we can't forget KP. Getting up at 0400 and scrubbing pots and pans, peeling potatoes, and preparing meals for over a hundred troops. Dead tired at the end of the day, the KPs slowly returned to the barracks. Tomorrow always came early, and they still had to shine their boots and prepare their uniforms.

The training became more serious when it came time to go to the rifle range. The DIs were a little easier on the men here. Most men enjoyed this time even though the day usually ended with a forced march back to the barracks.

As basic training neared the end, everything seemed to change. The physical training and road marches weren't as hard, the drill sergeants seemed less severe, and an esprit de corps had developed throughout the platoon. They were now able to work as a team. The harsh training had paid off. They were now soldiers.

Graduation was a proud day for everyone. They had made it; hard as it was, they made it. Drill sergeants called the troops together, announcing where they would be assigned and what their job, their MOS, would be.

Elroy Simmons

Elroy was on his way to his toughest assignment. He would accompany the 9th Infantry Division to Vietnam. The division left Fort Riley in December 1967, an entire division move, the old-fashioned way, like in World War II. They would travel by ship to the war zone.

Elroy and the remainder of the 1st Bn., 11th Artillery made the long nineteen-day voyage on the USNS *General Maurice Rose*, a transport ship that was launched in 1945. Like all World War II transports ships, it was not designed for the comfort of the troops it carried. The trip across the Pacific was uneventful by navy standards, but for men unused to life on the water, it had its moments. They encountered some choppy seas, and many men succumbed to bouts of seasickness. At the end of the voyage, most could not wait to get on dry land.

The *Rose* approached the coastline of South Vietnam on New Year's Eve, 1966. Everyone who did not have an assigned detail below decks was topside, straining to get their first glimpse of this war-torn country. What greeted them was the beautiful and lush greens of tropical jungle and long stretches of sandy beaches. What an exciting sight after the long, cramped sea voyage. It looked so peaceful and serene - how could a war be going on here?

The *Rose* docked at Vung Tau, a beautiful port city that sported a lot of French architecture, remnants of wars, and times past. Though the troops were getting used to the heat, all their equipment had to be unloaded and assembled in short order. The men struggled to get this all done at the double-time. They finished their preparations, and the next day they boarded convoys to their new home—Bearcat.

Bearcat was a French airfield in colonial times. After Japan took control of Indochina in World War II, they used it as an airfield. Early in the Vietnam War, the US Special Forces established a base there; now it would come under the control of the 9th Infantry Division.

As the convoy transporting the 1st Bn., 11th Artillery approached, they saw a desolate piece of ground covered with clouds of dust and construction machinery. The 15th Engineer Bn. was in the process of grading and constructing the base, which would remain in operation until 1972. Much to the dismay of the members of the 1st Bn., there were no buildings, tents, anything! They had to make do. This was war. For now, they would sleep on the open ground.

The 1st Bn. would have their 105mm cannons based out of Bearcat but would be sent all over Military Regions (MR) III and IV.

They would provide artillery support anywhere it was needed, but for the most part, they supported the 1st Brigade of the 9th Infantry Division. They moved their tubes to another base, Long Thanh North, to provide artillery support for Operation Silver Lake. On January 14, 1967, the operation began, and the firing started. They fired 443 rounds and suffered their first casualties when eight men were wounded. This was a wake-up call for the 1st Bn. The war was real, and men would get hurt and die here.

Elroy sent many letters to Barbara telling her about the situation in Vietnam and describing the severe living conditions. The tour in Vietnam was a difficult time for him as it is for all combat veterans. It was horrible, but the details of combat he kept bottled up inside.

In May 1967, his assignment changed. He took a position at Headquarters Battery of the 9th Division. While he was with the 1st Bn., 11th Artillery, they fired an impressive 60,685 rounds at the enemy.

The artillery followed the infantry and provided support wherever there was an operation. The living conditions didn't get any better in the field; it was always harsh. They were always vulnerable to enemy attacks from sappers, snipers, ground attacks, rockets, and mortars. But they did their duty and performed professionally.

On July 25, Elroy was once again reassigned. This time to the 84th Artillery, where he remained until his tour was up. They fired 24,854 rounds throughout MR III and IV. They covered as far west as the Cambodian border.

He made it through his tour unwounded, and in December, his time in Vietnam was up. Elroy traveled home on December 1, 1967, just in time to be with his family for Christmas. He seemed in pretty good shape when he got back, physically and mentally. As Barbara was quoted to say, "You know how you guys have your moments." And I am sure he had some issues to deal with, but he was in the army, and it was his career, so he was able to enjoy his time home with his family and prepare for the next assignment.

Elroy was given an extended leave before reporting back for duty. But, this time, he was able to take his family with him, and the next assignment was a good one—Germany!

Barbara and Elroy were able to bring all four children with them to Germany. The duty was excellent; they both enjoyed it. Barbara worked while they were there. That was something unusual at that time for American women in Germany to be working. Once again, the extra income helped with all the bills a family of six had. The Simmons family was able to travel a little, though with four children, traveling around Europe was difficult and limited.

Barbara enjoyed her time when the children were in school. Many times they had field trips, and she always volunteered to go along as an escort. On these trips, she was able to visit Luxembourg and some of the small towns in Germany.

They remained there for over two years, but all good things must come to an end, and Elroy received orders back to Vietnam. It was not a surprise; he knew he would be sent back. It was just a matter of time. He had made up his mind that he was going to stay in the army; it was his career. He had some misgivings about that, but he accepted that this was part of his job, and he had to do what he needed to do.

They came back to the States from Germany in April of 1970 and settled the family in Waukegan, Illinois. Barbara did not want to go back to East St. Louis even though they had family there. Elroy's sister was living in Waukegan and told Barbara how nice it was and how it was a great place to raise a family. So, there they remained while Elroy once again enjoyed his leave time and prepared to go back to war.

Elroy, Barbara, and the children went to East St. Louis to visit his mother for Mother's Day. When they returned to Waukegan, Elroy told Barbara that he wanted to go back for Memorial Day. Barbara told him, "Well, you can go, but you take the boys with you, and I'll take the girls with me because I'm going to Chicago."

He told Barbara that earlier his grandmother had told him to try and stay in Germany. She felt that was where he should be. Where it was safe. Unfortunately, she and one of Elroy's uncles had died while he was stationed there. When he went to East St. Louis for Memorial Day, he visited their graves. He told Barbara that while he was there, he saw his own grave. A vision? A premonition?

Elroy seemed anxious after this. He was always on the go like someone was pushing him. One time Barbara asked him, "Why are you going? Why do you have to go?" "I just have to go," he replied. One of the last times, she asked him, "What if something happens to you?" He looked at her and said, "You know exactly what to do," and walked out the door. He was running like death was chasing him.

He left the third of June, and the morning that he left, he kissed all the kids goodbye. He looked at his five-year-old daughter, Mickey, and told her, "I'll see you when I get back." She looked up at him and said, "You're not coming back."

This time Elroy did not have to deal with a long sea voyage. The war had changed, and everyone was now being shipped overseas on commercial airliners, at least most of them were. So, Elroy kissed his family goodbye for another year and once again left for war.

Denny Martin

Denny and Susie moved back to Iowa before Denny was sworn into the US Army on December 11, 1968. He reported for basic training on January 6, 1969, at beautiful Fort Polk, Louisiana. Not the best base in the army to serve your basic training, not that there was a good place!

Denny had no trouble completing basic training, hard as it was. The goal of the drill sergeants was to break you down then build you up. Denny remained thoughtful and self-possessed despite the efforts of the drill sergeants to reduce him to basic raw material. He kept his individuality, often speaking of Susie and the life they would have after his service was complete.

Denny was older than most of the recruits and better educated, an adult among a bunch of kids. He knew that he just did not fit the military mold. He knew it in ROTC, and he knew it now. As an example, once, he and a friend got utterly lost on a night compass course. The friend recalled standing with him in pitch-black darkness, agreeing that they were not cut out for this sort of thing. Neither was lifer material.

Tuesday, February 18th
Dear Grandmother and Grandfather

As of today, I have only 10 days left in basic training. However, that is not much consolation since I have received orders for "advanced infantry training" which is offered right here at Fort Polk. Incidentally, this infantry training is jungle oriented so there doesn't seem to be any question as to where I will be headed after my nine weeks of A.I.T. Needless to say, I was particularly discouraged by the news. It seems that my education meant very little to the Army.
Denny

After basic training finished, he remained at Fort Polk for Infantry AIT beginning on March 17, 1969. This was a serious precursor to Vietnam service. His home now was Co. E, 3rd Bn., AIT Brigade. Susie was able to come down and visit him at this time. The restrictions of basic training were gone. Their visits were short, but Denny was able to get some time off so they could be together.

Despite his self-doubts, the army recognized Denny's abilities, and he was selected for noncommissioned officer (NCO) training. This additional training would not stave off service in Vietnam, but it would delay it for a little while.

As AIT neared completion, Denny received his orders for Fort Benning as an NCO candidate. First, he would have a furlough home to Iowa and Susie.

The furlough was too short, but then, all furloughs are. It seemed that in the blink of an eye, it was over, and Denny caught a flight to Georgia and more training. After checking in on June 9, 1969, he was assigned to 75th Co., Candidate Brigade. The rigorous training to be an NCO in the infantry began. The training was hard—Vietnam was most likely the next stop, and they must be prepared, both physically and mentally.

Susie had finished her year as a student teacher and went down to Fort Benning to spend the summer; she rented an apartment off-post. Denny and Susie were able to see each other sometimes on the weekends and in the evenings through August. The condensed training schedule did not leave Denny a lot of time off, but they treasured their moments together. Denny graduated from the NCO Academy as a sergeant at the end of August.

Anti-war sentiment in the country was growing, and Iowa was no exception. Denny's sister Barbara was a part of the protests against the war, which caused a big rift in the family. There weren't many protests in Cedar Rapids, but there were in Iowa City. Later, Barbara was part of that. Denny didn't take part in any demonstrations against the war before he was drafted and certainly didn't now. He didn't have strong feelings against the war while he was in training; he only knew he didn't want to go to Vietnam. Susie didn't want him to go either. They just accepted it. It was what it was. They went with the flow. What else could they do?

On September 2, 1969, Denny was sent to Fort Lewis outside Seattle to join a basic training cycle. This was on the job training as an NCO cadre member. Susie went out to visit and still remembers going up in the Space Needle. The rest of the trip was a blank.

Of course, Denny received his orders for Vietnam after the cycle was over. Once again, he was given a short leave before he was to report for overseas movement to Vietnam. It would be the last time he would see his wife and family for a year. The leave began on November 14, 1969, and he was supposed to report to Oakland Army Depot on December 2. Denny left Iowa for the coast but decided to make a pit stop or two on the way.

Barbara had left home, and no one knew where she was. Denny figured she might be in San Francisco, so on the way to report for transport to Vietnam, he went to San Francisco to look for her. Yes, you read that right. He made his own detour while on active duty. When he arrived, Denny called his friend Tim Petersen, who was also in the army now and stationed nearby at the Presidio. He told Tim he was going to Vietnam and wanted to see him. Tim met him at the airport, and the first thing Denny said was that he was AWOL. Tim exclaimed, "You're what?" Denny said, "I'm AWOL! Everybody else was getting thirty days before they leave for that godforsaken country, and I'm going to take mine!" His attitude was, "What can they do? Send me to Vietnam?"

Denny never did find Barbara. It turned out she was back in Iowa.

He finally reported in on December 12 and was promptly busted from Sergeant to Specialist 4.

17 December 1969

Dear Grandmother and Grandfather,

I have been here at the Oakland California overseas reception station since the thirteenth waiting to be shipped to Viet Nam. It is a lonesome worried type of waiting. There are three formations a day at which they read out names of men who will within hours be boarding a plane for Viet Nam. It is impossible to tell when your name will come up. Other than the three formations & a few trivial details there is nothing to do but wander around this small post we are restricted to. Actually, the time has gone rather fast having spent most of it in their very nice little post library. However, I am certain that in time I will grow tired of this.
Leave once again was a life saver. I was home for a total of four weeks. Susie took the last week off and we went to Chicago and spent three enjoyable days wandering there. Leaving Susie turned out to be tougher than I anticipated, and I hope it will be the last time I ever have to say goodbye to her for a very long time.
Denny

Denny heard his name called and was manifested on a flight bound for Vietnam on December 19, 1969. Not the best Christmas present.

Carey Pratt

Leaving home for the army was a big adventure for some, especially those who enlisted on their own. But for those drafted with a wife and children, it was far from exciting. It was a duty they did not shirk, but, for most, it wasn't something to look forward to. For Carey, it was an obligation he felt required to perform. There was no talk of going to Canada and hiding from the draft. Like so many young Americans, he did what he felt was the honorable thing. He was very patriotic and he went.

Theresa accompanied him to the bus station in downtown Kokomo that cold January morning. Other inductees and enlistees were gathered for the first leg of their journey to learn to become soldiers—nervous chatter, cigarettes, bravado all hiding their apprehension. That was the pervasive attitude among the young men; many were just boys, some fresh out of high school, some never having finished high school. Some had been given a choice by a judge: army, navy, marines, or jail. Few with that choice ever chose jail, even during wartime.

Carey spent his last moments with Theresa in solitude within the controlled chaos. Then the time came. The last kiss goodbye. Board the bus for the four-hour ride to Fort Knox, Kentucky, and basic training.

Basic training began on January 28, seven days after being sworn in. Basic training was two months long. The old "temporary" World War II barracks that they called home were never warm. Every other window was left open two inches, letting in the cold Kentucky air. They trained on, despite the temperatures, learning the skills of soldiering. Skills that hopefully keep them alive when they reached Vietnam. At least, that was where most would wind up.

When basic training was almost over, their platoon sergeant called the group to gather around. It was time to find out what their next assignment would be. Those who enlisted for a particular school already knew, so there were no surprises there. Most enlistees had signed up for a specific job, usually a technical job that would keep them out of combat, or so they hoped. For the draftees, it was another story. They would now find out their fate.

Carey Pratt heard his name called out: MOS 11 Bravo 20 (combat infantryman), Fort Polk, Louisiana—Tigerland. The last stop before Vietnam.

Carey proceeded to Fort Polk directly from Fort Knox without any leave time. Like Denny Martin, he excelled at Fort Polk. He was well-liked and respected, a natural leader. The army knew a talented soldier when they saw one. He was offered additional training as an NCO candidate. If he were able to pass this course, he would graduate as a sergeant. NCOs who graduated from this course were called shake-'n'-bake sergeants. Short training, instant promotion, and then on-the-job training, OJT, at a training unit before shipping overseas to Vietnam.

Carey finished Infantry AIT at Fort Polk and was given a thirty-day leave before reporting to Fort Benning for training as an NCO candidate. The army was losing a lot of noncommissioned officers in Vietnam, and they needed replacements, so they pushed the candidates through.

Theresa was able to come down to Georgia to be with Carey, but their time together was limited. They spent their free time socializing with new friends, swimming at the post pool, and just being together.

Carey graduated from the course as a buck sergeant on September 12, 1969, and was then sent to Fort McClellan, Alabama, for on-the-job training as an NCO. The training was one thing; this was a time to put all he had learned to the test. Not a test like combat but a chance to use the skills he learned.

Theresa joined Carey in Alabama, but this was a lonely time for her as there wasn't a group of women in similar situations that she could relate to. It was here that she became pregnant. Carey and Theresa remained at Fort McClellan until the end of November when he received the inevitable orders for Vietnam.

Carey and Theresa weren't surprised when he received his orders. They knew it was coming. If the idea of going to Vietnam scared Carey, he did an excellent job not showing it. Theresa was scared enough for both of them. The war was on the news every night, and the casualties in 1969 were high. Most were infantrymen like Carey.

Carey finished at Fort McClellan and was once again given a leave. The couple arrived back in Indiana just before Thanksgiving; they would be able to enjoy the holidays with family. His mother had found the couple an apartment for their last leave. When Theresa saw the apartment, she told her mother-in-law that they couldn't stay there. The bed was like a sofa, and they could not sleep on it for the next month. They quickly found a three-room apartment for their last month together and loved it.

Christmas came, and the whole family had a wonderful time even though Carey would be heading to Vietnam shortly. It was wonderful to live like ordinary people and put Vietnam out of their minds—for the most part anyway.

Carey's leave was up before thew knew it, and it was time to go. Once again, Carey boarded a bus in Kokomo to take him back to the army and this time on to Vietnam. His mom was trying to get Theresa not to cry. Of course, sometimes you can't hold it back.

David Schultz

David arrived at Fort Bliss, Texas, to begin basic training on June 30, 1969. The usual routine at the reception station took a couple of days, and he joined his training company on July 2. Usually, there would be no duty on the upcoming holiday, but basic training would not wait. There was a war on, after all.

David adapted well to army life. He took whatever they threw at him and kept going. He quietly carried on and did his duty. Typical for David. He was younger than most at seventeen but not by much. Excelling at marksmanship, he qualified on the range as expert with the M-14 and as marksman with the M-16.

David graduated from basic training and left Fort Bliss on August 29 to travel to Fort Eustis, Virginia, for AIT. With aviation in his blood from the Civil Air Patrol and Air Force ROTC, he had enlisted in the army reserves for an aviation job. His enlistment agreement was for two years active and four years in the reserves, but he could pick his MOS. David was an intelligent young man, and he qualified for just about any job the army had. Training as a

Chinook CH-47 helicopter repairer was his choice. The army assigned the MOS number of 67U20 to this job.

David was not given any leave time before reporting in for his next phase of army life. His crash course training lasted a mere three months. This was not a whole lot of time to learn all about a complicated aircraft like the Chinook. But it would have to do. Replacements were always in demand in Vietnam. They would often end up serving as door gunners and possible crew chiefs.

It was no surprise that when the course ended, most of the students, including David, received orders for Vietnam. I am sure many hoped for Germany or an assignment in the United States. It was not meant to be. Like it or not, Vietnam was calling.

His orders allowed for a twenty-day leave before shipping out to Vietnam, so he packed up his gear and personal belongings and left Fort Eustis for Harlingen, Texas. He arrived home on December 9. He would be home for Christmas this year but would miss it in 1970. His tour would not be over in time for next Christmas.

He spent as much time as he could at the ranch with Donna. He continued to help out while home, driving the van and working on construction projects and just about anything else they needed to get done.

One day he borrowed a motorcycle. Donna still doesn't know who loaned it to him. They were just cruising around in the neighborhood, not going anywhere in particular, when David proposed. They talked about going to Mexico since they were right on the border. It would have been only a thirty-minute drive to get to

Reynosa, and they could have gotten married. Legally married. But Donna did not know where her birth certificate was and they couldn't get married without it. They would have to wait and marry when he returned from Vietnam. She was old enough to get married in Mexico, but since she was only fifteen, that would have brought a lot of trouble in the US. Donna's mother still did not approve of David. Marriage in Mexico would have led to horrible consequences for Donna after David left. Plus, living at home, waiting for her husband to come home would have been unbearable. They would have to wait for David to return home in a year.

Before leaving for Vietnam, David had a long talk with his mother. He asked her if she minded if he made the ranch the beneficiary of his $10,000 serviceman's group life insurance policy. If something happened to him, he wanted the money to be used to help finish the church. She simply told him, "It's your life." David changed the beneficiary to the youth ranch. When he told Reverend Morillo what he'd done, he said, "If I die, I want that money to build a new youth ranch, someplace kids like me can find a purpose in life. You know, Wally, I am not afraid of dying, and I don't worry about it since I know where I will spend eternity—in heaven."

A service was held for a parishioner who was going to Africa to visit his father. His parents had been divorced, and the father was doing missionary work there. They had a big celebration and an emotional send-off, but David's departure was quiet. He was going to Vietnam and war, but it seemed that they took little notice of him leaving for Vietnam, despite his gesture with the life insurance. After all the volunteering he had done at the ranch, it was almost like he was there one minute, and then he was gone. Was that oversight on the part of the ranch or just David's quiet way of leaving?

At home in Harlingen, David prepared for his departure. He packed his duffel bag, kissed his mother, told her how much he loved her, and quietly left. Donna did not have a car or any way to accompany him to the airport, so David left alone.

Just before the 1970 New Year, David began his journey to Vietnam.

Mike Vullo

Mike reported for active duty in the army on April 22, 1969. Being a draftee, he was only required to serve for two years. The problem was that his fate was entirely out of his control. Most draftees at this time were being sent to the infantry, combat medics, and artillery

Basic training was at Fort Ord, California. Not around the corner from his home but not across the country either. At least he wouldn't have to get used to a climate change while adjusting to military life.

At twenty, Mike was older than a lot of the inductees. Of course, like all new soldiers, he was given a battery of tests to determine his aptitude. Mike was smart, and he scored well. He and most of the other draftees were allowed to change their status and enlist for three years, becoming regular army as opposed to a draftee for two years. Because of his scores, he could pick almost any school the army had. The thought of being an infantryman or medic in

Vietnam did not appeal to him. Serving another year in a better job had great appeal. Without much hesitation, Mike signed on.

He chose to go to signal school and train as a weapons support radar repairer, a course taught at Fort Monmouth, New Jersey. Weapons support radar was commonly known as counter-battery radar. A counter-battery radar is a system that detects artillery projectiles fired by one or more howitzers, mortars, or rocket launchers. It analyzed the trajectory, pinpointing the position on the ground of the weapon that fired it. This system was critical in Vietnam, where rocket and mortar attacks were frequent. This tracking radar was always in the field with the artillery, and they experienced many breakdowns that needed a quick repair.

This was an excellent course for Mike, especially since it was twenty-seven weeks long, and he could have Kathi there with him the whole time.

Shortly before basic training completed, the platoon was called together by their senior drill sergeant, who read out everyone's orders. When he came to Mike, he called out, "Vullo, Fort Sill, MOS 13A20, Field Artillery." *What? Field artillery?* That wasn't what he signed up for. The first sergeant told him to deal with it when he got to Fort Sill. They would work it out—typical army, passing the buck.

Upon completion of Basic Training in June 1969, Kathi, her mother and sisters traveled to Ft. Ord for Mike's graduation. They drove back home after the ceremony to complete preparations for their wedding on 5 July. Mike had a thirty-day leave, they didn't have a lot of time to prepare for the wedding. Marrying into a

Sicilian family meant strong traditions and numerous guests from across the country.

Mike and Kathi honeymooned in a cabin at Big bear Lake in the San Bernardino Mountains. Their time was spent fishing and hiking in the lovely mountainside. They talked about the future as much as possible with their lives now controlled by the military and the war raging in Vietnam. The first thing was to get Michael's school assignment cleared up.

Mike proceeded to Oklahoma, assigned to Battery A, Enlisted Student Battalion, where he remained for three to four weeks, trying to straighten out this snafu. Eventually, the army figured it out and cut him orders for the right school at Fort Monmouth. Kathi was in the process of getting ready for the drive to Fort Sill to be with Mike when he showed up unannounced at her parent's home early in the morning the day before she was to leave for Oklahoma. He had been given time to get her and move to New Jersey. Kathi had no idea as he wanted to surprise her. They packed up their new '69 Volkswagen bug, loaded up their kitten, Tiffany, and drove to New Jersey. They stopped in St. Louis to visit her mother's sister and in Chicago to visit her mother's father. They almost lost Tiffany in Pennsylvania when she jumped out of the car. All in all, it was a great trip.

Once they arrived, they discovered that there were no quarters available on base. On a salary of $125 per month, the housing possibilities were minimal. But they found an apartment in the caretaker's quarters of a big house off-base. It was a studio apartment, and there was one big problem in this small space there was no stove. The kitchen consisted of a hot plate, a small refrigerator, and a sink—that was it! Luckily, it did have a bathroom. The rent was eighty-five dollars a month, and their car payment was forty-eight dollars a month, so Kathi had to find work quickly. They were young, and life was good—they survived just fine.

When Mike joined the newly started class, he quickly made friends with Mike Gandee. Gandee was in the same situation as Mike. He had been drafted but reenlisted for another year in the army. Mike and Gandee spent a lot of time together while at Fort Monmouth and became close friends.

This course usually had fifteen to twenty students in each class, and this one was no exception. As it neared completion, the question on everyone's mind was, where would they be stationed? Everyone expected orders for Vietnam, of course. They all waited with anticipation for their orders. Some wanted to go, but most were hoping for anywhere else in the world. Everyone was nervous and perhaps a little scared. No one would know for sure until they held their orders in their hands.

Their questions were answered at the afternoon formation. Everyone waited in anticipation as names were called and their next assignment given. Mike and Gandee were among the majority heading to the Southeast Asia war zone.

Mike and Kathi knew the dangers involved with service in Vietnam. This was the army, and some things were entirely out of your control. Vietnam was one of those things. At least it was a technical job and safer than most.

Gandee drove with Mike and Kathi back to California when school ended. They drove straight through, it took about three days. It was pretty crowded in Mike's VW beetle with three people and Kathi's white cat. Crowded it may have been but it did save on expenses for all. Kathi and Gandee got to know each other on that long drive.

Larry Butcher

The draft caught up with Larry just as he feared, and his induction followed on May 1, 1969. He was nineteen years old. His draft notice came a few months shy of the national lottery, which took effect on December 1, 1969. A few months made all the difference in Larry's case. If his notice had not come until December, he would have been spared from having to serve. When the lottery numbers were called, Larry's birthday was pulled as number 284. The magic number for those drafted in 1969 was anything under 195. He could have lived out his life in California unburdened by the war. Who knows why things happen the way they do. Sometimes fate takes hold of life. Sometimes for the better, sometimes for the worse.

Dale Iverson was a friend of Larry's, a classmate from fifth grade through high school. Dale was drafted right along with Larry. They were both inducted in Modesto and bused to Fresno, where they were sworn in. Welcome to the United States Army, boys! This is just the beginning!

Larry and Dale boarded a bus in Fresno for Fort Ord and basic training. Larry had already declared that he was a conscientious objector. Based on his religious upbringing, Larry refused to carry a gun. He did not shirk his duty or try to dodge the draft, but his religious convictions remained strong. The army always had a reputation for being hard on conscientious objectors. Time would tell how that worked out.

Larry and Dale were surprised to find they were assigned to the same company for basic training. Larry's status created problems, though. As his group began their training schedule, he was held back. Being labeled as a conscientious objector delayed his training again and again. He was put on KP duty over and over. Finally, he was released and received orders to Fort Sam, Houston, for training as a medic. Amazingly, Dale was also sent there for the same training.

Larry and Dale graduated from the course in September 1969, both with an MOS of 91B20, Combat Medic. As was typical, shortly before graduation, everyone received their orders for the next duty station. Both Larry and Dale were being sent to Vietnam. It shouldn't have been a surprise as there was a great need for medics in Vietnam after the heavy fighting in 1968 and 1969.

Larry was sick when he saw where he was going. The words of his grandfather flashed through his mind; "If you are drafted, you will die in Vietnam." For Larry, receiving orders to Vietnam was like a death sentence. For the first two days after he received his orders, he didn't talk to anyone and couldn't eat. He did not expect to return home alive. It took him two days to regain his appetite.

Larry and Dale both received a thirty-day leave before having to report to Oakland Army Depot for movement overseas.

Dale went home to his family, and Larry went back to his wife. The Butchers spent the next thirty days together in somewhat of a daze. The leave went all too fast; the departure date sped at them like an out-of-control freight train. No way to stop it, time going faster and faster.

Larry and Dale met up again when they both reported to Oakland Army Depot on a Friday in October 1969 for transport to Vietnam. They checked in at the Overseas Replacement Center; then Dale's mother picked them up and took them to her home in Modesto for the weekend. AWOL. Saturday morning, they went to church and once again spent the night with Dale's mother. On Sunday morning, Dale's mother drove them back to the Oakland Army Depot, and they went directly to the chaplain's office.

They told the chaplain, who happened to be a Lieutenant Colonel, that they had been AWOL. They just wanted to spend the weekend at home one last time before shipping out to Vietnam. He listened sympathetically and gave them both his business card. He told them what building to report to and told them to say only, "Call the Colonel," no matter what anyone said to them or what threats they threw their way.

Larry and Dale reported in, and the powers that be were furious but could do nothing. All Larry and Dale kept saying was "Call the Colonel." Finally, seeing their threats were useless, they issued them their jungle gear, and that was the end of it. They left the next morning by bus for Travis Air Force Base and their flight to Vietnam.

Harlen Metzger

Like Carey Pratt, Harlen jumped on the bus with a full complement of recruits from southwest Indiana—next stop, Fort Knox, Kentucky. His starting date for basic training was July 10, 1969. Exactly one year before the Chinook #65-07999's fateful day in Vietnam.

Harlen scored high on his battery of standardized military tests, so high, in fact, that an offer for officer candidate school (OCS) followed. Everyone knew that life as an officer versus an enlisted man was much preferred. However, being an officer had its drawbacks. First, you would probably wind up in the infantry. Then again, Harlen would probably wind up there anyway. Second was the length of service required. Harlen was informed that he would have to serve four years. Two years was bad enough, but four was more than he could handle. Harlen took a pass on OCS and would spend his two years as an enlisted soldier.

Harlen did well while in basic training. With graduation approaching, Harlen found out he was going to be promoted to private E-2. One step up from private, but because of the promotion, he was given a raise in his meager pay and allowed to wear one stripe on his sleeve, indicating his rank. It was an honor as few soldiers were promoted to E-2 upon graduation.

Harlen was given a certificate at graduation stating: *This accelerated promotion is made under the provisions of paragraph 7-19, AR 600-200, and is the result of your dedicated efforts, your exemplary conduct and attitude, and your demonstrated qualities of leadership. The officers and men of this organization join me in*

congratulating you as you receive this recognition of your
accomplishments during your period of basic combat training. 8
Sept. 1969

Brenda and Harlen's mother drove down to Fort Knox to attend his graduation. Harlen was with Brenda and his mom after the ceremony when he opened the envelope with the orders for his next assignment and course of additional training. He silently stared at them and couldn't believe what they said. Infantry, Fort Polk. He started to cry and looked at Brenda and said, "I am a dead man."

Harlen was given a twenty-day leave before having to report at Fort Polk. The training at Fort Polk was hard and intense. Not as hard as what they would be facing in Vietnam. Inevitably Harlen received orders for Vietnam. First he would have a leave home.

During the leave between AIT and Vietnam, Brenda and Harlen decided to get married. Before Harlen, Brenda had previously been engaged to a soldier who also went to Vietnam. Brenda was only sixteen at the time, and he was twenty. She didn't want to get engaged, but her dad told her that she should say yes since her boyfriend, Gary, was going to war. She waited for him while he served his tour. He was in the infantry also and was shot in the leg while picking up wounded soldiers. When he came home, he broke up with her.

Brenda told Harlen she didn't know if she would wait for him if they weren't married, as she had been through that already. So, the couple ended up driving to Indianapolis and used the address of a friend of hers to get a marriage certificate and asked a judge to waive the waiting period. They drove back to Evansville and found a justice of the peace to marry them. The knot was tied on December 5, 1969. The newlyweds drove over to the home of Harlen's brother Mike and his wife, Carol, and told them of their marriage. They were the only ones that knew.

Harlen didn't want to tell his parents as he felt they were already so upset about his going to Vietnam. So, the couple didn't live together from December 5 to his reporting to go to Vietnam on December 13. At a large family get-together before he left, one of his aunts asked Brenda if she wanted to get married into this family. It was kind of a joke. But Brenda was hurt that Harlen wouldn't acknowledge that they were already married.

A few weeks after Harlen left for Vietnam, Carol called Brenda and told her that Harlen's younger sister, Mariann, had pointed out in a picture that it looked like Harlen had on a wedding ring! The family had been contacting local counties to see if they had gotten a marriage certificate, without success. Brenda decided to tell them about their marriage. She was nervous about telling Harlen's parents, so she had a girlfriend accompany her. The two girls drove over to the Metzger's house to tell them. She met no opposition from them. Hank said it was a good thing as it gave Harlen a reason to come back home and also would prevent him from marrying a Vietnamese woman.

Brenda received a letter from Harlen saying he had gotten a letter from his parents saying they knew he was married. At first, he was stunned. Then he said it was OK and that his parents didn't give him a hard time. The marriage was now in the open. Now he just had to survive Vietnam.

Chapter 3

Vietnam

He who fights monsters should see to it,

That in the process, he himself doesn't become a monster.

And when you look long into the abyss,

That abyss also looks into you.

-Frederick Nietzsche

The Year of the Monkey, 1968, was over. It had been a violent year in Vietnam and the United States. The Tet Offensive saw heavy fighting throughout the country, sparking protests across the nation. US Casualties were high in 1968, including 16,592 deaths and 92,820 wounded. Constant TV coverage of the fighting created an enormous division in the country: there were the hawks, the doves, and the silent majority. Unfortunately, there was no end in sight. The war dragged on.

In 1969, the number of American military personnel in Vietnam peaked at 543,000. For the 25th Division in Military Region III, it was the drudgery of search and destroy, hunt the enemy and kill them. Body counts were what the generals wanted— big ones. Ground was not captured and held. It was just a constant dangerous cat-and-mouse game. It wasn't a game for the average grunt, but it was deadly.

Back in the States, Richard M. Nixon took the oath of office as the new president. Concerning Vietnam, he promised to achieve "peace with honor." He aimed to negotiate a settlement that would allow the half-million US troops in Vietnam to be withdrawn, while still allowing South Vietnam to survive. For the soldiers serving there, they believed they just had to stay alive until they were withdrawn or had finished their one-year tour. Despite the political rhetoric, the killing continued.

Early in his presidency, President Nixon authorized Operation Menu, the bombing of North Vietnamese and Viet Cong bases within Cambodia. This campaign targeted the NVA and VC base camps and sanctuaries hiding there. These targets were previously off-limits to American forces, at least officially. This bombing campaign began on March 18, 1969 and continued until the end of May of 1970.

In April of 1969, the total US combat deaths in Vietnam exceeded the 33,629 men killed in the Korean War. Approximately 25,000 more would die before it was all over. In Military Region III, the 25th Division continued to hunt the enemy. Skirmishes and booby traps were the order of the day.

On June 8, 1969, President Nixon met with South Vietnamese President Nguyen Van Thieu on Midway Island in the Pacific to discuss the withdrawal of American troops from Vietnam. They discussed Nixon's plan of Vietnamization-turning over the fighting of the war to the South Vietnamese. They also discussed the negotiating strategy with the North Vietnamese at the Paris Peace Talks.

There had been too much invested in the war-material, money, and American lives—to just call it quits. Nixon told Thieu that we must end the war honorably but end it we must. He told Thieu, "The war in Vietnam concerns not only Vietnam but the entire Pacific. The people of South Vietnam, however, have the greatest stake. If peace is inadequate, there will be repercussions all over Asia. There can be no reward for those engaged in aggression. At the same time, self-determination is not only in the Vietnamese interest but in the American interest as well. It would improve the prospects of peace throughout the Pacific."

The stage was set—time to get the hell out. On July 25, 1969, the president pledged to withdraw 25,000 American troops by August 31.

Another significant milestone happened in 1969. On September 2, Ho Chi Minh died of a heart attack. Twenty-four years earlier, on this day in 1945, just hours after Japan surrendered ending World War II, Ho Chi Minh declared Vietnam's independence from France. Vietnam would now be torn apart by a war that would last decades.

With troops being withdrawn and Ho Chi Minh dead, the hope was that the war would soon end. It didn't. The fighting, and the protesting, would continue for over three more years.

It was evident to everyone serving that the war was a lost cause. Now they fought for each other. There would be no World War II-type victories in Vietnam.

Larry Butcher

Larry Butcher arrived in Vietnam on November 1, 1969. As a trained medic, he could be assigned almost anywhere in South Vietnam. There were many possible places and jobs. Some were more dangerous than others. That was relative. There were no really safe places in Vietnam. The two most likely assignments were either at a hospital on one of the large bases or as a line medic with one of the infantry divisions. He found himself assigned to the 25th Division in Military Region III. More details on what his actual job would be would have to wait until he arrived at the sprawling base at Cu Chi, home of the Tropic Lightning Division. The troops called it the Electric Strawberry Division. The shoulder patch was a lightning bolt superimposed on a taro leaf. Since no one seemed to know what a taro leaf was, it became in their minds a strawberry.

Larry's assignment was HHC Company, 2nd Battalion, 14th Infantry. Shortly after arriving, he was attached to Delta Company, 2nd Platoon, where he would be a medic for the next six months. Their area of operation included Dau Tieng, Tay Ninh, Go Dau Ha, Trang Bang, Hồ Bò Woods, Boi Loi Woods, Cu Chi, Trung Lap, FSB Devin, FSB Pershing, FSB Patton II, Patrol Base Hunsley, Katum Airfield, and the Mushroom. This area was on the Cambodian border and infested with Viet Cong, NVA, and booby traps of all types.

While at FSB Patton II north of Cu Chi early in November 1969, he was befriended by PFC John Robinson, one of the grunts with 2nd Platoon. Larry had been with them for only about two weeks, and John took the time to explain the routines and what to expect. Recently everything had been quiet, calm, and no action or contact.

Larry quickly became acclimated to the heat and started getting to know the men he would be working and living with in Delta Company. Right away, he was offered a forty-five-caliber pistol to carry as a sidearm, which many medics did, but he refused. He was a conscientious objector and refused to carry a weapon. As he prepared to go on his first patrol, Jim Deppe, one of the other soldiers in his platoon, came up to him and asked, "Where's your weapon, Doc?" Butcher replied, "I do not carry one." Jim looked at him for a minute, studying him and then said: "Fuck you. If the shit hits the fan, you are on your own," and he walked away. Larry remembers that interchange today as clearly as when it happened. He walked over to him and said, "Jim, I am sorry you feel that way, but if it does hit the fan and you're wounded, I'll be there for you," and left it at that.

It wasn't long after that when Larry experienced his first casualty. On November 14, elements of the 2nd Platoon set up a night ambush on some rice paddy dikes. There were about six inches of water in the paddy, and everyone was trying to stay dry. Larry was out at the edge of the perimeter with John Robinson as he set up his position. John told him he thought he should be near the center with 2nd Lieutenant Darczyn and his RTO. So, Larry moved to that position for the night. At about 2200, he was startled awake by shouting: "Shoot! SHOOT!" Then gunshots and activity. It was pitch-black, no moonlight.

Artillery fired illumination flares for them so they could see. They found John sitting up in the paddy water with a sucking chest wound. Larry watched his friend's blood, mixed with paddy water, go in and bubble out with every breath he took. Larry quickly put a Vaseline gauze bandage over the wound and called for an urgent Dust-off. This was his first casualty as a combat medic in Vietnam, and it was his friend. When the Dust-off arrived with its landing lights on, the platoon all knew they were easy targets, and speed was critical. They placed John on a stretcher with the damaged lung down. He was given a morphine syrette for the pain. After John was on the helicopter, the pilot would not take off. In the confusion and darkness, claymore mine wires had wrapped around the skids, and if they took off, they would take the claymore mines with them. The Dust-off medic started shouting, "Get him off! Get him off!" Larry had a choice: take his friend off and watch the Dust-off leave without him or cut the wires.

Standing in the paddy water, he knew he was grounded, and there could be an electric charge created by the helicopter rotors. Knowing that an electric charge might set off the claymore mines, Larry took out his scissors and cut the wires. If the mines exploded, it would be the end of all of them. His luck held. After the wires were cut, the Dust-off took off for the 12th Evac Hospital in Cu Chi. The bitch of it was that it was friendly fire that got him. John had been accidentally shot by one of his platoon mates. The bullet entered his right lung and liver, causing massive hemorrhaging. He died later that night, at 0202 on November 15. He was nineteen years old.

Larry learned the next morning of the death. At that moment, he made himself a promise that he would never forget him, his friendship, or his kindness toward him. That morning was the only time he shed tears in Vietnam. You had to toughen up quickly. There was no time to mourn or even think about the dead and wounded. The environment was hazardous, obviously, and you had to keep on your toes and be ready at all times. Larry, like most medics, would now be called Doc, a moniker he would be known by for the rest of his life.

Patrols continued, men were wounded, the enemy killed. It all went on and on, seemingly without an end in sight. Delta Company carried on, plodding through rice paddy and jungle. The things they all feared most were booby traps. And in their area of operations, there were a lot. There was a constant turnover of troops due to wounds from these bobby traps.

The men of Delta would hump all day, and when they took a break, they would just sit on their asses and move around as little as possible, not wanting to accidentally trip an explosion that would kill or maim themselves or other members of the outfit. It was all about trying to get everyone home alive and in one piece.

On December 6, after only a short month in the field, Larry and his platoon were airlifted into the Hồ Bò Woods. Within minutes on the ground, a booby trap with a tripwire was discovered. A sergeant and the RTO stayed back to set a charge and destroy it. The call "fire in the hole in ten minutes" came over the radio. Larry looked at his watch, and within one minute, there was an explosion! "Medic!" someone yelled. Larry rushed back to them. The RTO had tripped a second booby trap they hadn't seen. Standing over him, Larry immediately called for an urgent Dust-off.

A forward observer officer (FO) was about ten meters from Larry. As he walked toward Larry, he reached his hand out and took hold of what looked like a dead stick. The FO grabbed the branch, and there was another explosion. He had tripped another booby trap. Larry was utterly frozen with fear! He was afraid to move his feet or even shift his weight. Another medic responded to assist the F O. Standing there, waiting for the Dust-off, Larry studied the ground. He looked around both of his feet, searching for tripwires or any evidence of another booby trap. Fear gripped him, but he couldn't stand there forever. Larry thought, *If it's my time…it's my time.* He forced himself to move and care for the wounded. He had a job to do no matter the risks. He had been immobile for only a minute, but it had seemed like hours. He brushed the fear aside and worked on the wounded men. When the Dust-off arrived, he helped load the men on it. The patrol continued.

Harlen Metzger

Harlen Metzger left the United States for Vietnam on December 13, 1969. The long flight over was quiet with the new replacements trying to sleep and not think of the year ahead of them. Twenty-two hours later, they arrived in South Vietnam tired, nervous, and as ready as they could be for what was to follow.

Harlen and the rest of the new troops were conspicuous in their brand-new jungle fatigues and boots. You could spot an FNG miles away. But the newness would soon be peeled away. They were herded like cattle off the plane into the hot, humid air of South Vietnam. After boarding olive-green buses with wire mesh covering the windows, they began the trek to the replacement center.

The men slowly became oriented to the tropical heat. Sleep was fleeting as most were too hot, excited, or exhausted to sleep. Harlen spent Christmas and New Year's Day at the replacement center waiting for orders. Finally, they came through: 25th Division out of Cu Chi.

Denny Martin

December 19: welcome to Vietnam. Now what? That was the question on everyone's mind. The answer? Twice daily formations, calling the names of those with orders. Endless work details in the heat. The smells of Vietnam. The aromas of the shit burners. Sweat burning your eyes and soaking your new jungle fatigues. Old hands catcalling you FNG, Fucking New Guy, holding up their hands and with the index finger and thumb close together, showing how short they were. Low man on the ladder.

OK, 364 days and wake up, then home.

Finally at one of the endless formations, they called out, "Martin, Dennis!" Orders were in, and it was time to begin his tour in earnest. His first helicopter ride took him over rice paddies and jungle to the sprawling base at Cu Chi. The 25th Division would be his home for the next year.

It was Christmastime and everyone back home was shopping, preparing for the big day! What a wonderful time! Of course, this wasn't the case in Vietnam, and it certainly wasn't the case for

Denny. After arriving in Vietnam, it seemed that Christmas was going to be just another day. Sure, there was some celebrating, attempts to bring the holidays to life-an occasional Christmas tree in a hooch or club. Many of the troops, especially those in support, enjoyed a well-deserved day off, a good meal, a couple of beers. Holidays in a war zone could be lonely times for those serving. In war you create a bond with those you serve with that most civilians will never understand. This camaraderie helped fight off the loneliness of being so far from home.

On December 29, Denny was assigned to Delta Company, 2nd Bn., 14th Infantry. Happy New Year.

Larry Butcher

It had been a long night, and Larry was beat. On December 23, 1969, 2nd Platoon was at FSB Venice East near Trung Lap for two days doing morning mine sweeps on the dirt road leading to the village. Larry didn't have to go on these sweeps as they were considered low risk. He could stay at Venice in a nice, safe (relatively) bunker. Larry asked the troops going on the road sweep to wake him up the next morning, December 24, because he wanted to take some pictures of Trung Lap.

When they woke him Christmas Eve, Larry was too tired and stayed on his cot. Just before they left, they went in a second time and asked him again if he wanted to go. Larry sat up on the edge of the cot for a few moments, felt exhausted, and lay back down. The pictures would wait for another day.

None of those conducting the sweep came back. Two mama-sans, two civilian women, with command-detonated claymore mines blew them away. Four Americans were killed, seven more wounded. Four ARVN South Vietnamese soldiers were also injured as well as four Vietnamese civilians.

Gary Trapman responded from FSB Patton II to care for the wounded. Forty-four years later, as Gary told Larry about the scene he and the others found, he had tears in his eyes. Larry told Gary that he always felt guilty that he wasn't there when his men needed him the most.

Despite the troop withdrawals, 1969 drew to a close with no end to the war in sight. The killing would continue.

In January 1970, the 25th Division continued to operate primarily north of Cu Chi in the western area of Military Region III. This was a relatively quiet time for the division. "Relatively" was the watchword. There was no quiet time in Vietnam, just some periods quieter than others. Casualties continued from sporadic encounters with the enemy. Booby traps were once again a constant cause of losses. You never knew when they would happen.

David Schultz

New Year's Day, 1970. PFC David Schultz arrived in the Republic of Vietnam. His entry was typical of so many other GIs: tired, excited, and scared as he left the plane onto the tarmac and was blasted by the tropical heat for the first time. It wasn't just the heat; it was also the humidity that assailed the some two hundred FNGs as they began the journey that day to the processing center at the sprawling base at Long Binh. Not all of those troops were new to Vietnam, though. There were some second and even third tour veterans in the crowd. To them, this was all old hat.

David spent only a few days at the 90th Replacement in Long Binh waiting for his assignment. On January 5 his orders came through. His assignment, the 369th Aviation Bn., 242nd Assault Support Helicopter Company (Muleskinners) at Cu Chi. Cu Chi? *Where was that?* he wondered. Wherever it was, he was anxious is get on with it and get settled in his new home.

He was put on a helicopter for the flight to Cu Chi which he soon learned was only about forty miles from Long Binh. The trip was uneventful, and it gave David his first real look at the Vietnamese countryside. They cruised above rice paddies with glistening water filling them, streams ringed with lush foliage, and the Saigon River. Small rural villages dotted the countryside, farmers working in the fields. Then there were the scars of war. Bomb and artillery craters dotted the landscape. Some older ones were filled with water; others were dry, more recent. The Vietnamese countryside was beautiful, and David quietly took it all in.

Arrival at a new base is always disorienting. The aircraft that brings in a new replacement is rarely from their assigned unit. The first step is finding your company, then getting checked in. Assignment to a hooch and stowing your gear follows, always being careful to lock up your belongings. There were a lot of men in the army ready to "borrow" your possessions.

David would be spending his year in Vietnam repairing Chinooks. There were always mechanical issues and, of course, battle damage. Quick repairs were required to get them back in the air, so long hours were the norm. David settled into the routine of working twelve-hour days six to seven days a week, keeping the Chinooks in the air. It was hot, dirty work, but he quietly did his job without complaint. Sleep was often interrupted by rocket and mortar attacks. Incoming fire would wake you up in an instant and send you to the floor or the nearest bunker. A Viet Cong sapper attack in February 1969 had destroyed several of the Muleskinner Chinooks and killed one man. Everyone at Cu Chi was aware of this attack even though it happened a year before. You had to stay alert to stay alive.

Carey Pratt

Sergeant Carey Pratt arrived in Vietnam on January 2, 1970, the day after David Schultz. Like David, Carey went to the 25th Division based at Cu Chi. There was one big exception, Carey was an infantryman, and he would be going out in the field.

Carey became a squad leader with Delta Company, 2nd Bn., 14th Infantry. At twenty-one years old, he was older than most of the troops in his squad, not to mention his company. Despite this as well as his training and OJT at Fort McClellan, Carey was pretty green. Smart, and savvy with the outdoors he adapted and learned quickly becoming an excellent leader in the field. He was looked up to and respected by his men.

Shortly after Carey arrived in Vietnam, Theresa found out she was pregnant. There was no way to tell Carey the news except by mail. It would take at least a week for the letter to reach its destination in Vietnam.

Early on in his tour, he was out with his squad on a night ambush patrol. The Vietnamese mosquitos must have been trained by the VC because they were always on the attack. Mosquitos weren't just a pest; they brought malaria and other exotic diseases. The military tried to control this by launching Operation Fly Swatter. In October 1966, a C-123 aircraft that had been spraying defoliant Agent Orange was given the mission of spraying insecticide, hoping to kill malaria-carrying mosquitos. The spraying continued throughout Vietnam until June 1972. These spaying missions were not without cost. In February 1971, a C-123 on an insecticide mission crashed near Phan Rang Air Base, killing five crew members.

Despite all the spraying, on this night, the mosquitos were out in force and on the attack. In the darkness, Cary was being eaten alive, and he decided to do something about it. He grabbed his mosquito repellant and started spraying it in his hand. Unfortunately, in the darkness, he didn't realize that the aerosol jet was pointed 180 degrees from where he thought it was. Instead of shooting the noxious fluid into his hand, it went straight into his eyes. This stuff was under a lot of pressure, and just the shot of it would've hurt. The liquid burned severely. Since they were out on patrol at night, he couldn't be medevacked. Poor Carey, he was forced to writhe in pain all night. Everyone felt sorry for him, but there was nothing they could do.

Denny Martin

This time next year, in 1971 Denny would be home with Susie and out of the army. Time to start counting the days. Denny was with his assigned unit in the field, Delta Company, 2nd Bn., 14th Infantry. He hadn't been there long but was already thinking about going home and getting out of the army. You couldn't blame him. He wasn't exactly happy about being drafted and leaving his wife and family to go halfway around the world to fight the Viet Cong and the NVA.

Denny was hoping for an early out from Vietnam and the army to go back to school. It was always possible to get out of the army early but difficult to leave Vietnam before your 365-day tour was up. Usually, the only way to leave Vietnam early was a serious enough wound to require medical attention in Japan or the United States. Not a good idea to get out of Vietnam duty that way. On January 3, 1970, Denny wrote this letter:

Mom & Dad

I guess Susie must have told you that I anticipate getting out of the Army in September so that I can go back to school. I don't think the Army will give me too much hassle about it. I guess it is a little too early to start counting the days but never the less I am certainly looking forward to being home in September.
Denny

Harlen Metzger

Delta, 2/14, was Harlen's new home. On January 7, he began his tour as a rifleman with Delta Company. After a short stint at Cu Chi, he was off to the field to join them. Initially, he was an assistant gunner for the M-60. Harlen was the biggest guy in the platoon, so he had to carry the most weight, at least while he was an FNG. Harlen did his job without complaint; that was the kind of guy he was. Not a whiner or complainer, and everyone liked him.

Their time in the field consisted of constant patrols and ambushes. A good day was when they could hunker down and hope they wouldn't have to engage the enemy. The war was going to end soon. No victory, just a withdrawal of American troops. Then the ARVNs were going to be on their own. As I said before, no one wanted to be the last person to die in Vietnam.

Night ambushes were always hard. Pitch-black, tons of mosquitos, and sheer exhaustion from having to hump in the heat all day. It was hard to stay awake for your watch, but they did it. They had to; it was too dangerous to fall asleep. Too risky for you and the entire platoon.

Harlen would quickly doze off when his watch was over, and when he did, he tended to snore. Every time he started to go to sleep, someone would shake him awake because they were afraid he would give their location away. He told one guy, "If you wake me up one more time, you don't have to worry about the gooks killing you because I will."

Denny Martin

Denny's letters took on a cynical tone as time went on. His frustration about the way operations were being carried out became apparent as he shared his observations home.

January 21, 1970
Mom & Dad

The company just returned from what could have been a bad operation. We went out two nights ago on a night raid of the local V.C. headquarters. We had to walk six kilometers (it turned out to be about eight) in the dark. There was a full moon and it was very open country but you still could not see well enough to detect booby traps which is what we fear the most in our area. To make matters worse our C.O. managed to get us lost and for several hours we were walking around at random. I don't think any of us know how we happened to stumble upon our objective. Despite the fact that helicopter gunships worked over the area for three hours after we sprang the raid at 3:30 am with machine guns & rockets, we only got six of the 30 V.C. suspected of staying there. Three and the six we found hiding in the brush when we swept through the area the next morning. It was certainly a flakey operation and I hope we don't do a repeat of it.
Denny

David Schultz

David and Donna wrote regularly. He told her stories about Cu Chi and the living conditions there and about the guys he worked with. He never told her about the dark side of the war. Donna told him about the ranch and the goings-on in Texas. She wrote to him that she had smoked her first joint behind Reverend Wally's house. David wasn't happy when she wrote about that but didn't make a fuss about it. He told her that before he joined the army, he had spent some time with his sister, who was a hippie and had the opportunity to smoke with her but didn't. His letters told her that a lot of people were smoking marijuana in Nam, but David would never try it. He just wasn't interested in it.

Donna's mother monitored all of Donna's letters, those she received, and those she sent. So, Donna would write a separate note, and once her mother read the letter, Donna would walk away, pretending to seal it and before she did, slip the note inside. She had written to David telling him there would be two letters inside if there was something she wanted to say but didn't want her mother to know. He would do the same. She was always the one who got the letter first and opened it and was able to retrieve his note before her mother saw the official letter, and that was how they communicated.

Donna missed David and was worried about his safety. She said a Rosary every night without fail while he was gone. Donna had been raised Catholic and prayed for him to return home safely so they could marry and share their life. David would be nineteen when he returned from Vietnam; Donna would be sixteen. They could get legally married then. They both counted the days.

At the 242nd, David was known as a quiet kind of guy, a loner perhaps? Still, he was always there if someone needed a hand with anything. He soon received a promotion to spec 4; it was well deserved.

Carey Pratt

Most of his experiences in the field during the first few months of 1970 consisted of patrols, night ambushes, and security sweeps near the Cambodian border. It was on one of these that Carey killed his first enemy soldier.

His platoon was on a mission, pushing through lush, green jungle. It could be beautiful if it wasn't such a possibly deadly environment. The sounds of the birds and bugs permeated the air. Slowly the moved forward, wary of any possible danger. Suddenly, a VC soldier popped up out of a spider hole that had been unseen by the troops who had passed it by. The enemy was ready to fire, but Carey was quicker. He quickly pulled his rifle to his shoulder and shot the enemy dead. The sudden crack of Carey's shot stopped everyone in their tracks as they hit the deck and prepared to fire. But the only shot fired was Carey's, and the man he fired at was dead. Carey wrote his wife, Theresa, about the incident. He felt guilty about killing a man, but he did what he had to do, what he was trained to do. When Carey saw the weapons on the enemy soldier, he realized that it had to be done. He or one of his fellow soldiers may have been killed or seriously wounded had he hesitated. Survival outweighed guilt.

Carey was an outdoorsman and hunter, a good shot with excellent instincts. He could spy a rabbit running through the woods better than most people. In one of his letters, written in February

1970 to his brother Bob, he said: "If it hadn't been for Dad, I would be in bad shape. There are guys here that didn't ever go hunting and fishing. They all stayed in the big cities. This is one of several ways I am more prepared for this place."

Denny Martin

Military life continued not to suit Denny. But he did his job and was well-liked by the men in his platoon. Him being one of the "old guys," the men looked up to him. Everyone respected him.

February 11, 1970
Mom, Dad & Scott

I was decorated today. I was sitting on the latrine when my squad leader walked by and handed me a pile of orders with a medal pinned to them. It turned out to be the Combat Infantry Badge which every infantryman assigned to a combat zone is awarded after completing some elusive requirements. At any rate, it arrived at a fortunate time because it turned out that latrine was out of tissue and the extra copies of orders came in handy.

Things are in a state of confusion here at Fire Support Base Devin. Earlier in the day we were unofficially told we were going out with a mechanized unit tomorrow for several days. However tonight I have gotten the word that the mission has been canceled, so once again we are left in the dark. Actually, that is nothing new because we rarely know what we will be doing from day to day. Believe it or not, I have gone out on missions without having been officially told about them. The word just sort of filters down almost

in the form of a rumor and we go from there. Well perhaps there is
some plan to all this madness but it certainly escapes me.
Denny

February 20, 1970
Mom & Dad

The Lt Colonel from our battalion came out today to award
some decorations. After awards he gave us a pep talk. In his closing
words he made the prediction that the 25th Division would be pulled
out some time between June and August. Of course this was only his
own opinion and certainly not the Armies but I believe that he
probably very close to being correct. However there is some doubt in
my mind as to whether or not this would have any effect on me. In
the past only individuals with more than eight months in country
were pulled out. Others were sent to different divisions. If the pull
out came in June I doubt if I would make it. If it came in July or
August I think I would stand a good chance particularly if it came in
the middle of August. At any rate it certainly gives me something to
look forward to.
Denny

Denny's hopes to get out of Vietnam with a shortened tour
were foremost in his thoughts. However, the war continued to be
fought by an ever-reluctant army whose troops just wanted to go
home. It was a war that the American public and politicians had
already given up on.

Hopes ran high throughout the American ranks in South Vietnam that their units would be pulled out as part of Nixon's withdrawal plans. The only questions left were how and when.

Larry Butcher

Larry and Carey Pratt became good friends right away. Larry had been in Vietnam a few months when Carey arrived. Larry didn't get close to many people because booby traps were taking a toll; a lot of men he knew had been wounded and evacuated. It was best not to have too many friends. Walking in the jungle or rice paddies, you had to be on constant alert. You could never let your guard down. There was a feeling of continuous stress for an infantryman in Vietnam.

But there was something about Carey. Their relationship may have started professionally as Carey had skin problems that had plagued him since before being drafted. So, he may have connected initially to the doc due to his skin issues, or maybe they just bonded. Carey was a good NCO and Larry a good medic. Both could be relied on when things got rough, and things did get rough.

Larry always carried his camera and took many pictures of Carey. while they were together. Carey asked Larry on one occasion to take his photo in front of a map of South Vietnam that was hanging on the wall while at Dau Tieng. It was one of Carey's favorite pictures of himself.

Harlen Metzger

Harlen and Brenda wrote at least two letters back and forth a week. She also sent him cassette tapes with recorded music, and sometimes she talked to him. He did the same with her. The most popular song back then was "Leaving on a Jet Plane," and that would instantly make her think of him. Occasionally when he was in the field on an operation, there were long periods when Brenda wouldn't hear from him. She would be so worried; she watched the news reports from Vietnam every day, hoping to catch a glimpse of him. Then she would be so relieved when a letter finally came. It was an emotional roller coaster.

Harlen sent her a lot of pictures of himself and others. There was a picture of him using his helmet to shave in, being on a boat, and another of a large building that the French Army had used as a headquarters. Pictures of the countryside, so different from Indiana, were included.

He told her about being cautious of anyone approaching as women and even children could be suicide bombers. He told her how disturbing it was that some of the troops took pictures of the dead enemy. He often talked about his best friend, Sgt. Carey Pratt. Pratt was from Kokomo, Indiana, and his wife was pregnant. He told her that many of the soldiers smoked grass. Although Harlen tried a joint, it didn't do anything for him, so he never started smoking it regularly, like a lot of them did.

Denny Martin

Denny also sent home photos. He sent pictures of the countryside, telling how pretty it was. Despite the dangers of being in Vietnam, Denny managed to find beauty in the midst of war. He complained to Susie about the heat and just being there in general. Like all soldiers, he was lonely.

Denny and Barbara also wrote often. Barbara was against the war and was part of the major demonstrations in Iowa City. Her participation in these did not cause any problems between Denny and Barbara. He knew what she was doing, demonstrating against the war. Denny just wanted to finish his time in Vietnam and come home to Susie and get on with his life.

Carey Pratt

Carey was a prolific writer and wrote many letters to his brothers, parents, and wife. He wrote mostly, describing what it was like, not necessarily in combat, but Vietnam in general. There was a lot of homesickness that you could read between the lines. He sent back gifts to everybody, even to nieces and nephews.

To Theresa, he sent tapes. This was the most high-tech way to communicate back then. You would talk into the mic of a reel-to-reel tape recorder and then mail the tape to your family and friends. No video, of course, but the voices told volumes. It was easy to detect excitement, sadness, stress, and homesickness in these tapes. So much more could be conveyed by the tone of the voice as opposed to the letter. Carey had a tape recorder or access to one that one of the guys had, and he sent about ten of these to Theresa. He told her how he felt older than the other guys. Carey was a twenty-one-year-old buck sergeant, and most of the soldiers under him were eighteen or nineteen. He never blew his own horn, but he did say how much he cared for the guys under him.

Larry Butcher

Larry's platoon humped one night to a position on the edge of the Hồ Bò Woods to be a blocking force. They put strobe lights in three steel pots and held them up to mark the triangular area of their position as the Cobra gunships tore the ever-loving hell out of the area in front of them. Larry held one of the steel pots with a strobe light and made sure the gunships could see it. During the gunship show, an infantryman from the South near him started shouting: "A rabbit, a rabbit!" He stood up and shot it with his M-16. Later, back at FSB Patton II, he cooked it and shared a small piece of Vietnam jungle rabbit with everyone the next morning. An unexpected culinary delight in Vietnam!

The grunts of Delta were good soldiers doing what they were told to do. The realization came that there was no way they were going to change anything over there, so their focus shifted to taking care of each other and coming home alive.

The fire restrictions seemed absurd at times. One day they were about to be airlifted into an area by the Michelin Rubber Plantation. As they were getting briefed, direct orders were issued that if enemy fire was received, they were not to return it.

One grunt said loud enough that the lieutenant heard him, "Fuck you; if I am shot at, I will shoot back." The lieutenant angrily said, "I will court-marshal you if you do!" They followed orders whether they liked it or not.

To the grunts, it was a fucking game. A deadly game they weren't there to win.

Harlen Metzger

Big, lumbering Harlen was known as a gentle giant. A friend to all. One day while back at the Cu Chi base camp, he accidentally pushed his hand through the screen door of the hooch where his platoon was billeted. Platoon Sergeant Ritz, a lifer without friends, got angry at Harlen and publicly dressed him down for his clumsiness. Harlen took it with complete apathetic silence, which pissed off Ritz even more. The yelling climaxed with Ritz slapping him across the face.

The entire platoon had been listening to this bullshit of Ritz's about the screen door, but when Harlen was slapped, the whole platoon ignited, rushing Ritz and yelling at him for his mistreatment of Harlen. Anger levels rose and resulted in an onslaught of punches until Ritz ended up on the floor being stomped on by the whole platoon. A passing NCO heard the commotion and interceded, putting himself between the fallen Ritz and the mob. The grunts were angry at their attack on Ritz being interrupted and may well have killed him, but they did respect this other NCO and weren't willing to hit him just to finish off Ritz. And so it ended.

It was a reflection not just of the platoon's volatility but of the esteem they had for the gentle and seemingly sensitive Metzger. Him getting slapped was a slap to all of them.

David Schultz

David quietly continued to do his job repairing the Chinooks of the 242nd. A new soldier named Rudy arrived at the company and shared the same hooch as David. David oriented him to the compound and made him feel welcome. The two quickly became friends. Like David, Rudy was from Texas.

David and Rudy talked all the time about anything and everything. Toward the end of April 1970, David told him that he had decided to volunteer to fly as a door gunner. He was bored working on helicopters, and the extra money for flight pay was a motivating factor. Rudy tried to talk him out of it, but David had made up his mind. It would be a few weeks before David flew, but his request was granted.

There was a contradiction here. David was very religious and flying door gunner may mean you have to kill. Was it just for the pay? Patriotism?

Carey Pratt

Carey wanted to meet Theresa in Hawaii for R & R, but he hadn't been in-country long enough to qualify. He pushed headquarters to make an exception. Theresa was pregnant and soon wouldn't be able to travel anymore. Reluctantly his request was approved, and he would be allowed to go on R & R. He was pulled out of the field and sent back to Cu Chi to pick up his orders and prepare for the trip to Hawaii. It was 1 May when he finally departed Vietnamese air space for the flight to Hawaii and Theresa.

Theresa had gone to a local travel agency that specialized in helping military people and their families with their R & R travel plans. Carey would have seven days to be with her, but there was a little glitch. They could only get her on a trip for ten days, not seven. So, she arrived early. Her flight landed at about three o'clock in the afternoon, but it was about eleven at night Indiana time. She was exhausted, so she lay down and fell asleep, waking up at eleven o'clock at night local time. Wide awake, she went downstairs, and the only thing open was a bar. She started to walk in there just to get a Coke, but when they found out she was just nineteen, she was not allowed in the bar. She said, "Well, what am I supposed to do?" They said they didn't know, but she could not come in the bar. So, she just walked around the hotel for a while, killing time.

Denny Martin

Denny's frustration with the army worsened. He didn't have much faith that those in charge knew what they were doing.

April 8, 1970

Mom & Dad

The Army continues to stumble along making blunder after blunder. Last night we sent half our platoon out on our nightly routine ambush patrol. It was just before sunset and they were just a few 100 meters from their ambush site when a strange 2nd Lieutenant and a platoon sergeant suddenly appeared before them. When questioned our A.P. learns that they are an A.P. (ambush patrol) from another company, from the same battalion and that they have five other ambushes set up in the same area. Somewhat unnerved our A.P. calls back to our company headquarters only to find that they also don't know what is going on. Finally, after fooling around, headquarters calls back and informs our A.P. that there has been a mix-up (something that they were pretty well aware of) and that they will have to move a kilometer to another A.P. sight. By now it is very dark and moving at night is about the most scary thing you can do. Not only do we have to worry about the enemy but also any American ambush that might be in your line of travel & waiting to blow you away.

When you consider there are at most four companies in the battalion on operation at one time, you would think that coordination would be reasonably easy. To say that last nights mix up was a pathetic blunder would be an understatement. It is really amazing that the two companies didn't end up shooting at each other. If it had been darker I imagine that is what would have happened. Our most dangerous enemy is not Charles but ourselves. Denny

Harlen Metzger

Poor Harlen was always getting stuck with uniforms so ill-fitting that he looked like Baby Huey. The Delta Company troops in the field didn't have their own uniforms, so every fifteen days, there would be a massive pile of cleaned uniforms dumped on the ground. They would disrobe and leave their dirty uniforms in a heap for pickup and then scrounge around for pants and shirts from among the clean pile. Harold Martin, who served with Harlen as well as Carey Pratt, recalled that once he got a pair of pants with the entire rear end cut out; he kept these and wore them without underwear (no one wore underwear) at an inspection at the base camp. You had to appreciate the humor in it; the Delta soldiers sure did.

Harold usually had no trouble finding something that fit, but Harlen was the biggest guy in the unit. He'd hunt and pick to find a shirt and pants he could get into. The result was often him ending up in a shirt way too small and pants that were 'high-waters.' Not exactly a recruiting poster look, but it provided some good laughs. He was a good-natured guy and took it in stride. This was a big part of the reason they were all so outraged when he got chewed out and slapped across the face without provocation.

Brenda sent Harlen a care package at Easter, and he wrote to tell her that all the candy was melted into one big glob when he received it. He shared it with his squad mates, and even though it was a melted mess, they loved it.

Harlen told Brenda that when he got home, he would never go camping again since he had to spend days at a time out in the open during monsoon season and had to drink water out of puddles. Harlen's idea of camping after the army would be fans instead of air conditioning, small televisions instead of large ones, cots instead of beds, lots of food-he wouldn't make allowances on that-and anything else to make life comfortable.

Carey Pratt

Theresa knew when Carey's plane was arriving but could not meet him at the airport. The R & R center was only about a thousand feet from the hotel. As the arrival time approached, Theresa walked over to the center to wait. Then, there he was. His smiling face was beaming when he saw her. He was here; he was safe.

The couple had a lovely week in Hawaii. Shopping, sightseeing, and just loving each other's company. They rented a dune buggy and drove all around the island. It was a perfect time, but all too soon it was over.

Carey and Theresa walked over to the R & R center for his trip back to Vietnam, and the sergeant in charge looked at his orders and exclaimed, "You were supposed to be here yesterday!" Theresa was afraid that he was in trouble and would be thrown in the stockade! The sergeant told Carey that the bus to the airport had already left. He would have to wait there until tomorrow. Theresa said her goodbyes and walked back to the hotel.

At eleven o'clock, Theresa walked back over there, thinking that maybe she could have lunch with him or at least visit. As she approached, she saw him in front of the building, sweeping. Typical army busywork. He saw her, looked up, and smiled. Theresa just stood there and waited, hoping for a chance to talk to him. This encounter was noticed by the desk sergeant who came out and called Carey over. He told him to go and have the rest of the day with his wife and come back in the morning. He was told that he better be there and on time. He was.

The next morning bright and early, Carey left. He boarded his flight and was whisked back to Vietnam. Life ahead looked perfect. His baby was due in August, just three months away. He just had to get through the rest of his tour and then home.

Back at Cu Chi, he found out his unit was in Cambodia, and he would join them there. The Cambodian incursion had begun on 1 May for the Americans. Carey and Theresa had seen it on the news in Hawaii.

Most of the supplies that the NVA and the Viet Cong received came down the Ho Chi Minh Trail through Laos and Cambodia or by boat through the port of Sihanoukville in Cambodia. When Lon Nol deposed Prince Sihanouk on March 18, 1970, he refused to tolerate the thousands of Vietnamese in his country. The North Vietnamese never acknowledged the presence of their troops in Cambodia.

Lon Nol decided to cut off the supply line from Sihanoukville and demand that the Vietnamese leave. This was a threat to the NVA supply lines, so they launched an offensive against Lon Nol's troops. Nixon decided to commit American troops and invade Cambodia. It was a big gamble, militarily and politically. The American public was getting very tired of the war and all of the casualties. They wanted the war to end. The incursion was an opportunity to capture large amounts of supplies and locate and destroy COSVN (Central Office for South Vietnam–NVA headquarters running the war).

ARVN forces had been involved in a series of incursions into Cambodia since the end of March with limited success. On April 26, Nixon decided to go. He gave his approval and authorization for a multidivision attack into neutral Cambodia. On April 29, 8,700, ARVN soldiers crossed the border into the Parrot's Beak area of Cambodia.

On April 30, 1970, Nixon addressed the nation telling of his decision to invade Cambodia. "This is not an invasion of Cambodia," Nixon assured the audience during his speech. "The areas in which these attacks will be launched are completely occupied and controlled by North Vietnamese forces. Our purpose is not to occupy the areas. Once enemy forces are driven out of these sanctuaries, and once their military supplies are destroyed, we will withdraw."

US forces joined the fight on May 1. Protests sprung up throughout the United States, especially on college campuses. At Kent State University in Ohio, a demonstration of about five hundred students took place on the morning of May 1. The students dispersed midday and planned another rally for May 4. During the days before the scheduled rally, tensions rose. There were accounts of threats to business by protestors trying to get the businesses to display anti-war slogans. There were unconfirmed rumors that the students were going to destroy the ROTC building and the local recruiting office.

Kent's Mayor Satrum met with city officials and a representative of the Ohio National Guard. Because of the threats, he believed that the city could not handle the chaos, so he asked for the National Guard to be brought in to preserve peace.

The decision was made to bring in the Guard at 1700 on May 2. A large demonstration was underway when they arrived at 2200. The ROTC building was set ablaze.

The protest on May 4 began at noon, with about 2,000 in attendance. The Guard tried to disperse the students, but when most refused to leave, they fired tear gas into the crowd. Students threw the tear gas canisters back at the National Guardsmen as well as rocks. Things escalated, and some of the Guardsmen fired their rifles into the crowd. Four people were killed and nine wounded.

Back in Vietnam, the 25th Division invaded the Fishhook area on May 6. Carey caught a ride on a helicopter into Cambodia to join his unit in the field. Everyone was glad to see him.

On May 14, Company D was on a reconnaissance operation when elements of Delta Company came in contact with a large enemy force. Deadly and accurate fire rained down on the prone men. Disregarding his safety, Carey exposed himself to a hail of bullets as he engaged them and placed suppressive fire on their positions. The men, awed by his example of courage came to life and returned fire with everything they had. The fighting finally subsided, the enemy dead or gone. The mission went on. Carey was awarded a Bronze Star with *V* for this action. Welcome back from R & R, Sergeant Pratt!

Denny Martin

The 14th Infantry entered into Cambodia, not knowing what awaited them there. Apprehensive, wary, and alert, they began their part in this operation. Denny took time to write and describe the change in terrain. He always appreciated the differences in landscape, and Cambodia was different than the jungles of South Vietnam just a short distance away.

May 4, 1970

Mom & Dad

The area we are in now is very uninteresting. It consists solely of wide-open grassy plains dotted with square bamboo hedgerows that once sheltered a house. The only variety of the landscape is an occasional swamp. There are no villages or houses anywhere near so we don't have any natives wandering around to keep us entertained. The combined situation makes it exceedingly difficult to keep my mind occupied despite the variety of books I brought along to read. At least R & R is rapidly drawing closer. Love, Denny

Mike Vullo

Mike Vullo arrived in South Vietnam on May 9, 1970, ready to begin his 365-day tour. It took five days for him to receive orders to proceed to the 725th Maintenance Bn., 25th Infantry Division at Cu Chi. He rode the first helicopter that had space and experienced his first ride over the exotic landscape of Vietnam. Pilots usually liked to fly low level when they had passengers new to Vietnam. His flight was probably no exception. It was always a little disconcerting for a new troop to be screaming along at tree-top level with the door gunners at the ready, scanning for any possible threats. Sometimes the pilots would fly over a "free fire" area and let the gunners fire their M-60s. That would be a great laugh for the seasoned crew but scare the hell out the new guys.

Mike's friend from Fort Monmouth, Mike Gandee, was assigned to the same outfit. Gandee and Mike graduated from the course together and reported for duty in Vietnam around the same time. They were surprised to find each other in the same outfit at Cu Chi. Mike arrived before Gandee due to an army snafu. When Gandee arrived, he was placed in an infantry unit by mistake. They were getting ready to deploy into Cambodia when someone figured it out. Much to his relief, he was reassigned to the 725th to do the job he was trained to do, repairing the weapons support radar system.

The weapons support radar was a large piece of equipment that was used in conjunction with the field artillery to detect incoming mortar and rocket fire. The operator would try to pinpoint where they were coming from or where they were heading so that they could give fire control the coordinates. Artillery or airstrikes would then try and silence the source of the incoming fire.

They would sling it under a Chinook helicopter and move it from firebase to firebase as needed. There were several of these scattered throughout the area. Of course, due to movement, heat, etc. they would break down and need repair. The repair crews were based out of Cu Chi, and when a call came in that one was down, a team of two would have to go in the field and fix it. They never knew where they were going. The repair calls usually came in the middle of the night. They would hop on a helicopter, and they would fly them to a firebase out in the middle of nowhere. They would repair the unit and try and find a way back to Cu Chi. Getting on-site was a priority, but getting back was not. They would try and catch a hop or a convoy or any way they could get back home.

Mike made friends with Frank Rodriguez while he was there. They were in the same shop but had different jobs. Whenever they were working together, they would always shoot the breeze. Frank liked Mike. He was somebody he could trust. Someone he knew could be a good friend.

Frank and Mike were both from Southern California, Mike from the Los Angeles area and Frank from San Diego. They swore to visit each other when they left the army.

Frank was a spiritual person. Not necessarily religious but spiritual. On the plane flying over the Pacific to Vietnam, he heard a voice saying, "Don't worry. You're not going there to kill or be killed. You're going there to learn." Frank thought, *Well, who's talking to me?* He looked around, and nobody was talking to him; almost everyone was asleep. Frank wasn't dozing or imagining things. The voice was real. He listened to it and thought about it for a long time. He believed what he heard.

Frank spent fifteen months in Vietnam. He did not fear death. He also knew he would never have to kill anyone. That gave him peace. He spent his time there with an unloaded rifle. He was told he wasn't going to kill anybody, so why did he need bullets? He never fired his weapon while in-country. The voice was right.

Denny Martin

Denny was all set for his R & R with Susie in June, but the army canceled it, most likely due to manpower needs in Cambodia. His disappointment and frustration were palpable. He continued to write home, but to add insult to injury, the only stationery he could get was army stationery!

May 17, 1970
Mom, Dad & Scott

    Please excuse the stationary but it was the only thing that I could find. I don't know why the Army insists on being military on everything you do.

    I certainly deserve a break after the canceled my R & R in June. It doesn't even look very bright for me going in July. I guess the summer months are popular times to go to Hawaii. Thanks for the book, Scotty it arrived while I was in Cambodia and had nothing to read.
Denny

Denny crossed his fingers and tried again for an R & R in July. The war continued.

May 23, 1970
Mom & Dad

    This morning we had a class on "mechanical ambushes" which is the G.I's answer to booby traps. It looks like we may have to start using them. I don't particularly like the idea because if you are not extremely careful about how you put them out, they can be as dangerous to you as they are to Charlie. Actually I think they are expecting a slow down in enemy activity and this is a desperate attempt to get a bigger body count so the division can prove its worth in the area.

    Turned in my new request for R & R for July 5. Hope this one goes through.

Denny

Despite the circumstances of being in Cambodia, Denny still pursued his education and thought of going home and resuming his life. He was hoping for a rear area job, but so was everyone else!

June 9, 1970
Mom & Dad

Most of my personal gear was brought out from Cu Chi including my correspondence course in biology. I have had a little free time and have completed another couple of lessons. I guess the only way my situation would really improve is if I managed to get a job in a rear area and wouldn't have to hump anymore – I am waiting but not expecting much.
Denny

Elroy Simmons

Elroy arrived back in Vietnam to start his second tour on June 15, 1970. His first tour was with the 9th Infantry Division, but this time his assignment brought him to the 25th Division out of Cu Chi. Elroy had no trouble acclimating to the Vietnam climate and countryside. He had been here before. Unlike the nervous FNGs Elroy took it all in stride.

Elroy checked in with Division HQ and joined HHB, 3rd Bn., 13th Artillery. Checking his record, they decided that he should perform another needed job other than running a section of cannon cockers. He was given the task of recruiting sergeant. He would travel around the 25th Divisions area of operations and try and boost reenlistments.

This job was perfect for Elroy. He was a Sergeant First Class now and had a lot of experience handling troops, having done tours in Hawaii, Germany, Korea, and Vietnam. He knew his way around the army and had a good handle on the type and location of assignments the troops could expect if the re-upped. It was a lot safer job than humping the boonies or running a platoon at some distant fire support base.

Denny Martin

Great news for Denny! His R & R to Hawaii with Susie was now confirmed. Back to civilization, for a week anyway. The hope of an early out still lingered in the back of his mind.

June 19, 1970
Grandmother & Father

The Army has finally given me a date so that I can go on R&R – July 13 through the 19th. Needless to say I am counting the days until then. We are hearing a lot of rumors that the 25th Division or at least part of it will be the next to be withdrawn. We are all hoping to be involved in it but I am certainly not going to hold my breath.
Denny

Larry Butcher

Larry had finished his six-month stint out in the boonies with Delta Company, and now he was at an aid station back at Cu Chi. Larry was a Spec 5 now, and the duty at Cu Chi was much preferred to being out in the field. He became good friends with 1Lt. Robert Klee, a Medical Services Corps Officer. They served together for about eight months. Being an officer, Robert looked out for Larry.

On more than one occasion, Larry and Robert visited one of the officer's clubs on the other side of the base, hoping to avoid running into any of the infantry officers Larry and Robert knew. After-hours the vehicle driver had to be in uniform, and Robert wanted to wear his civilian clothes. So, Larry put on Robert's officers' uniform and drove the jeep. One night they were in an officers club having pizza when three infantry officers who knew them well walked in. They stood in the doorway looking at the pair kind of stunned, for a moment, then came over, sat down, and had pizza with them. Not a word was said about that night ever again. They were just a bunch of "regular guys" enjoying pizza and beer.

Mike Vullo

Things at the 725th progressed at its average pace. The men continued working at the shop at Cu Chi and made forays into the field to repair broken equipment in place. Mike Vullo and Mike Gandee completed many of the trips to the field. A repairer named Melvin Chase joined the unit in June. Melvin wanted to get out to the field and see what it was all about. He would have his chance soon enough.

July 8 was Gandee's night off, and he spent the evening at the NCO club, relaxing with a few drinks. He returned to his hooch and crashed. In the middle of the night Mike came in and woke him up out of a sound sleep, telling him that a mission had come in. Gandee and Mike discussed it and it was decided that Mike should take Melvin, the new guy.

Vullo and Melvin caught a hop to Dau Tieng to repair the damaged radar. In the morning Gandee woke up and they were gone.

Chapter 4

Love Craft

When once you have tasted flight, you will forever walk the earth

with your eyes turned skyward, for there you have been, and there

you will always long to return.

-Leonardo da Vinci

In March 1966, the army purchased CH-47A, Chinook #65-07999. Shortly after that, it was sent to Vietnam. The tail number at that time was 57999, Boxcar Triple Niner. In the summer, it found its way to its first assignment with the 178th Assault Support Helicopter Company at Phu Loi.

By March of 1967, it had been grounded and partially cannibalized for parts. The 178th was going to move to Chu Lai in April and this helicopter needed to be flight worthy. Two guys new to the 178th Flight Platoon became its crew members: Flight Engineer Lyman Harvey and Crew Chief Dean Nelson. They worked on Triple Niner all day every day and fixed virtually everything that needed repair. The restored 999 now needed a name and nose art. The nose art they decided on was a lemon with tandem rotor heads, and they named it Mellow Yellow.

Mellow Yellow made it up to Chu Lai in a flight of fifteen and began combat operations as part of Task Force Oregon. During its time with the 178th· it flew many combat sorties and sustained hits from enemy ground fire. Despite the damage, it was always patched up and kept in the air.

This aircraft was later turned over to the 242nd Assault Support Helicopter Company, 269th Aviation Bn. at Cu Chi. It had different crews over the years as men rotated. The normal crew of five consisted of aircraft commander, pilot (co-pilot), flight engineer, crew chief, and a door gunner. The flight engineer and crew chief were assigned to the ship, and they were responsible for the maintenance of it. The gunner was a floater. They would go to different aircraft as needed. The gunners were normally volunteers from maintenance personnel or a myriad of other MOSes serving in the company.

In the early part of the book I mentioned that for the most part I would follow the lives and stories of seven men involved in the story of Chinook #65-07999. As the story progresses other men play an integral part. Now, the stories of others from the 242nd must be included.

Jim Calabrese

It was amazing how young everyone was - the pilots, crew, maintenance, and support troops. The pilots were usually only a year or two older than the rest of the flight crew. They were all kids. Kids who did their job no matter how hazardous or how many long hours they worked.

Jim Calabrese had been in Vietnam with the 242nd since June 1969. He was an old hand at performing maintenance on the company's Chinooks over long, thankless hours, six to seven days a week. One day in late January or early February 1970, two soldiers showed up to bunk in the maintenance hooch where all the mechanics stayed. They told Jim that they would only be there a few days as they were going to fly and would be billeted in the flight platoon hooch when space opened up. One of these men was Ross Bedient.

That week Jim showed them around the company area: important places, like the mess hall, mailroom, and supply room. He told them that when they flew, they would draw their M-60s at the back of the supply room where the company armorer was located. He then acclimated them to the basic layout of the Cu Chi base.

After they knew their way around the area, he asked them, "Why the hell do you want to fly? You get shot at." He told them that he flew whenever he wanted. He explained that he had an Air Medal and had flown on over twenty-five missions, even though he was a mechanic. That was better than flying every day and being assigned to a regular crew.

He couldn't talk them out of it; they wanted to fly. After they moved over to the flight platoon, he only saw them occasionally in line to get their mail or at the mess hall. Jim worked nights, and they flew days. He would get off anywhere from 0700 to 0900, and by then, they were usually in the air for the day. Night maintenance was the busiest. That's when most of the ships were on the ground and being repaired. Night maintenance worked from 1700 through the night. The work was occasionally interrupted by a mortar or rocket attack.

In the short time they spent together, Jim and Ross bonded. Both were from the Seneca Lake area in New York. It was typical for men from the same area to become friends. They shared familiarity of home.

Ross Bedient

Ross arrived in South Vietnam on January 18, 1970. Exhausted but excited after the long journey, he, along with all the other new arrivals, attended lectures and medical checks. Their shot records checked, malaria pills given, fluoride toothpaste issued—the usual incoming procedure.

Breakfast, lunch, and dinner were in a hot mess hall that served food that sometimes was unrecognizable. He attended the endless formations, waiting for his name to be called and assignment given. Finally, he was called-time to get his tour started. His assignment: the 242nd ASH at Cu Chi. He took his first ride in a helicopter in Nam as he proceeded to Cu Chi. The date was January 21.

Ross could have had a farm exemption if he had wanted it, but he decided to go in the army. His brother, Zane, had served a tour in Vietnam with the navy and tried to talk him out of going in the army. He told Ross, "That's a useless war over there. It is not one that's supported by the people of the United States. I've been there. And I don't believe in that war. It's a straight political thing." But Ross could not be dissuaded. He was going in.

At the time, he was engaged to Lois Trest, but that did not deter him from enlisting. Lois had a daughter, Sandy, who Ross adored. Ross treated Sandy like she was his daughter. The three were at the pool just before Ross shipped out when he picked Sandy up, hugged her, and told her that no matter what, he would always look out after her.

Ross enlisted in the army in June 1969 and went active on June 27. He attended basic training at Fort Dix and then was sent to Fort Eustis for training as a CH-47 helicopter repairer, MOS 67U20. Upon graduating from this course, he received his orders: Vietnam.

Ross knew he would be assigned to a helicopter company somewhere in Vietnam, and he had made up his mind that he wanted to fly. He didn't want to spend his tour working countless hot grueling hours repairing helicopters.

Rickey Wittner

Rickey joined the army, enlisting for a guarantee to be trained as a MOS 67U20, CH-47 helicopter repairer. His father was amazed at his choice. He said, "I don't understand that. You've never even been in one!" Rickey replied, "Well, I just like them." So that's what he decided to do.

His active service began on August 18, 1969. He and the other recruits were sworn in, received their final physicals, and boarded a bus in Houston for basic training at Fort Polk, Louisiana. While on the way, the bus was stopped. There was a spinal meningitis outbreak at Fort Polk, so their destination was changed to Fort Bliss, Texas. In Houston, they boarded a plane for El Paso and Fort Bliss. This was Rickey's first ride in an airplane.

Basic had the usual travails of learning the army way of doing everything, from how to wear your uniform to how to make your bed with crisp hospital corners to how to clean the barracks.

Basic finished in eight long weeks, and then it was off to Fort Eustis, Virginia, for AIT and training to be a Chinook mechanic, just like David Schultz and Ross Bedient. Training would take twelve weeks. The task of learning how to keep this complicated machine in the air seemed daunting at first. As it turned out, it wasn't as complicated as it appeared.

The class was from 0800 to 1700 daily, Monday through Friday and sometimes on Saturday. Graduation came quickly, and of course, he received orders for Vietnam. No surprise there. Rickey received a two-week furlough before he had to report for shipment overseas.

Ross Bedient

In short order, Ross was placed on flight status. The pilots loved flying with him. He was competent and always seemed to have a smile on his face.

Ross quickly rose from door gunner to crew chief. He had his act together and proved himself a trusted member of the flight crew. It wasn't long before he was promoted to be the flight engineer of Chinook #65-07999, named *Love Craft*. The name was painted on the nose of the aircraft and above it was a white horseshoe for luck.

Rickey Wittner

Rickey arrived in sunny South Vietnam in February 1970. Upon arrival, his planeload of new troops sat in bleachers for orientation. Across the fence, they could see soldiers who had finished their tour board aircraft for the flight home. To a man, they looked worn out and weary. They were not excited and energetic, like the new men in the bleachers.

Rickey received his assignment to the 242nd ASH at Cu Chi. He would be a part of the 1st Aviation Brigade supporting the 25th Infantry Division as well as any other local unit that needed their services.

He was to report to the 269th Aviation Bn. the next day. When morning arrived, he was placed on a Huey for the flight from Long Binh to Cu Chi. The trip was an exciting one for Rickey. He sat on the floor, feet out the door, as the helicopter low-leveled all the way, flying over rice paddies and farmers, jumping over trees and patches of jungle. Welcome to Vietnam.

After checking in with admin, he was assigned a hooch and waited for his hooch mates to get off duty. He spent the afternoon writing to his girlfriend and mother. At about 1400 another new soldier, PFC Ken Bookhammer, showed up, and they hit it off right away. Shortly after that, some of the flight crews started wandering in. One was Ross Bedient, a crew chief. He showed Rickey and Ken around the camp. They "borrowed" a jeep and went to the PX, returning it when they were finished. It was never missed!

After a couple more days of training and paperwork, Rickey found out that he would be working the ground crew. Rickey wanted to fly. He tried everything in the world to start flying. Being on the ground did not appeal to him. So, he politicked a lot with the flight crews and finally got one of them to consent to let him be a gunner. That is where you began. If you did well, you could progress to crew chief and then flight engineer.

Rickey's first flight as a door gunner was uneventful. He was flying from one base camp to another delivering supplies. After that flight, it would be a few days before he was able to get in the air again. The next time he flew, he was a gunner with Ross Bedient. He would fly pretty steady now, first as a gunner with Bruce Witwer. Bruce was a flight engineer and was losing his crew chief in a couple of weeks, and Ross would be taking his place. He wanted to see how Rickey and Ross got along. Things worked out perfectly. Rickey became his crew chief and Ross his gunner. Then they had a few problems with their ship. Bruce refused to let it fly it until it was repaired, and the heat came down. They wanted that helicopter in the air. Bruce was responsible for the safety of the ship and crew. He wasn't about to let it in the air until it was safe. A few days later, Bruce was back on the crew fixing the helicopters. They pulled him off flight status. That was when Rickey finely got the chance to be a crew chief. Ross would be the flight engineer.

Ross Bedient

It wasn't long before Rickey and Ross bunked together. They became close friends; being in Nam wasn't always all work and no play. Once a month, they were able to get everyone together and have some fun beer parties out at the edge of the flight line. For only two dollars each, they were able to fill a trailer with beer and ice.

Some would get drunk, others not, but everyone had a good time. It was a tradition to get the people who had started flying within the last month to stay in the trailer full of ice until they almost turned blue; holding one man down sometimes took everyone!

Rickey Wittner

Rickey was now a part of the crew of *Love Craft 999,* as it was called. It was unofficially called *Patches*, obviously, because of all the patched holes from VC bullets and shrapnel. The door gunners rotated in and out. They did not have a permanent one.

Love Craft flew many missions in 1970, mostly bringing in or taking troops out of the field. Sometimes they would get a break and fly a USO band to different areas to entertain the troops. Unfortunately, they usually weren't able to stay for the show. It was fly in, drop them off, and fly out on to the next mission.

The Michelin Rubber Plantation was in their area of operations, but they weren't supposed to fly over it. Supposedly this was considered to be a safe area, but most suspected it a haven for local VC and NVA troops. There were still French expatriates living in comfortable surroundings seemingly untouched by the war.

Nui Ba Den, the Black Virgin Mountain loomed over the countryside and was a natural landmark for navigation. There was an American outpost at the top and enemy all around on the slopes. Flights onto it were frequent, and each had its hazards.

Flying in Vietnam was always hazardous. There was no place safe in the skies of Vietnam.

Ross Bedient

The days dragged on, the flying was constant. It was May, and the Cambodian incursion had begun. That meant long hours for *Love Craft* and its crew. There were a lot of troops across the border in Cambodia, and they had to be fed, receive water, and constant replenishment of ammo. There were about 50,000 American troops involved as well as 58,000 South Vietnamese troops. The flow of helicopters crossing the border was never-ending. B-52s dropped tons of bombs on areas known as the Fishhook, Parrot's Beak, and Dog's Head.

On May 22 *Love Craft* was flying missions delivering ARVNs with Ross as flight engineer, Rickey as crew chief, and Ken as the gunner. As they landed and the troops started to get out, they began to receive small-arms and mortar fire. The VC wanted that ship down and did their best to accomplish this. Red hot iron and lead were flying everywhere, peppering *Love Craft*. The ARVNs got as far away from that helicopter as fast as they could. It was too big a target, and it was full of fuel.

One mortar landed about twelve feet in front and to the right of the nose, exploding in a bright orange flash and gray smoke. One of the pilots was wounded and bleeding, but there was no time to help him now. They had to get the hell out of there and get out now! The controls were damaged but still barely working. Ross, Rickey, and Ken were all shaken up but unwounded. The ship slowly rose and left the landing zone, shot at all the way. They limped, shaking, away a safe distance and landed, and the crew went to work. The pilot worked on the wounds of his partner while the rest patched what they could so they could try and bring the sick bird back home. They had significant damage but were in the middle of the jungle without air support; they had no choice but to try and get back in the air and return to Cu Chi.

They slowly lifted off, everyone holding their breath. Despite vibrations shaking the ship, somehow, they made it back to Cu Chi safely. There were over fifty hits in *Love Craft*, some superficial, some not. Repairs were quickly made, and it was deemed flyable. More missions were ahead.

May 31 was another heart-stopping mission. *Love Craft* was in a landing zone, trying to take off after dropping off cargo, supplies, and ammo. They received ground fire from the jungle tree line damaging the main rotor systems and flight controls. The ship shook with the hits but managed to get airborne and out of the kill zone. Once again, they beat the odds, and *Patches* made it home on a wing and prayer.

David Schultz

David started flying as a door gunner on June 18. He rotated from aircraft to aircraft. His assigned aircraft and missions were completely random. He could be flying milk runs all day or combat missions. It was the luck of the draw.

After David began flying, Donna received a letter that scared the hell out of her. He wrote to her that he felt there was a bullet out there with his name on it. Was it an omen or just the stress of combat flying? Despite feeling that, he continued to fly. Many men in

Vietnam had premonitions. Some came true and others not. The feeling of impending doom did not leave in either case.

Chapter 5

The Calm Before the Storm

"War is being reminded that you are completely at the mercy of death at every moment, without the illusion that you are not. Without the distractions that make life worth living."

-Francesca Lia Block, *House of Dolls*

Vietnam, like most wars, was a series of extreme boredom punctuated by moments of pure terror. Be it a sudden rocket/mortar attack (usually at night), a convoy or patrol ambushed, a helicopter crash due to mechanical failure or being shot down. These were all in the realm of possibility for everyone. The times in between were just dragged on. Tick off the day's one by one until the magic number of 365 was reached.

Larry Crozier

July 9, 1970 was another hot, steamy morning in South Vietnam. Boatswains Mate 3rd Class Larry Crozier and the other advisors of River Patrol Group 52 sat in the Saigon River astride the area known as the Mushroom, southeast of Tay Ninh. They began preparing breakfast with their Vietnamese naval crew. Grenade fish and rice. It was easy to catch fish in the Saigon River. You pulled the pin on a hand grenade and dropped it in the river. A boom and a splash! The fish then floated to the top, and you just scooped them up. Larry wasn't fond of fish, especially those that came from the depths of the brown Saigon River. The fish were terrible, but the large lizards they ate were worse. The Vietnamese would catch them and cook them up with rice. Everything they cooked, they chopped into bite-size pieces, so everything you chewed had bones in it. Given his choice, he would eat the fish over the lizards. But chow was chow. Squat with the crew, and breakfast was served!

Life was always exciting on the PBRs, the river patrol boats. When Larry first joined the navy, he was assigned to submarine duty. It wasn't his cup of tea. He wanted to see the world from on top of the water, not underneath it. He was based out of Groton, Connecticut, when he lucked out and received a reassignment to Panama. While stationed there, he met his future wife. They married and had a son. Larry spent two years in Panama then saw a show on PBRs in Vietnam and decided he wanted to do that. His brother was in the 11th Cavalry in Vietnam, and Larry wanted to see what it was like to be in combat. So, next stop—a PBR in sunny South Vietnam!

By the time he got to Vietnam, the boats had been turned over to the Vietnamese. US Navy personnel served on the PBRs as advisors, one to a boat. The PBRs patrolled the upper Saigon River where the water was shallow, and larger ships could not navigate. The PBRs were about thirty feet long and ten feet wide armed with three 50-caliber machine guns and an M-60 each. Of course, they also had an assortment of rifles, pistols and hand grenades. If the shit hit the fan, they had five minutes of pure firepower; then they had to get out of the kill zone.

Combat in the brown water navy was a unique experience that few Americans experienced. When the shooting started, the American advisors would get on the radio and call for support. Larry always thought they were just glorified radio talkers. An American calling for air support or artillery usually got a fast response, but a Vietnamese voice would not. A call for resupply or a Dust-off received the same result, fast for an American and slow for Vietnamese. The Vietnamese crew usually did whatever they wanted, no matter what the navy advisors told them, except when the shooting started. Then they were extremely protective of their counterparts who had American voices and the power of the radio.

In the upper Saigon River, they would usually have four boats working in pairs, a primary boat and a cover boat. They would patrol during the day and laager for the night. They would then call in their location as they never knew where they would be at the end of the day. But it was never in the same spot as the night before. Nine times out of ten, when Larry would call in their night location, nothing would happen. If they ended up changing it at the last minute and moving to a different spot, they would invariably run into trouble. It was uncanny. It was like the enemy knew exactly what was going on. Maybe they did.

The night would be long, hot, and full of mosquitos. Most of the time, it was spent in tense silence. Lying on the boat listening to the *re-up* frogs and the *fuck-you* lizards. The frogs' croaks sounded like "Re-up, re-up." There were big lizards in the vegetation near the shore that made noises sounding like "Fuck you, fuck you." The men sat there all night listening and wondering what the hell was going on. Larry would stare into the darkness, hearing "Re-up, re-up, fuck you, fuck you." He stared in the darkness, thinking, *I volunteered for this crazy shit, what did I get myself into?* Watch what you wish for.

Tomorrow was going to be a better day. They had radioed in for resupply of ammo, supplies, and fuel blivets. In the morning, they would find a good spot for the supply helicopter to hover and drop their load. It would take a good part of the day to refuel, and then another chopper could pick up the empty fuel blivets. Once fueled up, it would be time to move on to a new location.

242nd Assault Support Helicopter Company

July 9 ended like most other days at Cu Chi for the crews and personnel of the 242nd. The long day of flying was over, and maintenance on their Chinooks had just begun. The crew's jobs were not finished after the ships landed. They had to clean the interior of debris left by the resupply missions they had flown. Shell casings, if they had fired their M-60s needed to be picked up and disposed of. They could not risk loose debris that could be sucked into an engine intake. And of course, sometimes there was blood. If they had picked up any wounded or body bags, there was always an amount, small or large, of blood, other bodily fluids, and perhaps pieces of flesh. It was a dirty job, but it had to be done. Of course, the guns had to be cleaned. Gas checks had to be free-floating, and actions oiled. The risk of a jam could be the difference between life and death.

Rickey Wittner and Ross Bedient cleaned out *Love Craft* and checked it for any possible maintenance issues that may have popped up. The gunner of the day had the responsibility of cleaning the guns. Take them apart, dip them in solvent and scrub them down. The pungent smell of the cleaning solution would cling to his hands for the rest of the night.

Finally, it was time for chow and then off to the club for a few beers. Ross was in an excellent mood. He always seemed in a good mood, but this day was even better. After tomorrow's missions, he would be going on R & R. He was excited about going to Hawaii and seeing his fiancée, Lois.

Tomorrow would be another long day of flying even though the Cambodian incursion was over. All American troops were back in Vietnam, and things had been pretty quiet since their return. The NVA was trying to recover from all the supplies lost, not to mention replace all their casualties. Tomorrow would be pretty routine. Resupplies, in and out. An easy day.

Roy Harris

SP4 Roy Harris looked out over the firebase at Dau Tieng, his tour almost over. It seemed the same as it had since he arrived long ago. His thoughts drifted back to being drafted on February 24, 1969. He had to leave his wife, Linda, and start his army life with basic training at Fort Dix, New Jersey. It seemed like so long ago.

He was just twenty years old when he got called up. He had turned twenty-one two months ago, just before the Cambodian Incursion. He felt older than his twenty-one years.

Following basic training, he remained at Fort Dix for AIT. Like most draftees, he feared being sent to infantry training at Fort

Polk, but instead, he received orders for cook's school. No infantry! And a relatively safe MOS! He hoped he might go to Germany after AIT or another post in the United States. That way, he could bring Linda, and they could settle in and raise a family. But it wasn't to be.

As school approached an end in June, he received his orders. Vietnam. Not Germany or the US but Vietnam. Roy graduated as a cook on June 20, packed his duffel bag, and went home to his wife and family for a short twenty-six-day furlough.

Then Roy left his home in Bridgeport, Connecticut, and reported in at Oakland Army Depot for transport overseas, not knowing where he would be ultimately assigned in-country.

He arrived in South Vietnam on July 18, 1969. His one-year tour had begun. After processing at the 90th Replacement Battalion, he received his assignment to the 25th Infantry Division. Finally, on July 28, he was told to get his gear and board a Huey bound for Cu Chi and the 25th.

After his initial in-country orientation at 25th Division Headquarters in Cu Chi, Roy's assignment was Headquarters and Headquarters Company, 12th Infantry Regiment as a cook. There he would spend the rest of his tour cooking for troops in the field and those assigned to the bases of Cu Chi and Dau Tieng.

It was a relatively safe job in a country where nowhere was safe. Like everyone else in Vietnam, he was periodically subjected to rocket and mortar attacks. He adapted and got used to the job and the task of cooking in the ninety-plus-degree heat. The drudgery wore on, day after day. He was counting down until his 365 days would be up on July 17th, 1970. His short timer calendar was slowly filling in.

Now, on July 9 he had his orders in his hand. He would leave Dau Tieng tomorrow for Bien Hoa and process out of Vietnam. Home in a little over a week. He had done an excellent job as a cook and master at arms of the EM Club. He had already been awarded an Army Commendation Medal for his service with the 25th Division. But today he didn't think about awards. He just thought about going home to his wife. Perhaps when he arrived back in the States, he could get an early out. He would have about seven months left to serve on his two-year obligation, but the army was discharging many soldiers with less than a year to serve after their tour in Vietnam. As far as that went, all he could do is hope.

Robert E. Ivey

Master Sergeant Ivey was on his second tour in Vietnam. He was serving as an operations sergeant for the 12th Infantry. A career soldier, a man who knew his stuff; well-liked and respected by the men under him. It wasn't an easy job in 1970.

The war had changed, and so dad those fighting it. Morale had faltered when word came down about moving into Cambodia. The United States was withdrawing, pulling out, and now they would be going on the offensive in Cambodia? It made no sense to many of the troops in Vietnam. Every soldier in Vietnam knew the US was pulling out. To some, it seemed like a total waste of life. But the peace talks in Paris were stalled, and this incursion would ultimately prevent more American deaths. The end of this war was still a long way off. The word among the troops was to cover your ass and the ass of the man next to you. Come home alive, not in a body bag.

This type of attitude did not make Robert Ivey's job easier. He still had to follow orders, and as long as they were there, the enemy needed to be found and killed. Rumors that the 25th Division would be withdrawn before the year's end persisted. Maybe that rumor would be confirmed when he flew back to Cu Chi tomorrow. He hoped so. Whatever happened was out of his control. The important thing was his R & R. Tomorrow, he would be flying back to Cu Chi, then Bien Hoa, to begin the first leg of his transport out of here and a well-deserved week off.

Robert Oldham

Sergeant Robert Oldham was ready to go home. He was more than ready. It had been a long, draining, and tiring year. He was almost out of there. His tour had begun on July 22, 1969. Now it was almost over. Tomorrow he would catch a convoy or helicopter back to Cu Chi and begin out-processing. A few days after that, he would be on that Freedom Bird to the land of the Big PX. Eleven days and a wake-up. July 21, and he would be gone.

Robert Oldham had been drafted on February 4, 1969. A native of Caldwell, Texas, he completed his basic training at Fort Bliss.

Basic training finally came to an end on April 11, and he received his orders for his next assignment. He waited and listened for his drill sergeant to call his name. Finally, it came: "Oldham, 11C10, mortars." Mortars -it could have been worse. He could have been an 11 Bravo—infantryman. At least mortars should be a little safer. Little did he know.

Officially, he was trained as an infantry, individual fire crewman. The good thing was that the training was to take place at Fort Ord, California. A welcome change from dusty, hot Fort Bliss. The training course was nine weeks long and was taken seriously by the instructors and students alike. Life and death in the balance. Everyone assumed they would be shipping out to Vietnam as soon as the short training course was completed, and they better be ready. At least as prepared as the army could make them.

Orders came through for Robert Oldham and the other members of his class in late June. He wasn't surprised to see that he was to report at the US Army Overseas Replacement Station, Fort Lewis, Washington, on July 20, 1969. The course wrapped up on June 28, and Oldham traveled back to Texas for a short leave, where he said goodbye to his family, and then he was off to Vietnam.

Robert Oldham was assigned to B Company, 2nd Bn., 12th Infantry in the field as a mortarman. He didn't have a lot of time to adapt to the climate and the rigors of life in an infantry battalion. The most important things he learned was to stay alert, stay alive, do your job. And that was what he did. He wanted to be sure he would come home in one piece. One year, 365 days. Keep focused on July 21, 1970.

His exposure to combat operations would come soon enough. On the July 30, Company A, their sister company, lost two lieutenants. The 2nd Bn. was located at Patrol Base Dees. At 2205 hours, the battalion received ten rounds of 82mm mortar fire. They started falling outside the wire and walked them in. The third round exploded inside the compound. Lieutenants Harper and McArthur were running from their tent toward the command bunker when the mortar caught them. The same round wounded several mortarmen who were preparing the counter-mortar fire. Mortarmen like Robert Oldham. It could have easily been him.

On August 24, 2Lt. Skogerboe of his company was killed in action. Robert Oldham had only been in-country twenty-two days. He thought that being in mortars was safer than infantry. It might have been statistically but not by much.

Now his tour was almost over. Despite being a mortarman, he had been awarded the Combat Infantry Badge and an Army Commendation Medal for his service in the last year. He would put those awards on his khakis when he was at Bien Hoa for the flight home. Keep focused; the year wasn't over yet!

Thomas Campbell

Sergeant First Class Thomas Campbell had been in-country for the last five months—this tour. He was slated to head back to Cu Chi so he could go on R & R. It would be good to get out of there and see his wife again.

Thomas was a career soldier having joined the army in 1954. Starting as a mortarman like Robert Oldham, he served in Germany in 1955 and Korea in 1960. He rose to platoon sergeant in 1966 and served at a basic training company at Fort Ord, California. Vietnam beckoned, and he was transferred in 1967 and sent overseas. Upon his arrival in Vietnam, he joined Company C, 1st Bn., 12th Cavalry, 1st Cavalry Division as a platoon sergeant.

While with the 1st Cavalry Division, he was awarded the Silver Star for gallantry for an action on December 15th, 1967. He had been in-country for six months. During a combat mission near Tam Quan, his platoon became engaged with a numerically superior enemy force. Even though they were pinned down by heavy fire, Thomas organized his platoon and maneuvered it to an excellent defensive position directing return fire against the VC emplacements. Thomas then got up, completely exposed to the enemy fire, and assaulted one of the fortifications. With a hand grenade, he silenced it. The platoon rallied, seeing his example and attacked the remaining enemy positions.

Thomas was also awarded the Combat Infantry Badge and Bronze Star during his first tour in Vietnam.

Following that tour, he returned to Fort Ord as a senior drill sergeant. There he would impart the knowledge he gained fighting in Vietnam in the hope it would keep some of his young recruits alive. Recruits initially resented the harsh treatment from the drill sergeants, but as training went on, they saw the importance of it.

Orders came down for him to once again return to Vietnam as an infantry platoon sergeant. Return he did in January 1970. That was months ago, and now all he wanted to think about was going back to Bien Hoa tomorrow to begin the process of taking his R & R.

Lowell Ketchum

Sergeant First Class Lowell Ketchum was also on his second tour. For a career soldier, it would have been uncommon to serve only one tour in Vietnam. Lowell joined the Army in 1955, serving as a four-deuce mortarman. Between the time of his enlistment and his retirement, he served three tours in Germany and another in Korea. He enjoyed the army and rose steadily in the ranks.

His first tour in Vietnam was with the 1st Infantry Division in 1967. His assignment was with the 1st Bn., 5th Artillery Regiment out of Quan Loi. Quan Loi was north of Saigon, near An Loc and the Cambodian border, a highly contested area. He was there during the Tet Offensive in 1968.

It always amazed Lowell the way the war was reported back in the United States. His view of the Tet Offensive was a lot different than that of the newscasters. He said, "These newscasters sitting on their ass back in the states, or wherever, were talking about how we lost the war. That's the craziest thing, you know, they have no understanding of war at all. You take the Tet Offensive... Well, you know yourself, in a battle, in order to win, you have to own a piece of real estate that you didn't own before. You had to have killed more of the enemy than he killed of you. This didn't happen for the NVA during the Tet Offensive. They didn't gain anything. They were pushed back into North Vietnam. You know, every time Charlie marched his soldiers, we'd get stronger, that poor bastard. One day we chased them all the way from Quan Loi back into Cambodia. No telling how many people they lost, it was something else. But they didn't win anything."

Lowell began his second tour in March of 1970. This time he was assigned as a platoon sergeant with the 107mm mortar section of Company E and stationed at Fire Support Base Warrior. His mortar platoon provided support for the whole battalion. Following the Cambodian incursion, Lowell decided to reenlist for another hitch. The army had a program that if you re-upped while in Vietnam, you would get a free thirty-day leave. That was something he wanted to take advantage of. He knew when his time was up he would re-enlist anyway, so why not get a free leave and do it now? This way, he could use the leave to be home for Christmas. He had just heard some unsettling news from the sergeant major, who told him he thought that the policy had changed, and the offer of a thirty-day leave had been dropped, but he could not verify the truth of that story. No matter—tomorrow Lowell would find out, as he was to travel to Cu Chi on July 10 to reenlist.

Richard Green

Spec4 Richard Green had been in Vietnam since January. He was a grunt, 11 Bravo, infantry. He had already been wounded twice and received one Purple Heart. His first wound happened one night while on in an ambush position. Two enemy soldiers came down the path where their ambush was set up. Here they were waiting for any possible enemy activity. Selecting this position was about to pay off. As the two enemy soldiers approached Richard triggered a claymore mine that killed both of the soldiers. Somehow someone threw a grenade that hit the tree above him and landed, exploding about eight feet away. Maybe one of the enemy was alerted to the ambush and threw the grenade just before Richard set off the claymores. Richard was hit in the face by a piece of shrapnel. He was lucky; it could have killed him.

The wound was not severe enough to warrant a medevac at night. He stayed with the platoon until they finished their patrols and came back to base camp. His face getting sore, he sought medical attention, and the doctor removed the shrapnel and marked him fit for duty with a Purple Heart.

His second wound was a friendly-fire incident. It happened when he was in Cambodia. He was the point man and found a large supply area with machine guns, small arms, and rice. One of his good friends, the platoon medic, was looking at one of the pistols they found that day when it discharged. The round hit Richard's belt buckle, turned, and went in his hip and out his buttocks. He was medevacked, and it took them about three hours to sew up all the damage the bullet did.

There were so many wounded from Cambodia that they sent him to an MP barracks where he joined the company of soldiers who had superficial wounds. They were not provided with transportation to the chow hall, and the nature of Richard's wound didn't lend itself to a long walk, so he went hungry.

Two weeks later, he was marked "duty" and sent back in the field. He was still limping and bleeding but was told, "We need everybody in Cambodia," so he was sent back out. In late June, they withdrew back to South Vietnam.

Richard was slated for a promotion to Sergeant E-5. He jumped at this because he would be at the Division Sergeant School called Lightning at Cu Chi for two weeks. He would do anything to get out of the field. He had been out there for a long time. The time had come to join the school. He was sent to Dau Tieng for transport to Cu Chi.

Dau Tieng was a real treat. He had a comfortable cot and some relatively good chow. Tomorrow he would be gone for two weeks anyway. He was awakened in the middle of the night by a rocket attack on the perimeter. It didn't phase him. He just stayed in his bunk, thinking, *Wow, this is a cot; this is cool.* Everyone around him was scrambling, telling him, "You've gotta get under cover! We are being hit!" *Hell,* Richard thought, *this is about as safe as I've been since I got here. I'm not even getting out of bed! Shit, I doubt they are going to hit this building.* So, in bed he stayed.

Richard was a grenadier in his platoon and had been given the XM203. This was a grenade launcher affixed to the M-16 rifle. He was one of the bigger guys, so he had to carry it and the ammo it used. It was deemed that he should leave that weapon behind and take a standard M-79 grenade launcher with him to Cu Chi. Of course, it would be useless without ammo, so he had a vest with him containing thirty rounds of high explosive grenades.

He was supposed to leave, July 9 from Dau Tieng. But while waiting for a helicopter ride to Cu Chi, he found out a couple of guys from his unit needed to get back to the base camp and start their R & R, so he gave up his spot. It was OK; he would catch a hop tomorrow.

Denny Martin

Dau Tieng was a typical bustling Vietnamese fire support base. The 12th Infantry was headquartered there as well as other elements of the 25th Division. None of that mattered now to Denny. He was getting out of there for a week anyway. Tomorrow he would fly to Cu Chi, process out, pick up his clothes for R & R, and then be off to Ton San Nhut and the flight to Hawaii. Of course, he would have to visit the "Pee House of the August Moon" for a urine test. You couldn't leave the country with drugs in your system. Everyone knew that, so those who did use made sure to purge it before reporting. Denny didn't have to worry about that. He wasn't a user.

The whole process would take a couple of days, but that was OK. It was only the nineth and he was scheduled to fly out on the thirteenth. The next few days would be spent in the relative comfort of Bien Hoa. He would be out of the field and safe. Of course, there was always a chance of a mortar or rocket attack, but after being in the field, he could handle it.

Harlen Metzger

Harlen was relaxed being at Dau Tieng with his good friend Carey Pratt. They spent a pleasant evening chatting and sharing a laugh or two. Carey didn't have to go back to Cu Chi, but he wanted to celebrate Harlen's upcoming R & R with him. There were a few clubs on base, and they would find one and have a good time. Then Harlen would be gone, flying to meet Brenda in Hawaii, and Carey would go back to the field.

Carey Pratt

Celebrating with Harlen would be just what the doctor ordered for Carey. Cambodia had worn everyone out. Company D had been in the thick of it, as was evident from Carey's Bronze Star citation. Things had been pretty quiet since their return from Cambodia, but the stress never left. You were always on guard for an unexpected ambush. For the most part, the enemy was trying to regroup and resupply all their lost equipment. It would take them a long time to accomplish this as everything had to be brought down the Ho Chi Minh Trail. Not only was the trail fraught with dangers from accidents, but it was regularly bombed by allied air.

Right now, Carey didn't worry about all that. He was able to relax and enjoy the quiet of Dau Tieng.

Elroy Simmons

Elroy was still getting used to his surroundings, having only been in-country for a month, this tour anyway. As he was getting to know the area of operations, he was also meeting the men he would assist with their reenlistment plans. Tomorrow he would be heading back to Cu Chi to continue in his assigned job.

Mike Vullo and Melvin Chase

Mike and Melvin had completed all the repairs on the radar, and it was up and running, ready to once again track VC rockets and mortars. It had been a new and exciting experience for Melvin, the FNG. The helicopter ride to Dau Tieng had been unique and fascinating. The time on the new base doing the job he was trained for had been fulfilling. But now it was time to get back to Cu Chi.

For Mike, it was just another day on the job. Fly out, fix it, and try to get home. Mike's anniversary was just four days before on the fifth. He has been only married a year, and here he was, thousands of miles away from his bride. He had arranged a special surprise for Kathi, possibly through his sister Pam for their first anniversary. Delivered to her was a dozen roses!

He still had ten months to go on his tour. So far, he hadn't been in great danger. He wasn't in the infantry out in the bush. There were always risks when flying out to remote fire support bases. He was well aware of that. Today though was quiet, and if he could hop a flight back to Cu Chi tomorrow, he would be able to enjoy the comforts of the base: hot chow, relatively comfortable quarters, and a few beers.

Chapter 6

Inferno

God, I offer myself to thee to build with me and to do with me as

thou wilt.

-The Third Step Prayer

The morning of July 10, 1970 was hot, humid, hazy. The early-morning activities had begun. Night shift repair crews were shuffling into the mess hall for their breakfast/dinner, their work finished for the day. The pilots and crew members were having their early morning-breakfast. The usual joking around and playing grab-ass followed them out into the new day. The pilots got their assignments as the crew headed for their ship to prepare for the day's work.

For Ed Whittle, it was his third day as an aircraft commander. He had over two hundred hours of combat flying in Chinooks. When he hit the two hundred mark, he was selected as a candidate for aircraft commander. He had to fly with the unit's instructor pilot for fifteen to twenty hours; he would regularly give him emergency procedures, watching how he would react and what decisions he would make, how he would handle the people on the ground, how he would handle every situation as it arose. He passed all the tests they gave him, and his promotion to AC, aircraft commander, followed.

Today he was slated to fly with Robert Henry as his peter pilot. Robert had been in Vietnam since the previous April. They had flown together before and would fly together again. Both were comfortable being in the air together.

As they were preparing for their day's duties one of the other pilots called to Ed, "What are you flying today?" Ed replied, "Triple Niner." There was a pause. "Find something wrong with that aircraft, Ed," the other man said. "Something bad is going to happen." His tone was serious; there was no joking now. "Things come in threes; it can't go out without getting hit." Triple Niner was *Love Craft*. They didn't call it *Patches* for nothing.

Being young and invincible, Ed thought that this was all bullshit. He didn't believe in superstition. He just wasn't going to go there. He had SP4 Ross Bedient as the flight engineer. He mentioned the remark to Ross who thought that superstition of bad things coming in threes was a bunch of bull. If Ross wasn't afraid of flying in *Love Craft*, why should Ed be.

The regular crew of Ross and Rickey Wittner did a preflight inspection and made sure everything was as it should be. They were satisfied *Love Craft* was ready to fly. The gunner today was SP4 David Schultz. David was relatively new to flying but seemed to know his stuff. David walked over to the armory and drew two M-60s. He signed them out and began the long walk to the flight line with the guns. The handles cut into his hands, slightly numbing his fingers. Once he arrived at *Love Craft,* he set them inside and flexed his fingers to regain the feeling. He checked them carefully to be sure they were clean and ready to fire without jamming. Once he was happy that they were ready to fire, he secured them in their mounts. He drew additional ammo from supply while Ross and Rickey finished checking the ship. There was no such thing as too much ammo.

Armed with his clipboard listing the missions of all the ships in the company, Ed and Robert climbed into 999, *Love Craft* to begin the day.

Another crew was getting ready to take off for the day's missions from Tan Son Nhut near Saigon. They had an entirely different type of mission to fly. Their aircraft was an unarmed World War II vintage EC-47. It was piloted by a flight crew of the 360th Tactical Electronic Warfare Squadron. In the back were personnel of the 6994th Security Squadron. Their job was to locate and identify the enemy using airborne radio direction finding (ARDF) techniques and collecting intelligence information in support of ground combat commanders.

On this day, they would be flying missions off the Cambodian border, seeking enemy radio activity. The crew today would consist of four flight personnel and two electronic operators. One of those operators was Sergeant Thomas Hutchings.

SFC Lowell Ketchum couldn't seem to be able to get a flight from FSB Warrior to Cu Chi. There weren't a lot of flights going in and out of Warrior. Maybe if he were able to get to Dau Tieng, he would have better luck. There was always a lot of activity there, and flights to Cu Chi were frequent.

Later in the day, a Huey did arrive that was going to Dau Tieng. Lowell got on it.

The men slated to go back to Cu Chi slowly assembled at the airstrip, hoping to catch an early hop. They were all from the 2nd Bn., 12th Infantry. It would be a long, hot day of waiting. MSG Robert Ivey, SFC Thomas Campbell, SGT Robert Oldham, SP4 Roy Harris, and SP4 Richard Green were patiently joking around. It was a good day. Good days in Vietnam were rare.

Shortly they were joined by two other soldiers from the 2nd Bn. SP4 James Coleman of Company B and PFC Bruce Thompson of Company D. James was going home. His tour was up on August 1. and he would be processing out. Bruce was also going back to Cu Chi to go on R & R. Another straggler soon wandered over. PFC David Schwab. David was an infantryman, 11 Bravo. He was still an FNG, having been in-country only since early June, one month, give or take. For some unknown reason, they were sending him back to Cu Chi. Most likely a medical issue or some screwup in paperwork.

A few men of the 14th Infantry soon joined them. SGT Carey Pratt, SP4 Denny Martin, and SP4 Harlen Metzger. It was good to be out of the bush, even if it was for a short time. Carey would be heading back in a day or two while the other two enjoyed their R & R in Hawaii with their wives. Carey already had his R & R in Hawaii, and he knew how much fun they would have.

Some of the men were hungover from a little pre–R & R, or DEROS, celebration. Regardless, the prevailing mood among the men was a good one.

BM3 Larry Crozier waited for the radio to squawk confirmation that supplies were going to be delivered today. They needed food, ammo, water, and, most of all fuel for their PBRs. They cruised the upper Saigon River looking for a good spot to receive the materials. There had to be a piece of flat land near the river for the Chinook helicopter to deposit their sling load of supplies and three fuel blivets. The area where they were was called the Mushroom. A loop in the Saigon River made it look like a mushroom. The space inside the loop was heavily cratered by past artillery and bombing strikes. It had also been defoliated by Agent Orange, which contaminated the ground and river. Somehow there was still a village there and some jungle that had survived the ravages of war.

They had four or five different spots where they resupplied. They never refueled in the same location within a month. Too dangerous. Sometimes it would be a week between resupply. It all depended on how much fuel they used and if they had seen any action. They treated resupply missions like combat. You never knew what would happen or who was watching.

They had to pick a spot where the boats could cozy up to shore and bring in the supplies and refuel both boats. The location was critical—the shore had to be higher than the river. They could not be close to the jungle where an ambush could take place, and it had to be a spot where they hadn't been before. It had been about a week since their last resupply. The spot they used last time was farther downriver. The place they chose fit all their needs. It was a good one. Refueling was always dangerous. The blivets were connected to the boats by a rubber hose and gravity fed. It took a long time to do that, usually all afternoon. Refueling made for a stressful and tense afternoon. If there was leftover fuel, they would give it to the local children, who would put it in containers and take it to their village.

Finally, the call came in. They radioed the location for the drop. They were upriver from the small village of Ap Soc Lao and close to Ben Suc, not critically close to jungle or tree lines. No recent enemy activity was reported in this area. It was quiet. Now they would just wait a little upriver for the Chinook to get close; then, they would move into position.

The helicopter carrying Lowell from FSB Warrior to Dau Tieng finally arrived. He walked over to the group of men waiting for a ride to Cu Chi and instantly saw Ivey. They were friends. They had worked closely together at 2nd Bn. They started chewing the fat, talking about home, Vietnam, and the troops they led.

SFC Elroy Simmons soon joined the group. He was finished with his recruiting duties for now. He would continue looking for soldiers to re-up over the next year.

The tired pair of radar repairers SP4 Mike Vullo and PFC Melvin Chase walked over to the group, sat down, and relaxed, glad to hear that they would be able to fly back to Cu Chi and avoid taking a convoy, which was fraught with ambush hazards. Flying was best way to go: quick and safe.

Now they all waited for their ride to the World, R & R, or just a comfortable bunk.

Larry and one of his American counterparts, a seaman named Gonzalez, waited for the resupply bird to fly in and make the drop. They pulled close to the shore, and the two of them jumped onto dry land. Soon they could hear the Chinook coming, the familiar rotor sound splitting the morning air. The PBR left its mooring to move a little further downriver. This was standard operating procedure to avoid all the dirt and debris that would be thrown in the air from the rotor wash as the helicopter came to a low hover, dropping off the sling load of supplies and three fuel blivets.

The Chinook set down their load, and the two sailors unhooked them Everything was in place, and the Chinook was safely on its way to another mission. The first boat motored in close to shore and a fuel line hooked up. The boat had to be slightly lower than the bladders. It had to be that way as they had to use good old-fashioned gravity to transfer the fuel from the bladder to the boat. With the second boat providing cover, fueling began. They scanned the area, but nothing unusual was noted. Typical activity in the village—a piece of cake.

While everything seemed quiet and normal, it wasn't. The refueling was being watched. Undercover, possibly a reinforced squad of Viet Cong, quietly took it all in. Their squad normally consisted of thirteen men, but when the Americans crossed the border into Cambodia, they lost a few of their comrades, not to mention a multitude of supplies and ammunition. Today they had at least three rocket-propelled grenades and their AK-47s. They were likely part of the 9th Viet Cong Division and had seen it all before. These refueling procedures were pretty standard. Chopper comes in, drops supplies; then later in the day, another comes in and picks up what is left. They decided not to attack the navy boats but wait for the chopper to come in. They were in a good position, depending on the direction it flew in.

Late afternoon, 999's missions were complete, and they needed fuel. Ed and Robert Henry flew toward the Dau Tieng POL to fill up. The Chinook could hold approximately one-thousand gallons of fuel so it would take a little time.

After landing, Rickey and Ross filled the ship with fuel so it would be ready for the next day's missions. As they prepared to take off for Cu Chi, they received a call from the control tower: "999, we have some passengers here going to Bien Hoa and Cu Chi—can you take them?" Ed replied, "I will take them to Bien Hoa then Cu Chi." Bien Hoa was just a hop, skip and a jump. They were full of fuel and would have no problem delivering them there before heading back to Cu Chi. If they had been flying a combat mission, they would never pick up the passengers, but now the day was done. It was about 1800—it would be and easy flight to Bien Hoa and back to Cu Chi to wrap up the day.

The Chinook flew over to the tower area and landed. The fifteen troops joined the five-man crew, settling in place on the red jump seats lining both sides. Ross made the call over the intercom: "We have fifteen and five." Twenty souls on board.

Lowell and Robert Ivey were the last to board. They made sure everyone got on safely; then they climbed in. They both went to the front of the aircraft to sit down. Lowell always went to the front of the aircraft, any aircraft. During his first tour, he boarded a

Caribou and was the last man to board. It was during the monsoon, wind blowing, and heavy rain. They flew in at a steep angle to land at a remote airstrip. The pilot swung the plane around at the last minute. As he lined up for the landing, Lowell flew down onto the ramp. Fortunately, he did not fly out! He was banged up and airsick, but OK. So when he boarded the Chinook, he went way up front and sat himself down in a jump seat.

Harlen made sure he was seated near the open cargo hatch in the floor. He had grown up around heavy machinery, and his dad had always taught him that if anything happened to make sure he could jump clear. Being near the cargo hatch seemed like an excellent place to be.

Richard boarded and saw there was a lot of room on that ship. He made his way forward and sat in one of the jump seats by the hook and the open hatch in the floor. He thought, *Well if I gotta get out of this place, this is where I'm gonna be.* His training and feelings of self-preservation told him that this was the spot to be, so that was where he sat down.

When all the troops were on board, they took off for Bien Hoa and Cu Chi.

The flight was uneventful until a radio call came to *Love Craft* from another Chinook of the 242nd. This ship was farther south and was slated to pick up the empty fuel blivets. The problem was on board there was an IP (an instructor pilot) giving a check flight. He had too many hours in the air and had to get back to Cu Chi. Ed and Robert Henry had the closest aircraft and were instructed to take this mission. The area of the pickup had been very quiet and considered pacified at that time—no action. This would be a milk run, something they had routinely done. Just an average slight delay in picking up the empty blivets and head out. They had no choice but to divert and do the pickup.

They would never have gone on a combat mission with passengers. If there were a perceived threat, Ed would have refused the task no matter what the consequences might be.

A Chinook is not a quiet machine. It makes a lot of noise and can be heard from a far distance, especially if you are waiting for it. Larry and Gonzalez left their boats and walked over to the empty blivets and prepared to hook them up to the Chinook when it arrived. The Vietnamese sailors would not get under a landing or hovering Chinook. They thought it would come down and squash them.

The PBRs backed away upriver from the pickup point. The backwash from the powerful rotors would blow loose ground debris onto the boat, not to mention anything on the boat that wasn't tied down would be swept overboard.

Larry watched the Chinook in the distance as it approached. It would be quick and easy. The ship would hover, he and Gonzalez would hook up the straps attached to the empty blivets and off they would go. Easy-peasy. He popped a smoke grenade and waited.

Another group of eyes watched the approaching chopper. Viet Cong eyes. They prepared for the arrival by spreading out in the closest jungle tree line. RPGs ready, AK-47s prepared to fire. Now they waited in tense silence.

As *Love Craft* approached the pickup zone David was at the left window sitting on the toolbox they kept there. With his M-60 machine gun at the ready, he scanned the area for possible threats. Rickey did the same from his gun position on the right. Peaceful, everything looked quiet—nothing out of the ordinary toward the river and treeline.

Richard looked down the hatch at the ground and saw that they were going down to pick up a cargo net and rubber blivets. Now he became tense and extremely apprehensive. He thought, *What the hell is this guy doing?*

When they took off from Dau Tieng, Ross was at his position at the front of the ship by the right gun, and Rickey was at the back by the rear cargo door. Ross walked to the end of the ship, where Rickey was and said, "Tex, let me call this load in." This was Ross's last mission before going on R & R to see his girl. It was no big deal as they swapped back and forth all the time.

As they passed over the village, something looked different to Rickey. It took him a moment to figure it out. No children were running around the village. No adults either. Where was everyone? What the hell?

Before he could warn the pilots he saw a puff of smoke from the tree line. He keyed the mic but before he could speak, the RPG struck the ship. It was 1840.

The Viet Cong had waited until the ship was entirely in range and right over the mostly empty fuel blivets. Then they fired the first RPG. With a *whoosh* and a trail of flame, it struck the right engine pylon, exploding in an orange flash and igniting the full right fuel tank.

Everything happened fast now. Rickey saw two more puffs of smoke as the second and third RPGs screamed toward 999. The AK-47s opened fire at the hovering helicopter.

Up front, Ed heard the first *whoomp* as the RPG hit but had no idea what it was. Then he heard more *whoomps*. The aircraft started to list left, and Ed added right cyclic to try and correct it. He thought the *whoomp* was from mortar tubes firing, but no one on the ground had told him there would be outgoing mortar fire. He keyed his intercom and yelled, "What's going on? Where are those mortars? Where are those mortars?" Nobody answered him. He was still frantically trying to correct the aircraft, but the aircraft wouldn't correct. It just kept floating down and to the left. Now, everything seemed to go into slow motion.

He looked out his left window and saw the rotor blade. "We're gonna contact the ground!" He thought he was dead. Instinctively he stiffened his arm out the window and then thought, *Well, that's dumb, get your arm back in here.*

The second RPG hit in front of the number one engine, and the third hit right beside the door in which Rickey was standing. He grabbed his M-60 by the butterfly grip to hang on, but when the third hit, it took the gun mount with it, so he had nothing to hang on to. The chopper rolled over and hit almost on its left side. As the helicopter rolled, Rickey was flung to the other side of the ship near where David had been standing. He smashed his left leg against the toolbox, splitting the leg muscles.

Inside the aircraft, it was chaos. Somebody screamed, "We're hit; we're going down!" Lowell looked toward the back of the ship, and all he could see was a ball of fire rolling toward him, the men in the rear screaming and already engulfed in flames. He thought, *Bud, you've had a great life, but it's all over. It's ashes to ashes and dust to dust.*

Robert Oldham and Thomas Campbell were sitting together at the rear end of the Chinook. When the first RPG hit, they were peppered with shrapnel and burning JP-4.

The burning ship came down on the mostly empty fuel bladders exploding in a ball of fire. The fuel bladders immediately caught fire, adding to the intense inferno that now engulfed the crashed helicopter. Larry saw it coming down and ran like hell away from it. The rotor blades acted like a scythe cutting through the air. He outran the whirling blades and ball of fire, but then he went back. There were holes in the side of the burning chopper either from the RPGs or from the Chinook's own melting skin breaking apart.

Larry waved at the PBRs to come to the crash site then ran toward the back of the chopper to help the survivors.

In the cockpit, things happened in split seconds after the RPGs hit. As the Chinook went down, Ed saw his home, friends, and family waving at him. And then 999 hit the ground, and there was a big, loud crash and the tearing sound of ripping metal. The rotor blades struck the ground disintegrating and sending pieces flying everywhere. When he came to, he could hear the transmission going, "Rrrrrrr," the last few gears stopping. The rotor system was gone; it was just the hubs. Everything went black; he thought, *I'm dead.*

The third RPG had broken the nose off the ship, landing it upside down with the pilots in it. Ed found himself upside down, his head on the dirt. The center console and the forward pedestal were so close to him that even though he tried, he couldn't move. Robert Henry was also upside down. He sat in a confused daze trying to figure out where he was. He couldn't move. Then he realized he was strapped in so he undid his seat belt falling down on what was the top of the cockpit.

Ed saw red liquid dripping, like hydraulic fluid, and he thought, *Geez, that's hot. Where is that coming from?* He put out his glove, following the hydraulic fluid up, and he discovered that it wasn't hydraulic fluid at all; it was blood from his head. He had a massive gash across the left side of his forehead.

He knew he had to get out of there and fast. He reached up and grabbed what turned out to be a hot hydraulic line, and it came off and sprayed hydraulic fluid on him. He removed his helmet because the mic cord had become tangled, not allowing his head to move. He struggled out of his chicken plate to try and get out through a broken window next to him. He heard his copilot yelling, "Help! Help! Help!" Ed looked over at him and hollered, "Hey, are you OK?" Robert Henry replied, "Yeah," and Ed said, "OK, let's get out of here," and the next time he looked over there, his copilot was gone.

Robert Henry had crawled out through a broken window. He staggered away from the wreckage and felt a wetness on his leg. *What the hell?* he thought. He reached down and found a large cut on his leg. What he was feeling was blood.

Lowell hadn't been strapped in, and that probably saved his life. As the ship impacted the ground, he was projected across the aircraft injuring his shoulder and a couple of ribs. He also took a good hit on his head and had no remembrance of the events right after 999 crashed. Robert Ivey was blown out of the ship into the dirt.

Two thousand feet above this scene, the EC-47 of the 6994th Security Squadron was flying. One of the pilots looked down and keyed his mic: "There's a 47 down there taking fire!" Thomas Hutchings looked out his window and saw an RPG hit the ship. He watched it explode and drop to the ground. To him, it looked like the front was destroyed. He watched as the passengers scurried from the burning Chinook into the brush and river. This wasn't the first shootdown he had seen, but it was the most unusual because there were so many troops running from the wreckage.

Richard Green was sitting by the hook, looking down at the ground when the first RPG hit. All of a sudden, *BOOM*! The fire from the burning fuel roared through the ship, and it started to go down. Richard thought, *Well, this is how it's gonna end, huh? Well, it's been a good life up to now.* Then he was engulfed in flames, and the ship hit the ground, hard and tipped partially on its side.

When the third RPG hit, Rickey was thrown out of the helicopter. When everything stopped, he realized he was on the ground and away from the chopper. Suddenly he was hit in the back of the head by a piece of the rotor blade which cut his helmet in half knocking him back on the ground. That helmet saved his life! As he stood again, the broken helmet was falling off his head, so he threw it on the ground.

Inside the chopper, amid flames, Richard Green looked for a way out. He saw some daylight –a hole in the side of the ship. Somebody was staggering around in shock in front of him, blocking his way. He just pushed him through the hole in front of him. As he pushed, he yelled, "Get the hell out of here. Let's go." He ran out of the ship, entirely on fire - with thirty high-explosive grenades strapped to his body.

Harlen Metzger was also sitting by the hook. He heard the first explosion and saw the flames rolling toward him. He braced as the Chinook impacted the ground; then, with his back toward the fire burning him, he jumped through the hatch in the floor. He hit his side hard on the way out, bruising a kidney and rupturing his spleen. He was halfway out when the ship rocked, pinning him under it. When it rolled, he scrambled free and back into the ship, but the fire was too hot, so he tried again but was pinched under the rocking helicopter. He had no choice but to stay and crawl out from underneath away from the fire. Harlen's instincts had taken over. His father's instructions echoed in his mind. *Jump clear!* He was almost crushed but made it out alive.

Harlen had taken his rifle with him, and despite his burns and injuries, he started firing into the tree line where the rockets had come from. The VC were still there, firing at the burning helicopter and running troops. Harlen made it to the river and saw one of the black soldiers in the river drowning. Harlen grabbed him and pulled him out, saving his life.

Rickey's first instinct at this point was to find Ross. He knew he was somewhere in the chopper, which was burning uncontrollably. Not only was it on fire, the ammunition, and grenades the men carried as well as the belts of M-60 ammo from 999's guns started to cook-off. There were still men trapped inside, screaming. Ignoring the fire and exploding ammunition Rickey ran into the burning wreckage looking for Ross. He couldn't find him, but he found others and helped them out of the wreckage. He put out the fires on their bodies with his hands, burning them. The Nomex gloves were supposed to be flame resistant, but they burned right off Rickey's hands. He kept finding burned and burning soldiers but not Ross or David.

Then he heard Ed screaming for help. He was trapped in the wreckage. He could only get his hands out through a hole in the window or chin bubble; he couldn't tell exactly which was which do to the fact that the cockpit was smashed and inverted. He saw the Robert Henry and Rickey and yelled, "Hey, hey, hey!" They saw his hands sticking out, and they ran over and grabbed each of his arms and started to pull. Ed hollered, "Wait, wait, wait. My legs are caught." They tried to free his trapped foot but couldn't.

They ignored his pleas and just kept pulling. Pulling. The aircraft was now in pieces, and the burning fuel and melting magnesium were flowing into the cockpit. For him to not burn alive, they had to keep pulling, not caring if his legs were injured or even removed in the process. Finally, they pulled him free. There was no time to try and stop the bleeding from his head wound because the VC were still firing at the downed helicopter.

The PBRs jumped into action and fired all of their fifty-caliber machine guns into the tree line, suppressing the VC fire.

They began bringing the boats up near the crash to rescue the survivors. One of the navy advisors made an urgent radio call for gunship support. "Anyone in the area!"

Larry and Gonzalez were in the thick of it. They saw the nose of the helicopter come off and land upside down. The enemy was firing from the tree line, but they disregarded the incoming rounds and made three trips to the burning ship, rescuing the injured and extinguishing their burning clothes.

Larry took it all in, almost as though it were happening in surreal slow motion. There were soldiers with their clothes completely burned off. One soldier's eyelids were burned off. His mouth was moving, but Larry was sure he would not make it. He grabbed men, herding them away from the fire and toward the river. As he grabbed some, their skin came off in his hands.

He saw a man on fire coming toward him. He threw him on the ground and jumped on him, putting out the flames, and yelled, "How many guys were in the crew?" He yelled back, "I don't know; I'm not part of the crew." Larry looked back at the ship and saw men running out of the fire through holes in the helicopter. He and Gonzalez herded them away from the fire and incoming rounds. Then there were guys coming everywhere.

Richard Green's clothes were on fire, and he knew if he didn't get to the river, the high-explosive rounds in his vest would start exploding. It was about twenty or thirty yards to the river. He ran as fast as his feet could carry him and jumped. Somewhere along the way, he had lost his M-79 but was still completely weighted down by the ammo in his vest. The rest of his clothes were burning off. When he hit the water, the flames went out, but he sank like a rock. In his haste, he had jumped too far into the river. He struggled to keep his head above the water and started yelling for help.

One of the soldiers, Bruce Thompson it was believed, ran over, and grabbed Richard, pulling him out of the water, keeping him from drowning. They stayed low by the bank because there was still fire coming from the tree line.

Denny was severely burned in the crash. He crawled free of the burning wreckage but then did something so characteristic of Denny. Despite the intense pain of the severe burns covering his body, he went back in to try and rescue some of those still trapped. He helped someone out and went back in again. That trip was his last; he didn't make it out.

Rickey helped Ed to the river to be picked up by the boats. He was still bleeding profusely from his head wound. Despite his injured leg and burnt hands, Rickey ran back to the burning Chinook to look for Ross and David. He saw no sign of Ross, but he knew where David should be, and he would try and find him. There was wreckage, burning fuel, and melting aluminum everywhere, so it was hard to pinpoint the exact location. It became impossible to search anymore for David. He just hoped he made it out somehow. The heat was intense; ammo continued cooking off; the smells of the burning fuel, burnt flesh and cordite assaulted his senses. As he turned away from the conflagration, he heard another soldier hollering for help. He grabbed him by the shoulders and led him to the boats.

All of a sudden, two Cobra gunships were on station firing miniguns and rockets into the tree line. As they were doing so, the boats arrived to pick up the survivors. One of them ran aground so the injured could climb aboard. Another boat arrived to do the same. As Ed was preparing to board one of the ships, he saw Ross running toward the water. His Nomex flight suit was burned entirely off him. All you could see was his boots and where the elastic from his shorts had seared into his body. The burnt skin was just falling off him. Somehow Ross saw Ed and started screaming, "Mr. Whittle, Mr. Whittle, it's not your fault. Mr. Whittle, it's not your fault." Rickey never saw this as he continued looking, with his stinging eyes and burnt hands for Ross in the burning wreckage and rescuing others as he found them.

Those not seriously injured started helping those who were. The incoming fire from Charlie had stopped. The Cobras had done their job—the VC di di mau'd out of there.

Lowell Ketchum was wandering around the burning mess in a daze. He was burned and had taken a severe blow to the head. He walked around the front of what was left of the aircraft and met Robert Ivey. In the blast, he had been blown through the door and had a bad shoulder injury but no burns. Lowell was still smoking from his burns, and Robert Ivey was bleeding from his wounded shoulder. They both slowly walked toward the river and the boats.

Carey Pratt was completely engulfed in flames. He had been sitting at the back of the cabin with Harlen's gear on the floor between his legs. When the RPG hit, it broke open the fuselage, spraying burning fuel over everyone sitting there, including Carey.

Covered in flames from his head to his toes, he either staggered out of the fire or was helped into the clean air where he collapsed, his clothes gone, burned off. He was carried to the boats.

Roy Harris and Elroy Simmons had been in the rear near Carey and suffered the same fate. They also were somehow able to escape the conflagration and made it to the boats badly burnt.

When the Chinook crashed to the ground, Melvin Chase was able to escape alive. Realizing his partner Mike was still inside the helicopter, he ran back into the burning and melting wreckage, found Mike, and dragged him away. Melvin was severely burned, but Mike was much worse. Melvin helped the smoldering Mike toward the boats, praying that both would live.

Robert Ivey arrived at the river ahead of Lowell and jumped in. The water was too deep, and he sank like a stone. He tried to use his arms to get to the surface, but because of his shoulder injury, he had only one hand. When his feet hit bottom, he pushed himself up as hard as he could to break the surface. Fortunately, there was a branch there that he caught hold of with his good hand and was able to haul himself out of the water. He survived the crash but almost drowned in the river just feet away from rescue.

Larry kept herding the dazed survivors onto the boats. He had no idea how many there were; it was too chaotic. On one of his trips to and from the wreckage, he saw a corpse, wholly burned and smoking but still recognizable as a man. The smells made a lasting impression, much more that the noise filling the air. The smell of a battlefield is one you never can forget. It wasn't just the smell of burning JP-4 and melting aluminum. The coppery smell of blood, the acidic bite of the smell of vomit and the horrible smell of burnt flesh combined with the smell of the rockets that exploded in the tree line were overpowering. The survivors would never forget it.

There was still an occasional round or grenade going off from the flames and heat. Four or five men were in terrible shape. They were carried and put in the boats. The ARVNs helped. It was time to get everyone out of the area.

Ed took one of the radios from the ship and began calling one of the 242nd ships that he'd seen on a test flight nearby. It didn't have any guns, but it did have two pilots and a flight engineer on board. He asked them to relay the call to flight operations and tell them what was going on. Then the boats went downriver to get to a safe place for the wounded to be medevacked out.

Larry gave one of the less wounded soldiers his radio and map to call for help from any aircraft in the area.

Rickey was still on the shore. He had done all he could to rescue the wounded. Now he turned back to the river and the boats. The boats were pulling away as he ran toward them. Reaching the river, he jumped in and started to swim. One of the boat crew saw him and turned the boat around to pick him up. He was aboard.

The boats headed downstream to the second curve in the river, away from the kill zone. In a few short minutes, two Hueys flew in to pick up the wounded. They hovered amid the elephant grass, and the most severely injured were loaded first. Harlen, though badly wounded, was apprehensive about getting on another helicopter. Truth was, he had no choice

Waiting to board, Richard was in shock, and his clothes completely gone, burned off, but there were men in a lot worse shape than him. They should have boarded first. But the only seat left was in the door, and everyone shied away from the door. Finally, Richard said, "Well, no one's gonna sit in the door. I'll sit in the door. I'll go." And then he was out of there. He was on the first evac out because he sat at the door, naked as a jaybird.

Chapter 7
Caring for the Wounded and Recovering the Dead

Only the dead have seen the end of war

-Plato

Two helicopters were carrying sixteen burnt, battered, shocked soldiers. They made the flight from the Mushroom to Cu Chi in short order. As they flew in to land at the 12th Evacuation Hospital, there was a host of medical personnel waiting; they knew they had a mass casualty complement arriving. The wounded were quickly offloaded and immediately triage began. SP4 Roy Harris, PFC Bruce Thompson, PFC David Schwab, SGT Carey Pratt, PFC Melvin Chase, SP4 Mike Vullo, and SP4 Ross Bedient were the most severely burned and immediately brought into the hospital.

Upon arrival at the hospital, Rickey Wittner tried to get away and go back to the barracks despite his injured leg and burnt hands. He ran into his friend Ken Bookhammer who was at the hospital looking for him and Ross. He made Rickey go back for treatment. The doctors and nurses were working on everyone, trying to keep them alive. Looking at the burnt and mangled bodies, Rickey got scared. He couldn't find Ross anywhere, and this bothered him even more. Later, he found a nurse and asked her where he was. She told him that they had taken him to the 3rd Field Hospital in Saigon for care that only they could provide. After they stabilized him he would be moved to Camp Zama, Japan then to the Brooke Hospital Burn Center in San Antonio.

Rickey was given a bed to lie down and rest while those more severely injured were treated. One of the 25th Division's officers came in and started to grill Rickey on how many people were on the helicopter. Rickey gave them his count of fifteen passengers, but he kept pressing him to change his number as it was thought there should be sixteen plus the crew of five. There was supposed to be one more man on there according to their count. Finally, the company commander of the 242nd jumped in and said, "No, no, no, no. We're not going there anymore. You asked him; he's answered you! Enough!"

But the questions on the count continued with Ed Whittle. The medics were trying to clean up his head wound so they could stitch it. The XO from the 242nd asked him for the count: "Fifteen and five." Ed replied. Fifteen passengers and five crew. But he kept grilling him: "How many people were on that airplane? How many people?" "Fifteen and five." He said, "Whit, Whit, really. Come on; we're trying to find out how many bodies we are we looking for." He replied, "No, no, no. That's right." Finally, they left him alone.

Robert Henry was one of the last to be taken care of. The cut in his knee needed seventeen stitches to close. He would be pretty stiff for a while but he was alive and relatively unscathed.

Rickey was admitted to the hospital because of his hands and left leg. In the bed next to him was SFC Lowell Ketchum, still unconscious. Lowell came to the day after the crash. He looked over at Rickey and saw that his hands were bandaged due to his burns.

Rickey looked Lowell and said, "They did a job on us, didn't they, Sarge?" Lowell still kind of out of it from the blow to the head he received in the crash, said, "Who did?" "Charlie. I'm sure sorry." "Why? Did you help them?" Rickey replied, "No, that was my aircraft."

SP4 Harlen Metzger limped into the hospital. The doctors told him to lie down. He had a really hard time doing that—his back was covered in burns, and his spleen was ruptured. Whatever he did, it hurt. He saw his friend Carey on a gurney, but he was so burnt it was almost impossible to recognize him.

July 10, 1970 was Larry Butcher's twenty-first birthday, and he was celebrating. He was in the NCO Club when SSG Jerry Conn came in with some bad news. "A Chinook was shot down, and some Delta guys were on it." That was all he knew. He didn't know who they were if they were dead or what. It was a shock to the men celebrating Doc's big day.

Once the boats made sure that all the survivors had been dusted off, they returned to their normal duties. Two of the PBRs continued down the river completing their patrol. It was starting to get dark now, so the two containing Larry and Gonzalez traveled back to the crash site where they sat on the riverbank, keeping watch. It was an eerie night. Normal river sounds permeated the air while things in the village were quiet. The smells of burnt metal, flesh, and grass filled their nostrils. They could also smell the melted magnesium and cordite from the exploded ammunition.

They had no idea how many bodies would be found in the morning. They hoped none; maybe everyone got out. The dawn would tell. For now, it was quiet. No VC activity: no one was disturbing the wreckage.

Things were still hectic at the 12th Evacuation Hospital. Mike Vullo, Carey Pratt, Ross Bedient, Roy Harris, Bruce Thompson, David Schwab, and Melvin Chase were all evacuated to Tan Son Nhut and the 3rd Field Hospital less than two hours after the crash. They required a higher level of care than the 12th Evac was equipped to give them.

The helicopters carrying the soldiers arrived at the 3rd Field Hospital at approximately 2030, on July 10. Medical personnel were waiting for them and immediately went to work. The hospital had no official ID on these men as their clothes had been completely burned off and their dog tags melted or missing. Identification would wait; now they had to try and save their lives. Mike Vullo was immediately taken into the operating room. He had first, second and third-degree burns covering 90 percent of his body. In actuality, the only part of his body not affected was the front of his torso. His body was grotesquely swollen and the flesh on his arms, legs, and chest greatly distended. In the OR, an escharotomy was performed to prevent the collapse of the vascular and lymphatic structures. These surgical incisions were made on his arms, legs, and chest to relieve this pressure.

Carey was actually in worse condition than Mike. His burns covered 100 percent of his body. He was wholly charred and swollen. He also needed immediate escharotomy incisions on his legs, arms, and chest. The staff worked furiously to keep him alive, but it seemed it might be futile. Nevertheless, they did everything they could.

Ross had burns over 50 percent of his body, including his entire back, the back of his arms and legs, his face and neck, as well as parts of the fronts of his arms and legs where the fire had circled around from his back. They started IVs and antibiotics. He was in better shape than Mike and Carey, so there was hope he would live.

With the dawn of the next day came the sound of helicopters as the army sent a platoon in to secure the crash site and begin the grisly task of searching for bodies. Their first task was to patrol for any marauding VC who may still be lurking in the area. None were found. They then searched the area targeted by the Cobras, looking for bodies or blood trails. None were found. The VC knew that it was only a short matter of time before gunships would arrive on the scene. Typical ambush: hit-and-run. Live to fight another day.

Finding the bodies in that tangled mass of destroyed machinery was very difficult. According to the reports by Rickey and Ed, four men were missing who were on the helicopter when it crashed. These turned out to be SP4 Denny Martin, SFC Thomas Campbell, SP4 Robert Oldham, and SP4 David Schultz. The only one that they knew should be in there was David. At the time, the rest were unknown. The fire was so intense it was like a crematorium.

Graves registration (GR) personnel flew in when once the site was deemed secure. GR personnel took photos and sifted through the melted aluminum looking for human remains. It was hard to find them; they were infused under the remains of the rotors and engines.

Eventually, they located the remains of four bodies. All had been burned completely, like match sticks. Identifying them would be a difficult task for the mortuary personnel. Two bodies were located toward where the rear of the helicopter would have been and one midships. The lower extremities of the bodies they found were missing. The intensity of the flames had incinerated them. The fourth body was up front near where the helicopter came down on the fuel bladders. He also was severely mutilated, his skull crushed, brains leaking. Some of the local villagers, mostly children, came out to explore the area but were shooed away by the security troops.

The four were placed in body bags. The team then continued searching in case there were others killed in the crash that they weren't aware of. They found no one. The site was clear.

A helicopter arrived to take the four body bags to Cu Chi and the GR Collection Point. There they would try and make preliminary identifications. They knew that there were two black and two white soldiers missing. None were readily identifiable. The men working at the collecting point would contact the units of the missing men and gather up their personnel files and any other information that might identify them.

Their work finished, the troops assigned to secure the site left and went back to war, leaving the remains of *Love Craft* where it lay.

While in Vietnam, Lowell was always worried about losing an arm or a leg. When he came to the morning of July 11, he looked down, and there was a cage over his legs covered with sterile sheets. He was sure his legs were gone. Finally, he worked up enough nerve to lift the sheets…and saw he still had his legs. They weren't very pretty, but he still had them.

Later that morning, the hospital commander, a full-bird Colonel, pinned a Purple Heart on Lowell and asked how he was doing. He replied that his shoulder was killing him. The colonel asked, "What did the Doctor say?" Lowell replied that he hadn't seen a doctor. Shortly after the colonel left, the doctor, a very red-faced major came in. The colonel had chewed his ass big time. The major asked Ketchum, "What in the hell are you talking about; you haven't seen a doctor, Sergeant? I came in, and you were the last man that I saw because you wouldn't let nobody touch you until everybody on that aircraft had been looked at." Lowell had been out of his head but was still doing his job as an NCO. He realized then what had happened and said, "Doctor, you go get the colonel and bring him back here, and I'll apologize in front of you. I had no remembrance of nothing until I woke up this morning." "That's all right; don't worry about it." The major laughed. "You know," he said, "we didn't find anything wrong with your shoulder, but I'll send you back to X-ray."

Lowell was still a little foggy about the details of the whole crash. There was a black kid in the bed next to him whose hands had been severely burned. Lowell looked over and asked him, "Did you see me? What was I doing?" He said, "Yeah, I seen you. You were in the back of the boat, and I was up front." He continued, "The front was raised, I think. Anyway, you got up and came up there and made me get down in the boat." Lowell was pleased with himself that he was still trying to do the things that an NCO should do.

Larry Butcher made it over to the 12th Evac to see his friends from Delta Company. Carey had been evacuated to the 3rd Field Hospital at Tan Son Nhut. Larry had been told that Denny was missing, but he knew Denny Martin only in passing because he wasn't in Larry's platoon when he was out with the grunts. Larry visited with Harlen, who was still coherent despite the pain meds. He told Larry that when he got out, the fire was so hot, there was nothing he could do. He was in pain; it was impossible to look for Carey. He was lucky to get out alive. When Larry left, he got physically ill and threw up.

MSG Robert Ivey, SP4 James Coleman, SP4 Richard Green, SP4 Harlen Metzger, SFC Elroy Simmons, Lowell and Harlen remained at Cu Chi. For the time being, their wounds would be treated there. Ed, Robert Henry, and Rickey were treated and released; their injuries were not deemed serious.

Word started circulating among the troops what had happened. The men of D Company, 2nd Bn, 14th Infantry, were outside Dau Tieng when word came down that a helicopter was shot down carrying three D Company troopers. Information was sketchy except that the aircraft they were on was at a hover, took enemy fire, and crashed. Denny, Carey, and Harlen were on board. Denny was missing. All Bill Bullock, one of Denny's friends could think of was how much Denny had been looking forward to his R & R in Hawaii with his wife.

Dan Krehbiel was in the same platoon as Carey and Harlen. They had been in the field and just returned to Dau Tieng from a multiple-day ambush patrol when SGT Mike Tolbert gave them the news that both were in a crash and seriously wounded. It was a somber day for the platoon. Both men were well-liked and respected. They could only hope they would both live. There was no time to contemplate that for long. There was a war on, and it wouldn't stop for mourning.

At the 725th, Mike Gandee was on guard duty when someone walked by and casually said, "Mike was in a crash." The person told Gandee that Mike Vullo and the new guy, Melvin Chase, had caught a hop on a Chinook coming back to Cu Chi, and it was shot down. He didn't know anything else. Mike Gandee was in shock.

Jim Calabrese had three days left in-country, and he was going home. But even though he was short, he still had work to do at the 242nd. He and a soldier from the parts supply were detailed to drive a truck from Cu Chi to Tan Son Nhut to pick up parts for their Chinooks. This was a long drive, and it was far from safe. Jim couldn't believe it. "Here I am with three days left, and I'm riding in this frigging truck. What am I doing?" Well, they made the trip without incident, and when he got back, he heard that Ross and David Schultz were shot down. David Schultz was missing and presumed dead, and Ross was in the hospital.

The four bodies of the missing soldiers arrived at the graves registration collection point by helicopter on July 11. The 242nd reported one soldier missing; the 12th Infantry had two believed to be on that helicopter; and the 14th had one. Their personnel files were requested from their parent units, and the grisly task of trying to get a preliminary identification of the men began before they would be sent to the mortuary at Tan Son Nhut.

An NCO or officer went through everything the men owned. Everything had to be screened for anything that might prove upsetting to the next of kin. They looked at every photograph and read every letter to be sure there was nothing that might be deemed inappropriate. Per army regulations, anything screened out would be destroyed. All remaining personal effects would make their way to the mortuary for additional screening and shipment to the next of kin.

The collection point personnel checked the bodies for anything that could identify them, such as tattoos and scars, but the remains were charred. No evidence of any identifying marks could be found.

One soldier wore charred remnants of Nomex trousers and a shirt with a partially obliterated name tag saying "Schltz." He was marked BTB (Believed to Be) SP4 David Schultz. The other three were unidentifiable to the personnel at the collection Point.

Despite the desperate efforts of the hospital staff, Mike Vullo succumbed to his wounds. He died of cardiac arrest the day after the crash, July 11, at 2150, approximately twenty-four hours after arriving at the 3rd Field Hospital. The pain was over now. His suffering would shortly be transferred to his family. His body was moved to the army mortuary for embalming and processing for the trip back home.

Processing and record collecting of the missing men took several days. On July 13, the job of the men at the collection point was finished, and they could now send the bodies to the massive Tan Son Nhut airbase. A priority request was made for a helicopter to transport the remains of the four dead soldiers for their final trip out of Cu Chi.

Upon arrival at the collection point helipad, the bodies were placed on the waiting helicopter. The available records were given to the helicopter crew with instructions to give them to the mortuary personnel when they landed. The flight was a relatively short one, the day bright and cloudless. The helicopter took off and flew over the lush jungle vegetation and glimmering rice paddies. The crew was silent, with no joking or idle chatter. They treated this flight with the reverence that was its due.

They approached Tan Son Nhut at approximately 0930, flying over the crowded city of Saigon. They received clearance to land. The mortuary was kept away from the troops as much as possible. It was considered to be demoralizing so.

As the intensity of the war increased, so did the need for a better and larger mortuary. A new one had been built at the end of the flight line. The locating landmark was an old church right outside the wire. The casualties of the crash would be prepared here for their final trip home.

As the helicopter landed, it was met by mortuary personnel who removed the four bodies and brought them inside. The time was 1005.

Frank Rodriguez didn't hear about the crash right away. It was a day or two later when someone came up to him and said, "Hey! Did you hear what happened to Mike? He was... The helicopter he was on got hit with an RPG round, and it crashed, and it burned, and Mike didn't make it." His buddy from Southern California. The guy he was going to visit when they got back to those sun-soaked beaches. It was always a surprise when you heard of the death of a friend. But you didn't dwell on it. You absorbed it and moved on.

Carey remained in critical condition, struggling for life. That struggle ended on Sunday, July 12· at 0450. His body just could not fight anymore. The official cause of death was respiratory and renal failure. Back home in Indiana, it was 4:50 p.m. on Saturday, the eleventh. The next morning his family would go to church not knowing he was gone.

Ross was also still fighting to stay alive. He was in and out of consciousness and able to talk on occasion. So, the medical personnel knew who he was, and the word was sent to the 242nd that he was still alive.

The hospital was struggling to get Ross stable so they could fly him to the burn unit at Camp Zama, Japan. Two days after the crash, on the twelfth Rickey received permission to fly to Tan Son Nhut and be with Ross. Ross was lying in a rotatable Stryker bed, and when Rickey went in to see him, he was lying facedown. Rickey immediately noticed that Ross was having difficulty breathing. He told the nurse, and she told Rickey, "Sit on the floor so he can see you and talk to him." The nurse must have known what the probable outcome would be.

Ross was semiconscious and pretty drugged up but was able to talk to Rickey. They spoke about the crash, Rickey's burnt hands, and what happened to David Schultz. Rickey told Ross that he would be OK; he would recover and go home. But it just wouldn't work out that way. At 0530 on July 13, while they were talking, Ross stopped breathing. His body could not fight anymore. Rickey lost his good friend. The official cause of death was listed as pulmonary aspiration and cardiac arrest. Rickey left him and caught a hop back to Cu Chi. The war went on.

Back at the 242nd, Jim Calabrese was preparing to fly out of Cu Chi for Bien Hoa and home. He was ready to board a helicopter out of the hell of Vietnam when the company commander called a formation. Since Jim was still there, he fell in with the rest of the company. The CO told the company that Ross had just died. Jim felt horrible. Here he was about to board a helicopter for home, and Ross was dead. Ross and David Schultz. Gone. Now he would leave, but the memories of his tour in Vietnam would linger for the rest of his life.

Things had calmed down at the 12th Evacuation Hospital. After a couple of days, Elroy Simmons, Robert Ivey, James Coleman, Richard Green, Lowell Ketchum, and Harlen Metzger were stable enough to make the trip to the burn unit at Camp Zama, Japan. An Air Force Caribou flew them to Tan Son Nhut for the flight to Japan.

As Lowell was being taken off the plane, the pilot said, "Now, don't drop him like you did the last guy." Lowell raised up and said, "What the hell?" The pilot laughed and reassured him that he was only joking. Not funny.

Rickey, Robert Henry, and Ed would recover within the unit at Cu Chi. They survived, but none would ever be the same.

Chapter 8

Mortuary

Who wishes to fight must first count the cost.

-Sun Tzu, *The Art of War*

Mike Vullo's battered body was placed on a stretcher and loaded on an army ambulance for the short trip to the mortuary. It was the middle of the night, but the constant roar of jets and helicopters taking off and landing filled the air. It was a quiet, somber drive past metal and wood buildings, some bustling with activity, some silent. Yellow incandescent lights gave glimpses into the work going on inside as army and air force troops performed the mundane tasks that were always needed at an airbase in a war zone. It wasn't a far drive, but it was a lonely one.

The ambulance drove through the open gate in the chain-link fence surrounding the mortuary compound, past two hundred empty, waiting transfer cases that would soon be filled with the broken hearts of mothers, fathers, family, wives, sweethearts, and friends of the dead of Vietnam. The metal building stood, waiting—the last stop in Vietnam for many soldiers, too many soldiers. An NCO met the ambulance, and they gently moved Mike's body inside and onto a waiting table. All remains were treated with utmost reverence. The sharp smell of embalming fluid filled the night air. It was 0155 on

July 12. The work of positively confirming his identity now began. They knew who he was, but there could be no mistakes made. No one left Vietnam without their identity being confirmed beyond a shadow of a doubt. Mistakes had been made in the past, and there could be none now.

The mortuary personnel tried to take his fingerprints, but the extent of the burns made this extremely difficult. Finally, a print of his left index finger was obtained at 0725. This print was sent immediately to the FBI for positive identification. Confirmation from the FBI was received on the July 13 at 1125 that this was, in fact, SP4 Michael P. Vullo. Now the family could be informed that he was gone.

Just a little earlier that hazy, hot morning, the sound of an approaching Huey, one of many flying around Tan Son Nhut, stood out to the mortuary personnel. This bird had human remains as cargo—four bodies from the graves registration collection point at Cu Chi. The four had died together and now would possibly be sent home together. They would have to be processed, identified, and embalmed before the trip home. It was 1005 on July 13.

The Huey settled down on the pad by the mortuary, personnel waiting to move the bodies inside. They were brought in, one at a time, and laid on the cold, white porcelain tables. The room was all white, like an operating room. The partially shuttered windows let in the bright Vietnam sunshine. That plus overhead lights made the room as bright as day. It was quiet, except for the sounds of wrinkling body bags as each man was placed on his examination station. The smell of burnt flesh filled the room, but the mortuary personnel were used to that. It had happened before—too many times.

The charting now began. The bodies were examined for any scars, tattoos, or identifiable marks. Of course, there were none visible. Obtaining fingerprints was attempted. Not an easy task for the mortuary personnel. The charting form contained a figure, front and back, on which all injuries observed were noted along with any identifiable marks.

The first body was believed to be that of SP4 David Schultz. He was the only missing crew member, so the remaining Nomex and name tag made it seem likely. But a positive ID must be made. The misspelling of the name was probably a mistake when a Vietnamese tailor made his name tag. The body was completely charred and missing his lower legs. Both arms were broken. He most likely died instantly when the helicopter came down on the side where he was sitting on the tool chest. He was unidentifiable otherwise. They were able though to get a fingerprint of his right thumb, which was dispatched to the FBI for identification. After the exam, he was placed in the refrigeration room.

The remaining three soldiers were much more challenging to identify. The remains of all three were incomplete, not recognizable, mangled, mutilated, and burnt. But they could not, in no uncertain terms, send the wrong body to the family. Of the three, they knew that two were classified as Negroid and one Caucasian. The Caucasian was believed to be SP4 Dennis Martin.

Denny's body was now under examination. His fingerprints were unobtainable. When he went back into the burning helicopter, he must have been caught by the collapsing rear rotor assembly. His skull was crushed, and he had numerous fractures of his arms. His legs were missing, having been burned off in the ensuing fire. The bones of his lower extremities were crushed. Identification would have to be by other means.

They knew Denny had been a passenger on the ship. The remains were those of a Caucasian male, and he was Caucasian. The estimated height based on the left humerus was 67.3"; Denny was 67" tall. The remains had brown hair, based on an axillary sample under the arm, and Denny had brown hair. The tooth chart prepared for this set of remains was in excellent agreement with the dental records and X-rays for Denny and contradictory with associated casualties. Thus, he was declared identified at 1240 on July 15. He could now be embalmed and sent home.

The remaining two now had to be examined. Once again, fingerprints for both were impossible to get. The bodies were incomplete. The legs of both were missing. Both had portions of the torso missing, most likely from the RPG blast. Skulls were fractured and incomplete, and both had burned.

Identification for both was based on available dental charts as well as skeletal and anatomical comparison. The estimated height for one was 70.8"; SFC Thomas Campbell was 71" tall. The estimated height of the other was 66.7"; SP4 Robert Oldham was 66" tall. Thomas was declared identified at 1220 on July 15. Army dental records for Robert Oldham were not available, so they were requested from his dentist back home in Texas. When they arrived, it was noted that he had gold crowns that were identified on his remains. He was finally declared identified at 1050 on July 24.

The remains of SP4 Ross Bedient arrived at the mortuary forty minutes after the other four. There was no doubt who he was, but following regulations, a positive ID must be made. His hands were not burnt, maybe the Nomex gloves actually helped. His fingerprints confirmed his identity at 1610 on July 15. He could go home now.

The remains of Carey Pratt were sent to the mortuary on the July 13 at 1115. His life's hopes and dreams were gone. He never lived to see the birth of his child. His right hand wasn't burnt and prints of all but the little finger were taken. Based on his records, he was positively identified at 1355. The notification of death could now be made.

The job of mortuary personnel was tough. It was the only job in the army that you could quit. Dealing with death every day took its toll on these men. Yet they treated every set of remains with complete respect and reverence. They treated them all like they were family.

Chapter 9

Camp Zama, Japan

Never think that war, no matter how necessary, nor how justified, is

not a crime.

-Ernest Hemingway

July 13 was just another morning at the Tan Son Nhut airbase in Vietnam. The busy flight line activities were well underway. A C-141 cargo plane was being made ready for the flight to Japan. Racks of litters were clean and had fresh linen. The five-hour flight to Camp Zama would begin as soon as the wounded and sick were on board. At Zama the seriously wounded troops would receive stabilizing care before their trip back to the States.

Ambulances at the 3rd Evacuation Hospital loaded up their wounded and seriously ill troops for the short drive to the airfield. Some soldiers arrived by Caribou from Cu Chi for the flight. SFC Lowell Ketchum, SFC Elroy Simmons, SP4 Richard Green, SP4 Roy Harris, PFC David Schwab, PFC Bruce Thompson, and PFC Melvin Chase were among those being sent to Japan for further medical treatment. All were in serious or critical condition.

Upon arrival in Japan, they were gently removed from the plane and, once again, placed in waiting ambulances. All were examined and allowed to rest. Of course, they were all on pain medications, so their recall of the next few days was foggy.

Richard Green's arms were swollen and gigantic, almost three times their usual size. He didn't know if it was from the infection or the burns. Second and third-degree burns covered about 80 percent of his body. His right arm was especially bad. The doctors were concerned that they might have to amputate it. They went so far as to tell him that he needed to start learning to write with his left hand as soon as he was able. He did write a couple of letters home left-handed. But after that, his right hand started to come around a little bit, and they decided they were going to try to save it. After a couple of surgeries to graft skin onto it, his hand was saved.

Several of the survivors of the crash were sick from being in the river with their open wounds. The exposure to the dirty river water resulted in infections and, in several cases, hallucinations. One of the privates kept asking a doctor if he wanted to play with his yo-yo. Lowell stopped the doctor and asked what is wrong with the private. The doctor told him about getting a disease in the Saigon River. Lowell said that he was in the same group, and he was OK. The doctor told him that it affected some people, and others it didn't.

The doctors and nurses continued to work hard to stabilize all of the burn patients. Medications, fluids, and bandages were the order of the day. No matter the length of their efforts, they couldn't save everyone.

Elroy Simmons spent his thirtieth birthday, July 15 at Camp Zama. He was burned over three-fourths of his body. He was a strong man, but the burns were too numerous and severe. Pneumonia set in, and he passed away on July 19.

Richard remembered knowing that there were others from the crash in the ward with him. He didn't remember a lot due to all the pain medication he was on. He did know that a couple didn't make it. He heard that one died from infections. He didn't remember exactly who. He recalled that everyone had a malaria type of bacterial infection that caused illness and fever.

SP4 Harlen Metzger finally arrived on the seventeenth. He was recovering from the removal of his spleen, a bruised kidney, and his burns.

On the July 20, SP4 James Coleman arrived. He would be one of the first to be evacuated to the United States, leaving on July 25.

In the worst shape was Roy Harris. According to Lowell, they had to remove one of his arms it was so severely burned. A partition separated Lowell's bed from Roy's, and he heard him stop breathing several times. Each time they fought to bring him back, but finally, on July 26 he passed.

The next day, Lowell Ketchum, Richard Green, Harlen Metzger, David Schwab, Bruce Thompson, and Melvin Chase were placed on a hospital-modified C-141 and flown to the United States. There they would continue their recovery.

Lowell could not say enough about the hospital staff at Camp Zama. "They were the hardest working people I ever met in my military career. It was great the way they took care of you. It was all top-notch, a bunch of the best people I ever met in my life. Very concerned, very hardworking, you know, they'd come in in the morning all bright, and they'd leave there at 5:00 p.m. with their asses dragging. I doubt that any of our men ever in the world got the medical attention that we got. It was phenomenal; it was great."

Lowell remained in the hospital at Camp Zama until the end of August. During that time, he couldn't hold down solid food. Couldn't stand the smell of it. He lost thirty pounds.

Chapter 10

Notifications

What we have once enjoyed, we can never lose. All that we love

deeply becomes part of us.

-Helen Keller

Casualty notification duty was probably one of the most
difficult assignments in the service. Each branch had personnel
assigned to this duty. They would cover a specific geographic area,
usually one they could access by car in a four-to-five-hour drive.
Often, they were assigned from a local base or reserve center. It was
a tough and taxing assignment that most would have preferred never
to have had.

A notification was a process of specific tasks, all of which
had to be accomplished efficiently and compassionately. In the
Vietnam years and beyond, all notifications have been done in
person. In World War II and Korea, the notification was by telegram.

The notification process all began when the casualty
notification officer received a message or phone call telling them of
a casualty in their area. They would receive the name of the victim,
the general description of the cause of death, their address, and the
name and relation of the next of kin. When they had complete
information, the notification officer would have a specific amount of

time allotted to make the notification. At the end of that period, a confirming telegram would be sent. Time was of the essence. If, for some reason, the officer could not make the notification during the allotted time, they would call in a request to delay the sending of the telegram.

They never went alone. A chaplain/clergyman or doctor/medic would accompany them. There would be a senior enlisted man if the casualty were not an officer. They had to make sure they had a vehicle from the motor pool (usually an OD green army sedan) and, if need be, a driver. Once they were assembled, and with all the proper information in hand, they could begin the drive to the family. No matter how close the family lived, it was a long, quiet drive.

When the military sedan drove up to the house, anyone who saw it knew it was bad news. In small towns, it was common knowledge who was serving in the military. In cities, those living on the same street knew. Word traveled fast either way.

Once they arrived at the home, the team would ring the bell or knock, ask for the designated next of kin, and give them the news. If the specified next of kin were not home, they would inquire about their whereabouts and proceed to find them. They would not tell anyone else why they were there. They never knew what would happen when they drove up to a house soon to be racked with grief. The reactions were as varied as the families they met.

There would be a personal notification for anyone who died in the service, whether it was in Vietnam or not. Combat related or accident. War zone or assignment in the States or overseas. If someone were seriously wounded and in a hospital for over forty-eight hours or evacuated out of the country, the family would also be notified. Of course, when the family saw the sedan drive up and military personnel exit, they dreaded the worst. Their son, daughter, grandchild, husband, wife, brother, or sister had been killed. This wasn't always the case, and many of those seriously wounded lived to come home.

The family would be given any information available about the circumstances surrounding the death or injury of their loved one. This was always in general terms: gunshot, helicopter crash, vehicle accident, etc. They would answer any questions the family had about the cause of death if they knew the answers. They would never make guesses or conjectures. Just facts.

The whole process would then be explained to the family. They would tell them when the body would be brought back and get information on any preferred funeral home. If someone were escorting the body home, they would be given that information.

They would go over all the paperwork involved, government burial benefits, life insurance details, if any, and disposition of personal effects. They make sure the family understood that they would be available to assist in any way with all the arrangements.

Harlen Metzger

Brenda knew she would be spending her life married to Harlen, so she decided to quit the University of Evansville. The thought of incurring more debt from school loans was terrible, so she left and took a job. Brenda worked at an insurance company as a secretary and policy writer. On Friday, July 10 she was in a wonderful mood. Sunday she would be leaving for Hawaii to meet her husband for his R & R. Everyone she worked with was excited for her. They even put "Aloha, Brenda" on their marquee.

Saturday morning was a sunny, clear day in central Indiana. The tranquility of the day was interrupted when the green sedan pulled in front of Hank Metzger's home. When Hank saw the car pull up, he thought his son was dead. He ran out of the house in his underwear, yelling, "No, no, no!" Finally, they calmed him down. They were looking for Brenda. After a bit, Hank was able to tell them that Brenda had moved. It seemed that Harlen had not updated his next-of-kin record. Hank didn't even know her new address.

Brenda was at her apartment, packing for the flight to Hawaii when the phone rang. It was Hank. He told her that there was an army officer there who needed to talk to her. Hank put the officer on the line. He told her that her husband had been in a helicopter crash. It had been shot down, but Harlen was still alive. He was in a field hospital in serious condition. The officer told her that they didn't know her current address, and they were trying to stop her before she got on a plane to Hawaii. That was why they went to Harlen's parents' house. She was informed that a representative would keep her up to date. Horrible news and even worse hearing it over the phone.

Brenda drove over to her in-laws house, where she found Hank beside himself. He kept saying that they were lying, and Harlen was dead. He was sure they were playing a hoax to try to ease them into it. Brenda kept reassuring him over and over him that they wouldn't do that.

She started receiving telegrams the next day. The first one said "Your husband, Specialist 4 Harlen Metzger, was involved in a helicopter crash and received second and third-degree burns to fifty percent of his body, a ruptured spleen, and a bruised kidney." They said he was in a field hospital and would be sent to Camp Zama, Japan, shortly. In the days before computers, Brenda looked up information on burns in the encyclopedia. She learned that when someone had second-degree burns over fifty percent of their body, there was almost a 100 percent mortality rate.

A couple of days passed before she received a second telegram that said Harlen actually had second-degree burns to forty percent of his body and was still in serious condition. Hank got hold of his congressman and asked if he could intervene to provide additional information.

The congressman's office did check on him and provided Hank with the same information he already knew. The congressman told Hank that they would follow up with any news he received.

Brenda had taken a couple of days off work to prepare for the trip to Hawaii. Her office called and told her that she might as well come in as it might take her mind off the situation. She contacted Western Union and had them put in a note to deliver any telegrams to the office. Every time a telegram arrived, all her coworkers gathered around to see what it said. She would then call her in-laws and give them an update.

One day a week after Harlen was wounded, she received a letter in the mail from the chaplain who had seen Harlen in the field hospital. He said Harlen was in high spirits and seemed to be doing well. She also received his personal items in the mail in a small box. It contained his wedding ring, address book, and some miscellaneous items.

Finally, a telegram came notifying her that he was now in Japan at the Camp Zama burn ward. It contained a phone number that she could call and actually talk to him. She was excited and called her in-laws and told them she was going to call him. The phone number that was on the telegram was the wrong one, but whoever answered the call gave her the correct one. Just as she was getting ready to phone, his parents showed up. They lived about twenty miles away but made the trip in about fifteen minutes! Through another town and around traffic, they sped over.

The family called Harlen and the nurse gave him the phone. He spoke to them in a monotone voice. He was on a lot of pain meds and groggy. His dad had told Brenda that he could get them on a military transport to Japan in two days. Brenda told Harlen that they would come to Japan to see him. They would take care of him if need be and make sure he got the best care possible. Harlen was surprised that his dad would do that. The family spoke with him one at a time and were relieved that he was able to speak. Harlen told them that a general had come by and pinned a Purple Heart on his pillow.

Carey Pratt

Theresa was home where she lived with her parents on Saturday, the July 11. She was in the kitchen, drying a plate at the sink, when the doorbell rang. She walked over to the kitchen door, and from there she could see though the living room window, to two soldiers in uniform standing at the front door. Her brother was in the army and had just returned home from a tour of duty in Korea, and her first thought was that they were friends of his. Her brother answered the door.

She turned back into the kitchen, but something told her to go into the living room. Standing there were two soldiers, both officers, one a doctor. The look on her brother's face was one of grave concern. They told her that her husband, Carey, had been seriously wounded. He had been burned over 95 percent of his body. She was shocked. Here she was just twenty years old with a baby due next month, and now her husband was in critical condition and horribly burned. He was supposed to be coming home in December.

Theresa and her mother drove with the notification officers to Carey's parents' house to tell them the bad news. When they arrived, they saw Carey's dad and brother walking toward the house from the river, fishing poles in hand.

Carey's father, Dick, and brother, Thomas, had been fishing in the Kokomo River, joking and having a good time. It was a beautiful day. They were walking back to the house when about halfway Dick stopped. He spied the olive, drab army sedan with a white star on the door, a soldier in dress uniform standing there, and said, "Oh no."

Dick knew immediately that something had happened to his son. When they approached, the officer introduced himself and asked if he was the father of Sergeant Carey Pratt, who was serving in Vietnam. He nodded. The officer told him regretfully that his son had been seriously wounded in combat in Vietnam. Dick bowed his head and said nothing at first. Then: "What happened? How serious are his wounds?" The officer replied that yesterday, July 10, at approximately 1830 hours, the helicopter in which he was a passenger was shot down and exploded upon contact with the ground. Sergeant Pratt suffered third-degree burns over 95 percent of his body. He was now in a field hospital in Vietnam, being cared for.

Theresa and her mother stood, silent and still in shock. Carey's mother and grandmother came out of the house and rushed over to the group pleading, "What's wrong? What's wrong?" Carey's dad was so distraught that he was unable to speak. Finally, they were told what had happened. At first, it didn't register, and they had to be told again. Carey's mom, in her anguish, said, "Why wasn't it one of the other boys?" Theresa found out later that she meant one of the other soldiers, not one of her sons.

Each withdrew into themselves to try and understand what they just heard and come to grips with this devastating news. The burns were likely fatal, covering that much of Carey's body. But there was always hope, and now, hope was all they had.

Not being able to do anything else, the family prepared dinner. Tomorrow they would go to church and pray for him. There was no joy in the Pratt household on this night.

Their hope was destroyed the next day, on the July 12. Carey's brothers had asked that in the event of Carey's death to please call them, and they would notify their parents and grandmother themselves. That call came to them, bringing the bad news that Carey could not fight any longer, and he had passed into eternity that morning. Brothers Thomas and Bob had agreed that if the worst happened, they would go to Theresa first and tell her. They drove to Theresa's parents' house, where she was staying. They were greeted by her mother, who was distraught and crying. The casualty notification officer and chaplain had already been there and given her the bad news personally. That was proper protocol. The spouse was always notified first.

Theresa was eight months pregnant, and when told of her husband's death, she began wailing, sobbing uncontrollably. She retreated to her room and wouldn't come out. Bob opened the door where Theresa was sitting on the bed, her legs pulled up encircled by her arms, crying hysterically. When she saw Bob, she reached out both arms to him. They embraced, and he held her as she wept.

Theresa's doctor was summoned. He had been in the military himself, so he knew what she was going through. He came to the house and tried to calm her down without success. He gave her a shot; it took a while to take effect. When she started to calm down, she looked around at everybody there and said, "Tell me this isn't true." It was so hard to think. They were about to have a baby, and he was not going to be around. She had fallen more in love with him and knew that this baby was a part of him, and now he was gone. So much was going on in her mind. She heard the doctor say, "I saw this a lot."

Concerned that they had not yet told their parents, when Theresa regained her composure, Bob and Thomas drove to their home. As they pulled into the gravel drive, their dad was standing in the garage, the overhead door open. He watched his two sons' approach, a look of dread on their faces. Thomas walked straight to him and said, "Dad, he didn't make it." His hand drooped, and he mumbled, "What a hell of a way to go." He and Thomas embraced and stood in stony silence for a time. Bob went into the house to tell his mom.

Mike Vullo

Usually, the family was notified the same day the soldier died. Mike's identity was confirmed on the morning of July 13. Notification of his death was delayed because the army did not have the correct address of his natural mother. That was finally obtained on the fourteenth. The sad process of telling the family their loved one was gone could now begin.

Kathi was living with her parents in their ranch house on Sequoia in Brea, California. She and Mike had purchased a horse before he was sent to Vietnam, which they boarded at a local ranch about ten miles away. Kathi worked there, giving riding lessons along with doing some general office work to help pay for the boarding of the horse and other expenses she had. Michael's pay as a Spec 4 even with hazardous duty pay was pretty low, and they still had a car payment, insurance, etc.

The fourteenth was just another day at work for Kathi, like so many others, but today would be different; she was about to become an aunt. Her sister Diane was about to give birth to her niece. A new life was beginning.

Kathi's twelve-year-old sister Debbie was at home alone when the doorbell rang. She opened the door and was met by two soldiers in uniform. They asked if she was Kathleen Vullo. "No, she is at work. What is this about?" They asked for the address where she was working and bid their leave to drive and see her.

Kathi was giving a riding lesson when she saw the olive-green military sedan pull into the property and drive up the hill to the barn and office. She saw a soldier get out of the car, young and blond resembling Mike. "What is Michael doing here?" she wondered. He hadn't been gone long enough to be home, even for a surprise visit. Then the loudspeaker barked, asking her to please come to the office. Something came over her and told her that wasn't Mike. It hit her. She knew right away. When she arrived at the office, the two soldiers took her aside and told her that her husband was dead. Killed in a helicopter crash and had been dead for three days.

Kathi was in a fog; she had to get home and tell her parents. Everything was a blur. She drove herself home in their 1969 Volkswagen bug. She couldn't remember if the soldiers offered to drive her home, but she suspected they did. She decided to drive herself. Both of her parents were working, but she needed to call them and give them the horrible news. She needed them now.

Her dad worked for North American/Rockwell, and her mom worked at the Red Cross. She phoned her mother but had a terrible time getting her on the phone. She had to call several times as her mom was in meetings. Finally, she told them it was a family emergency, and they brought her to the phone. She was so upset by the news that she had to have her boss drive her home. She worked in Santa Ana, so it took her a while to get there. She must have called her husband, Kathi's father, as he arrived home shortly after her mom.

The casualty notification officers were there, and one thing they asked of them was that they tell Mike's family themselves. They drove over to Mike's father and stepmother's house in San Gabriel. When they arrived, it was apparent that the casualty notification team had already been there and told them. However, Mike's grandmother, who raised him, did not know. When Mike's father told his mother that Mike had been killed, the pain and anguish she displayed was indescribable. Then everyone broke down.

Mike's mother was living in Nebraska at the time, and Kathi did not recall who notified her. She did come back to California to attend all services, though.

Kathi's sister gave birth that afternoon. They did not tell her that Mike had died until the next day.

Kathi was in shock. The thought of everything that needed to be done now was overwhelming. How could she take care of all the details while dealing with the grief? She was only eighteen and wouldn't turn nineteen until this coming October. Her father stepped in and took care of most things having to do with the funeral and military paperwork. He had been in the honor guard when he was in the service, so he was familiar with the protocol of what would happen. The next two or three weeks were a blur.

One thing Kathi did request was for Mike Gandee to escort Mike's body home. The army had no problem making those arrangements.

Denny Martin

Susie's preparations for her flight to Hawaii were complete, and she was packed and ready to go to the airport. It would be wonderful to see Denny and in Hawaii! His R & R was a full week. Today would be a long day of traveling, but she was excited to get out of her apartment in Cedar Rapids and begin the adventure. The flight left about 10:00 a.m.

Susie was living in a fourplex, and her aunt was living in the unit above her. Suddenly, at about 6:30 a.m., there was a knock on the door. Who would be knocking on the door at this early hour? She looked out the window onto the street and saw a car but didn't think anything of it. They knocked again, and finally, she asked who was there. The voice on the other side of the door identified himself as a representative from the army. He said that he needed to talk to her. She asked to see some ID, and he showed her his military ID card through the peephole. She opened the door to see a soldier standing there in his dress greens.

She let him in, and he broke the bad news that her husband had been in a helicopter that crashed, and he was declared missing in action. She was in shock and kept repeating, "Well, I'm supposed to be going to Hawaii. Today's the day I'm flying over there." She just couldn't comprehend what was happening.

Susie called her aunt upstairs, and she came down. Susie called Denny's parents and her parents, and everything just sort of blew up. They all came over, and the casualty notification officer explained to everyone what they knew, which wasn't much. At this point, no one knew if he was dead or alive.

Now they had to find Barbara and tell her what was going on. Barbara was estranged from her parents. They didn't even know where she was. Barbara was a free spirit, a hippie living in her first apartment in Iowa City, just thirty miles away. They called a friend of Barbara's who they thought would know where she lived. Her friend knew that Barbara was in Iowa City but didn't know her exact address. So, she drove from Cedar Rapids to Iowa City, looking for her. She asked around and eventually found her apartment.

She came to the door, and Barbara answered. She told Barbara that Denny had been shot down and was missing. Barbara couldn't believe it. "What, are you making some kind of joke?" She didn't believe her but was finally convinced it was true. Barbara didn't have a car, so her friend drove her back to Cedar Rapids and her parents house.

When she arrived, she found that they still didn't have much information. There was a crash, a helicopter or a plane and Denny was missing. They just had to wait for more details, and the waiting was horrible. Denny's mother kept saying, "I know he's dead. I know he's dead," and Barbara kept saying, "No, no. I don't think so. No, don't say that. I don't think he is."

The confusion and horrible heartache continued for four interminable days. Then, on the evening of the fifteenth the casualty notification officer once again came to visit Susie and the family. He told her the news they had been dreading hearing. Denny was confirmed killed. He didn't have many new details on what happened. Just that Denny was on a helicopter going back to base camp that had been shot down. The doctor who her aunt worked for came over and gave Denny's mom and Barbara a sedative to help them calm down. The family started to arrive to offer their support relatives and cousins doing what they could.

The casualty notification officer often visited during this time, helping with all the arrangements and paperwork. Susie was in a complete fog during this challenging period. The officer told her that it would be a closed casket. Denny's remains were not viewable. The identification was by dental records.

Susie later remembered a nightmare she had had when she and Denny were in a Wilmington hotel before he was sent overseas. In the nightmare she saw a picture of Denny lying in a coffin. She knew it would happen. She had kept telling herself, "No, it's just fear." This sort of dream or premonition was horrible but not uncommon.

Susie requested that Denny's college roommate, Tim Petersen, escort his body home. Tim was still in the army stationed at the Presidio, working as a company clerk for an outfit that was handling undeliverable mail coming back from Southeast Asia. Tim had graduated from college in March of 1969 and immediately went to work of the Minnesota Conservation Department. It took three months for the draft board to catch up to him, and he had to report in June of 1969. Because of his bad hearing, he was sent to clerk school, and that ultimately kept him out of Vietnam but not out of the army.

Tim's outfit was considered a light-duty outfit. All they had to do was sort mail. Many of those in his unit had already served in Vietnam. Some had been wounded. Many were just bitter as hell, because of the way they felt the war was being fought.

Susie had planned to see Tim and his wife before going to Hawaii to meet Denny. Those plans changed. She called Tim after being notified that Denny was missing. Tim and his wife were distraught. They also waited and hoped for more information on his status.

Susie made that call to Tim on the fifteenth. Sue was devastated. She told Tim that Denny was dead and she was going to request that he be the one to escort his body home.

Elroy Simmons

Barbara Simmons was home that Sunday, July 12. It was a hot, sunny afternoon. The OD army sedan drove up to the apartment building on Julian Street in Waukegan, Illinois. Two uniformed army officers got out, one a chaplain. They entered the lobby and looked at the row of bells for Barbara Simmons.

They found it and rang the bell, and when she answered it, she looked at them and took it all in. She said, "You can tell me anything but not that he's dead. I can't accept that." Their news was terrible, but not the worst it could be. He was wounded; he had been burned. A helicopter crash. It all ran together. For now he was alive, and that was all that counted. She had four children she had to take care of, a tough burden for a twenty-nine-year-old woman.

Being a military wife, she knew that anything could happen. Elroy had already served one tour in Vietnam and come home unscathed. Although she knew that he could be wounded or killed, she was not prepared for the arrival of the two army officers standing in her apartment.

Now, she had to tell the children. She told them the truth, that their father was severely wounded in Vietnam. She was wanted to make sure they heard it from her, not someone else.

Once Barbara pulled herself together, she notified her sister-in-law, who lived in the area. Immediately she came over.

The officers informed her that a notification was going to be given to Elroy's parents in East St. Louis later that day. Barbara told them that her mother-in-law had heart problems, so they dispatched an officer and a doctor to inform them. They told Barbara they would keep her informed of any progress in his condition and left her alone to deal with her thoughts and fears.

Elroy's brother, Dwight, was newly married and living in East St. Louis. He had been married on June 27. Brothers Lacy and Randall were both in the service, Lacy in the army in Vietnam and Randall in the navy. Dwight and his bride were enjoying a quiet Sunday afternoon when the phone rang. It was his sister. She told him there was a problem at the house, and he needed to come over right away. He lived a short six blocks away, so he jumped in the car and drove over. That was when he found out that his brother had been wounded and was in the hospital in Vietnam. This was a tough pill to swallow as his first tour in Vietnam had been much more hazardous than this one.

Barbara began receiving telegrams about Elroy's condition shortly after the notification of his being wounded. He had been transferred up to the burn ward in Camp Zama, Japan. They were doing everything they could to keep him alive. Once he was stable, he would come home to the United States and the Brooke Army Burn Center in Texas.

On the morning of Sunday, July 19, the doorbell in Waukegan once again rang. Barbara answered the door and saw the army officer and chaplain. She knew right away what had happened. They informed her that her husband was dead. They discussed all the arrangements that were being made to bring his body home for burial. Barbara told them she wanted the body brought to East St. Louis, not Waukegan. That was where the family was; she felt he should be buried there. She chose the Jefferson Barracks National Cemetery in St. Louis.

She called the children together—all four were under the age of ten—and explained that their father gave his life for his country and that they should be proud of that. They took the news very hard. It was hard for Barbara also, but Elroy had served in Vietnam and Korea before, and in his absence, she ran the family and raised the children. Despite her great sorrow, she had to carry on.

Elroy's parents were heartbroken.

David Schultz

Donna hadn't received a letter from David in several weeks and was ecstatic when one arrived on July 10. He was good; he was safe. She had been very worried about David. He had volunteered to go on flight status and was now flying as a door gunner. She didn't know exactly what type of missions he flew on, but she did know it was dangerous. She prayed for David's safety, saying a Rosary every night while he was gone. She would not sleep until she did.

Donna anxiously awaited for David to return. They would be married, and she would start having babies, a lot of them. She wanted to become a baby machine. When family or friends would visit, she would take care of their children and fantasize about what it was going to be like with David and children of their own.

Donna would be sixteen in November and David nineteen in October. They could get married when he came home in January. Less than six months away. She had to keep praying for him.

On Saturday, July 11, Donna was bored and decided to get out of the house and away from her mother, so she walked over to the ranch. It was already hot and would only get hotter. The high today was predicted to be ninety-five and sunny—a typical July day in this part of Texas.

Donna casually wandered up to the old white house and saw the pastor, Wally Morillo, quietly talking to two or three of the kids who frequently hung out there. It was unusual to see Wally just standing there talking; he was always busy doing this and that. As Donna walked over and joined the group, she heard Wally quietly say, almost in passing, "Oh, by the way, I heard David is missing in action." Donna stopped dead in her tracks, a wide-eyed look of disbelief on her face, and said, "What do you mean he is missing?" Wally replied, "Well, the helicopter he was on was shot down behind enemy lines, and he's missing."

Missing? Missing? What does that mean? Are they trying to find him? Donna was in shock. She received a letter from him yesterday morning. How could he be missing? This was a nightmare! She turned and left in a daze, slowly walking into the hot sunlit street. This couldn't be happening. She received a letter yesterday. And how could Wally say that in such a matter-of-fact way? He knew how close they were; everyone at the ranch knew.

Donna was scared and confused. She had no one to talk to, and Wally wasn't interested in comforting her or even addressing it with her directly. She went home right away and told her mom but didn't get much of a reaction from her, either. Why didn't Wally call her and tell her privately? He had her phone number. Maybe because of her young age, they didn't take their relationship seriously.

From that moment on, it was like she was walking in a dream, no a nightmare. It was surreal. She was in shock, trying to handle something that she had no idea how to cope with it. On top of that, she was not getting any support from anyone.

Donna remained in a fog until the end of the month. Then things got worse. With his identification finally confirmed, the family was notified that his status had been changed from Missing in Action to Killed in Action.

The notification came on Saturday, July 25 when an army staff car pulled up in front of David's mother's house. Wally was also notified as he and the ranch were the beneficiaries of David's life insurance policy.

Later on the twenty-fifth, Donna called Wally to see if he had heard anything more about David and was told that he was now confirmed to have been killed. Gone.

Ross Bedient

Approximately three hundred miles northeast in Dundee, New York, the Bedient family was enjoying their Saturday. It was a sleepy gray day with a light rain shower in progress when the staff car pulled up to their house on Seneca Street. The two soldiers brought terrible news to Ross's parents. He suffered burns over 50 percent of his body in a helicopter crash and was being treated at an army hospital in Vietnam. They assured the family that everything humanly possible was being down to care for their son. They would keep them informed of the care and progress of their son. Now all they could do was pray.

The telegrams began to arrive the next day, Sunday July 12, informing them of the progress of their son. It wasn't looking good. He was in critical condition. He died on Monday, the thirteenth. His parents were notified that he was gone. Amid their grief they told the army representative that Ross's older brother, Zane, was a career navy man and stationed in Morocco. The soldier told them he would arrange for Zane to be notified. They would call their other son,

Gerry, themselves and tell him. He was living in St. Augustine, Florida, so that contact would be easy.

Chapter 11

Transport Home

Only a moment you stayed, but what an imprint your footprints have

left on our hearts.

-Dorothy Ferguson, *Little Footprints*

It was time to bring the men home. Those alive and those dead. The physically healthy who survived their tour seemingly unscathed and those with mangled bodies whose scars would remind them of their time in Vietnam until the end of their days. It would take two and a half more years until all came home. Some never came home. Some who were missing in action would remain in Vietnam long after the war was over and forgotten. Some of those who returned to their families would be back in Vietnam every night.

The dead and wounded from that small action on July 10 were prepared for transport. They wouldn't all go home together; some took longer than others. Those seriously wounded could not leave Japan until they were stabilized. The dead would come home when their identification was confirmed without a doubt and their remains prepared for shipment.

The dead from that crash weren't alone. Although the war was winding down in July of 1970 and troops were being withdrawn, the killing continued. On that fateful day of July 10, four soldiers died, SP4 Denny Martin, SFC Thomas Campbell, SP4 David Schultz, and SGT Robert Oldham. In addition to them, eighteen other soldiers and marines died in Vietnam on that day. On July 11, SP4 Mike Vullo passed on, and five other servicemembers lost their lives that day also. On July 13, SP4 Ross Bedient and SGT Carey Pratt lost their lives in addition to nine other soldiers and marines. They were joined in the army mortuary in Tan Son Nhut and Da Nang with the other casualties for their final trip home.

At the mortuary in Tan Son Nhut, the silver transfer cases that would transport the dead were stacked neatly, five high, rows of forty waiting for the remains of those who would lose their lives over the course of the next months. The war was approaching the end. Units were being withdrawn. Though the writing was on the wall, about 10,000 of the 58,000 -plus deaths would happen between 1970 and our final withdrawal in 1973.

The dead would leave Vietnam on air force C-141 cargo planes. The bodies were embalmed to whatever extent they could be. Each was wrapped in white sheets then placed in a plastic bag that was then secured tightly around the body. The transfer case would be marked with the name of the occupant and the paperwork attached on the outside. They were then secured on aluminum pallets and loaded into the aircraft.

Sometimes an escort accompanied the body from Vietnam home, but this was not usually the case. Most escorts would meet up with the body in the States. When an escort did accompany the body home, he spent the long flight sitting on a jump seat looking at the transfer cases. It could be his buddy, his brother, or maybe even his dad. No matter who, the aircrew treated the escort like a king, at least to the extent they were able. The flights carrying bodies were long and lonely for everyone involved. The crew and escorts just stared at those cases for hours and hours—each alone with his thoughts.

Those who were from east of the Mississippi would be flown to Dover Air Force Base, Delaware, and those west of the Mississippi would be flown to Travis Air Force Base in California then transferred to the Oakland Army Depot. That was where the final preparation of the remains would be. For a burn victim, the body would be wrapped in bandages concealing his burnt flesh. They would then be clothed in a dress green uniform as much as could be possible, with their ribbons, badges, and insignia affixed. The body was then placed in a casket that was locked. He was now ready to be transferred to their appointed funeral home. For most, another flight was needed to get them there.

Carey Pratt and Mike Vullo were on the same flight from Tan Son Nhut to Travis Air Force Base on July 14.

Thomas Campbell and Denny Martin would also make their final journey from Vietnam together. The transfer cases containing their bodies were loaded on a C-141. Other bodies that had been released from the mortuary would join them. The destination was Travis Air Force Base, then Oakland Army Depot, then home. The date was July 16. Ross Bedient left Vietnam on the sixteenth also, but he was bound for Dover Air Force Base. He may have been on the same flight as the others and transferred to another plane at Travis, but that is unknown.

Elroy Simmons left for home from Camp Zama on July 20. David Schultz's final flight from Tan Son Nhut began on July 25. The remains of Robert Oldham accompanied him. Roy Harris' body was released from Camp Zama and flown home on July 28. Harris was the last one to make that final flight.

The wounded from the crash were prepared for the long flight to the United States. They would fly on specially equipped C-141 transports. The planes were fitted with racks holding rows of litters, enough to carry fifty-four wounded. There were nurses and medical personnel on board to care for them during their trip home. They had one goal—get them home safe and alive. They did an outstanding job.

The first of the wounded to leave was SP4 James Coleman, who boarded a flight on July 25. His final destination was Fort Bragg, North Carolina, where he was admitted to the hospital and placed on medical hold. His wounds were not severe enough to warrant him being sent to the Brooke Burn Center at Fort Sam Houston in San Antonio. He would remain at Fort Bragg until his two-year service obligation was up in February of 1971. MSG Robert Ivey followed him to Fort Bragg on July 27. He was also placed on a medical hold. After his release, he was assigned as an ROTC instructor at the Virginia Military Institute.

The remaining survivors left Camp Zama on July 27. SP4 Harlen Metzger, SP4 Richard Green, PFC Melvin Chase, PFC David Schwab, and PFC Bruce Thompson came home together; their final destination was the Brooke Burn Center in Texas.

The survivors suffering the effects of their injuries were gently brought on board the specially fitted C-141 transport. All were groggy due to the pain medications they were on as well as other drugs to help them sleep during the long flight across the Pacific. The flight crew and medical personnel made them as comfortable as possible. Although they were still in pain, their war was over.

Richard Green described himself being pretty drugged up during the fight home. He remembered waking up once or twice on the flight from Japan to San Francisco, the nurses going from patient to patient checking on their well-being.

Richard remembered someone asking if they were going to get off the plane in San Francisco. The response was "No. They aren't treating our guys well there." After refueling, they took off for Fort Sam Houston.

SFC Lowell Ketchum's flight was very smooth and comfortable. The plane landed to refuel, and Lowell was amazed at the soft landing. He never felt the plane touch down. After they came to a stop, he was talking to a few men who were standing around him, and he said, "Man, they must have their best pilots on these aircraft. I never even felt this thing hit the ground. That was the best landing I ever made."

One of the men spoke up and said, "No, we're not the best." He continued, "We try harder, but we're not the best pilots." Lowell had no idea he was talking to one of the pilots. The flight continued to Maxwell Air Force Base in Montgomery, Alabama. The landing there was typical, a bit of bouncing then touchdown. It wasn't a bad landing; it was just a normal landing. When they rolled to a stop, the pilot came back looking for Lowell. He wasn't happy with the landing. As he searched for Lowell, he was overheard saying, "Where's that guy who thought I was a great pilot?" He apologized. When they had wounded aboard, he knew a hard landing could cause a lot of pain.

All were now home.

Chapter 12

Funerals

Death leaves a heartache no one can heal, love leaves a memory no

one can steal.

-Irish proverb

All of the victims of the crash received a funeral with full
military honors. The number of troops performing the ceremony
varied from two to seven plus a bugler if available. The size of the
detail depended on military manpower and availability. With so
many Americans in uniform during the Vietnam period, there always
seemed to be enough troops around to perform this task. In many
cases, local Ready Reserve troops rendered honors. Personnel
selected for this detail were generally well trained. It was not an easy
job to perform. It had to done right. There would be no do-over. The
honor detail and service is designed to show the highest regard and
respect to those who dies while on active service. All participants
must be in proper dress uniform with correct insignia attached.

There may have been small variations for each funeral, but
basically they were the same. The funeral honors detail included at a
minimum the folding of the flag, the presentation of the flag, and the
playing of taps. In most cases but not all, it also included a firing

party to render a final twenty-one-gun salute. The escort would play a large part in the service.

The flag was always draped over the casket at the funeral home, whether the casket open or closed. Those for the men involved in this incident were all closed. If the funeral detail was large enough, the honors squad would act as pallbearers. If not, the family selected the pallbearers.

The casket would remain under cover of the flag even in the hearse to the cemetery. The pallbearers would carry the casket to the grave. The honor guard would be at attention. The immediate family would be seated beside the site while the guests would gather around and behind them.

A final prayer would be said by the family's minister or military chaplain. The honor guard would lift the flag off the casket and pull it taught, holding it tight over the casket. The rifle party then would fire a three-round volley, and when that was complete, a lone bugler would play taps. If a bugler was not available, a recording would be played at a respectable distance from the grave.

The honor guard would ceremonially fold the flag and the highest-ranking member present it to the closest next of kin, saying the words: "On behalf of the President of the United States, the United States Army, and a grateful Nation, please accept this flag as a symbol of our appreciation for your loved one's honorable and faithful service."

The service would then be concluded.

Carey Pratt

The body of Carey Pratt returned to Kokomo on July 18. He had been posthumously promoted to staff sergeant, a final recognition of the quality of the noncommissioned officer he was. Carey was the 1,169th Hoosier to die in Vietnam. More would die before the war ended. Large numbers like this desensitize us to the loss of even one person. Thinking about numbers like 1,169 from one state or 58,220 total American deaths throughout the war, the enormity makes us forget the individual. Each individual must never be forgotten.

Theresa was eight months pregnant. The stress of Carey's death could cause a premature birth at any time. Under normal circumstances, the visitation at the funeral home would be on the nineteenth with the burial on the twentieth but they decided to delay. July 20 was Theresa and Carey's anniversary. It would have been their second. She just could not bury him on their anniversary. It was bad enough that the visitation would now be on that date, from 2:00-9:00 p.m. A sad way to spend your anniversary, all while carrying a baby who would come into the world without a father. Hard to fathom.

The Peacock Funeral Home handled all the arrangements in conjunction with the army. The casket was obviously closed. Theresa wanted to open it and view the body. Carey's brother Bob knew how difficult that would be for her so he volunteered to accompany her. Bob was the closest brother to Carey. John Peacock, the owner, said that he would go with her but Bob said no, it would be him. Theresa decided in the end that she couldn't put herself or Bob through that, so they did not view the body. She regretted that decision afterward. Could the military have made a mistake? Was that really her husband in there? They wouldn't have recognized him anyway. Though he was dressed in his uniform as much as possible, any gaps or bare skin were wrapped completely in white linen.

The visitation was well attended with people near and far filling the chapel to pay their respects. The funeral the next day was also crowded. Friends, and strangers who had also lost a loved one in Vietnam came from miles around.

The funeral was set to begin at 1:00 p.m. on the twenty-first. The mayor decreed that flags be flown at half-mast in Carey's honor. Carey was to be buried in Knox Chapel Cemetery, a small cemetery in the countryside of Point Isabel, Indiana. The cemetery was about a half-hour drive away. The plot had been purchased by his grandfather when Carey's twin sister died. There were eight plots for immediate family members.

Theresa's mother was by her side the whole time, helping her, offering support.

The honor guard carried Carey's casket to the grave. The mournful notes of taps echoed across the cemetery and nearby cornfields. The flag was folded and presented to Theresa. Then silence. Carey's duty to his troops and country was finished.

Theresa felt God put a calming feeling on her after Carey died. It lasted a few weeks. It was the only way she could get through it.

Shannon Rae Pratt was born on August 9, 1970, in Kokomo at 3:16 p.m. This beautiful girl came crying into the world weighing six pounds, ten and a half ounces.

Ross Bedient

The navy gave Zane an emergency furlough to go home for the funeral of his brother. It would not be an easy trip. His younger brother was dead, and he didn't get along with his father. Ross had had a much closer relationship with their dad. Zane and Gerry were both born during World War II. Their father, Francis, was sent to Europe. Francis' brother, also named Zane, was killed during the Battle of the Bulge. After the war, the family struggled financially, but by the time Ross was born, they were in a better position. As Ross grew, the time Francis had to devote to his son increased. When Ross entered his teenage years, he and Francis were able to spend good time together-quality time he wasn't able to spend with his older sons. Ross was like an only child as his brothers left home at a young age, Zane at eighteen and Gerry at twenty.

Zane arrived home to find his father completely distraught.

There was a delay bringing Ross's body up from Dover. No one knew why. The snafu was taking its toll on Francis and Madeline. His father was always crying, which made his wife cry. Zane felt sorry for him. Francis was so overcome with grief that he couldn't sleep. Zane knew that his father needed to get some rest, but how?

The family doctor was a crusty old man. Zane went to see if he could get some sleeping pills to put in his father's coffee so that he would sleep. He was waiting for the doctor when he heard the doctor yell as loud as he could from his office, "Send that damn idiot in here!" Zane entered his office, and the doctor said in response to

Zane's request, "That's against the law." Zane persisted, "Well, I understand that, but, you know, I'm trying to give him some rest. He's not sleeping at all because they weren't taking care of my brother's body like he thought they should have, OK?" He gave Zane three pills – "samples." He said, "Just take it out of the capsule and stir it into his coffee."

Zane's father didn't drink whiskey, but he did drink a lot of coffee. When his dad wasn't looking, Zane emptied the contents of all three capsules into his coffee and finally, he slept.

Then Zane called Dover to ask what the hell was going on. His brother's body was there—why wasn't it being brought home? The wait was horrible for everyone.

He was informed that they didn't have an escort to bring the body home. Zane called the commander there and said he would fly down and escort the body home. Finally, they found a master sergeant who was able to serve as escort and bring Ross home.

The body finally arrived at Weldon Funeral Home in Dundee. The family held a viewing there on the July 22 from 7:00 to 9:00 p.m. The casket was closed, of course, concealing his badly burnt body. Many of his family, friends, and acquaintances attended to pay their respects. Two of Ross's friends from high school came by, but Francis would not let them in because of their long hair.

A service was held at the funeral home the next day at 2:00 p.m. Afterward, Ross's body was transported to Hillside Cemetery where he was laid to rest. His father never got over the death of his youngest son.

Mike Vullo

In the middle of another workday at Cu Chi, SP4 Mike Gandee was called in to the battalion commanders office. Following proper military protocol, he saluted the CO and reported in. The commander put him at ease and told him that SP4 Vullo had died as a result of a helicopter crash while traveling back to Cu Chi from Dau Tieng. Gandee knew he had been in a helicopter crash, but this was the first time he was hearing the details. He hadn't been told that his friend Mike was dead.

Mike's wife, Kathi, had requested that Gandee be the funeral escort for Mike's body. He was given TDY (temporary duty) orders and told to prepare for his trip back to the States. He would receive complete instructions when he arrived at Oakland Army Depot. He would leave Vietnam the next day, July 18.

Gandee jumped on a helicopter for the flight to Tan Son Nhut. He wasn't the only passenger on the Chinook; there were a couple of body bags there too. Gandee spent the flight looking at the body bags, wondering if his friend was in one of them. There were no identifying marks on the bags.

Upon arrival at Tan Son Nhut, he was put on a flight manifest as a priority passenger. The plane was full of soldiers rotating home. They cheered as the plane lifted off, their tour over. Gandee still had a long way to go on his tour. His flight home now was grim. Nothing he was looking forward to.

After arriving at Travis Air Force Base, Gandee was taken to Oakland Army Base for further instructions on being an escort as well as connecting for the first time with Mike's body, which had arrived at the mortuary on July 14.

Gandee was given a pamphlet explaining his duties and outlining how he was supposed to conduct himself. He was told that the remains were not viewable. It was stressed that he tell the family that. He was given TDY orders authorizing him to go to Alhambra for the funeral as well as a week's leave afterward to visit his parents.

Paperwork and instructions complete, Gandee boarded a plane for the short flight to Los Angeles. His friend's body was on the same flight, in the hold, resting in a casket encased in a cardboard box. Upon arrival, the stairway was pushed up to the aircraft, and all the passengers disembarked. Gandee made his way down the stairs, and when he reached the bottom, he was pulled aside and escorted to the cargo ramp. There he awaited the unloading of Mike's body. As the box containing Mike's casket slowly left the plane's hold on the conveyor, Gandee came to attention and saluted.

The hearse from the funeral home was there, waiting to transport the body and Gandee to the mortuary in Alhambra. Gandee checked into a motel and called Kathi, telling her that he had arrived and where he was staying. Kathi would not hear of him staying at a motel and insisted that he stay with her and her parents. She would not take no for an answer and drove over to pick him up. This may not have met with the approval of the army, but that was just too bad. He grabbed his bag and left for Kathi's family home.

Gandee was glad he was there to offer his support, but it was extremely stressful at the same time. Kathi and her parents were so very upset but trying to hang on as best they could. It was good he was there.

The next day, on July 22, Mike's mother, Cherie, went to the funeral home to see if she could view the body of her son. Once again, she was told that his remains were not viewable. There was speculation that perhaps he was viewable, but that wasn't the case. His face and body had been severely burned. It would have been horrible for her to see him in that state. In any case, his head was wrapped in white bandages, and he wore gloves.

That night the family held a Rosary at the funeral home. Acting as escort, Gandee was in uniform. Mike's entire family, as well as Kathi's, visited Mike one last time. It was a horrible time for all. Unlike someone who dies at ninety, having lived a full life, Mike was only twenty-one—life was just beginning. Many tears were shed that night and would be shed for a long time into the future.

Kathi had chosen to bury Mike at Rose Hills Memorial Park Cemetery in Whittier. Rose Hills donated a burial plot to anyone who was killed overseas. While making the arrangements, Kathi bought a plot for herself next to him.

The next morning a Mass was held in the church where Mike and Kathi were married in Brea, California. Like all funeral Masses, it was a solemn affair. As an escort, Gandee was given a script and instructions on everything he was to do during the burial. He was supposed to stay in the back of the church so he could be the first one out the door after the Mass. There, Gandee would await the casket as it left the church, but Kathi insisted that he sit in the first row with her. He acquiesced to her wishes. Following the Mass,

Mike's body was wheeled out of the church accompanied by the military pallbearers. Gandee quickly left the church and saluted the casket as it was wheeled past and into the waiting hearse.

Gandee rode with Kathi and her family in the limousine to his friend's final resting place. There Mike was to be laid to rest with full military honors. Upon arrival, the casket was placed on the gurney and wheeled to the grave. Once the ceremony was over, taps was played, its eerie, sad tune wafting across the cemetery mixing with the crying of those in attendance. The flag was removed from the casket, folded, and given to Gandee to present to Kathi. He did so and then stood back, and saluted. This whole ceremony was tough for everyone, including Gandee. He froze in his salute, caught up in the extreme sadness and grief of the moment. Finally, the soldier in charge of the honor guard said, "Order arms," and Gandee lowered his salute.

When the service was over, some of Mike's friends approached Gandee, asking him if Mike really wanted to be over there fighting that war. Gandee replied yes, as he felt he should, being the representative of the army. But Gandee thought they knew he was probably lying. He didn't think Mike wanted to be there in the first place.

Kathi's and Mike's parents questioned Gandee about what had happened. He told them all that he knew—Mike had been a passenger on a Chinook helicopter that was shot down, and he died of his burns. He also told them why he wasn't with Mike at the time.

Mike Gandee left the grieving widow and parents for a week home with his family. Then, it was back to the war in Vietnam.

Two weeks after the funeral Kathi received a one-half carat, tiffany set, diamond engagement ring. Mike had purchased it through the PX somehow. They had decided to return her original engagement ring when Mike was drafted, knowing money would be tight on military pay. She found the receipt for the ring when his belongings were returned.

Denny Martin

SP4 Tim Petersen was called into the orderly room and given travel orders to be the escort for his friend Denny Martin's funeral. He was given two days to do it. Tim reported and received his instructions on his duties and how to act while performing as an escort.

He was directed into a room with other soldiers who were to escort the recently killed. It was a morbid scene. Nobody asked any questions. It was all business. No compassion at all. "Here are your orders. Here is what you do and what you say." Tim just sat there and silently listened. It was still a shock that Denny was gone.

The basic protocol was to bring him home and tell the family it was a closed casket. He did not know anything about the circumstances of Denny's death so he would not be able to answer any questions about that. He was informed that Denny had been posthumously promoted to sergeant.

The escorts didn't talk to each other during the meeting or after. Everyone was captive to their own thoughts. Tim didn't know whether they knew the servicemen that they were escorting or not, but he certainly did.

Orientation over, he was bused to San Francisco airport and boarded a plane bound for Cedar Rapids. The first leg was a four-and-a-half-flight to Kansas City, where he would change planes. There was a short layover. While Tim was standing looking out the window at the plane he would shortly board, he saw a cargo trawler carrying a box toward the aircraft. Inside the box was a casket. The box was labeled with the name "MARTIN." Tim thought, *God, I hope that's you in there, Denny.* Then he thought, *I hope that's not you in there, Denny.'* He knew how the army could screw things up. If Denny was dead, he hoped that was, in fact, his body being transported. But he, like many others, hoped there had been a screwup and that Denny wasn't dead but instead captured or in a hospital somewhere in Vietnam.

Upon arrival in Cedar Rapids, a representative of Turner Chapel Funeral Home was waiting with the hearse to take Denny to their chapel. His body had already been prepared, wrapped in bandages, and dressed in full uniform. The casket was not to be opened. They would have visitation the following day, the twenty-fourth and then he would be buried on Saturday the twenty-fifth.

The family met at the funeral home before visitation opened to the public at 6:30 p.m. Denny had been dead for fourteen days. It was explained to the family that it was a closed casket. *Remember him as he was. Don't have your last remembrance of him be the way he is now.*

They looked at the casket. They didn't even know if anything was in there. The family had been told his dental records identified him. Not seeing the body made it all the more difficult. It was unreal.

It was horrible for his parents not to be able to see him one more time. No parent should ever bury their child.

Occasionally, Susie would have that little feeling like, "Oh, they've made a mistake." You do hear stories every once in a while of a mistake. In reality, she knew this was real, but there was that inkling of a feeling that maybe, just maybe… It just didn't seem real, perhaps because she couldn't see him. It didn't seem like it happened because she never had that finality of viewing him.

On the morning of the funeral, a limousine picked up Susie for the ride to St. Paul's United Methodist Church in Cedar Rapids for the service. She wore a pale-yellow pants suit, which she realized probably wasn't an appropriate color for the burial of her husband. But she wore it in the hope it would lift her spirits. It didn't work.

The casket was at the church with a display of red roses on top. Sobs broke out periodically, punctuating the service. After the final blessing, the honor guard placed the flag-covered casket in the hearse for the short drive to Cedar Memorial Park Cemetery. The grave was part of four plots previously purchased by Susie's parents for themselves and their children. They gave one the plots to their daughter for her husband's burial.

The open grave awaited them when they arrived. It was a sunny morning, low seventies. The beauty of the morning was overshadowed by the sadness of the day. Family and friends gathered around the grave, and the ceremony began. Flowing the prayers, the flag was held above the casket; then the three-gun volley salute fired. It startled everyone who was not aware of military protocol. They were buried in their own thoughts…and then the loud *crack* of the rifle fire. As soon as the rifles fired the first volley, everyone started crying. Barbara thought it was absolutely horrible, a shock she wasn't expecting.

The folded American flag was presented to Susie and slowly Denny's casket was lowered into the ground. The only sound was the forlorn tears.

Tim's duties were over. He phoned his commanding officer to seek permission to stay a few more days and visit with Susie and Denny's family. Permission was denied. They would not allow him to stay even another day. They told him to get on a plane and fly to the Presidio.

When he arrived at the Presidio, there was no follow-up. No one talked to him about the possible psychological consequences that this experience would have on his life.

Tim always wondered if the army made a mistake; maybe it wasn't Denny they buried. Later, when the POWs were released in 1973, he kept checking for Denny's name. The long list of names was published in the *San Francisco Chronicle*, and he went through it with a fine-tooth comb, thinking that somebody might have screwed up. He just hoped beyond hope that Denny was one of those people that survived. It was not to be. It was not to be.

Elroy Simmons

Elroy's body was brought back to the United States via the Dover Air Force Base. There they prepared him for burial. He was wrapped in white cloth and wore white gloves; his full uniform resplendent with all his ribbons and badges properly attached. When he was ready, an escort was assigned to accompany the body back home.

Barbara decided to bury Elroy in the St Louis area rather than Waukegan. Their families were there, and that was where he grew up.

The casket was picked up at the airport, and it and the escort were transported to the funeral home Barbara had selected. When the body arrived, Barbara was notified, and she went over to the funeral home with Elroy's father and two of his brothers. Once again, the family was told that it was a closed casket. Barbara would not hear of that; she told them that she needed to see him; she couldn't deal with a closed casket. She said, "I've got to know." So, against their wishes, they opened the coffin. All exposed skin was wrapped in white bandages. Barbara looked down at him and knew it was him. Even though he was unrecognizable, she knew.

Dwight could not believe his brother was dead. Could they have made a mistake? Without seeing him, he had his doubts that that was Elroy in the casket. Maybe he was in shock, but he just didn't think that was him. Then he saw Elroy's Mason ring. It now sunk in. Elroy was dead, and this was his body.

As a child, Elroy was playing and fell up against a potbelly stove burning his face. He had a scar there and was very self-conscious about that. Had he recovered from the helicopter crash, he would have had a tough time living with the burn scars. That was no longer a concern.

A wake for Elroy was scheduled for July 29. The escort was present throughout the wake and funeral. The family thought he did an excellent job in a tough situation. Elroy would be buried the next day.

The burial, like all others, was a somber affair. The funeral procession proceeded at a slow and steady pace to Jefferson Barracks National Cemetery. The honor guard flawlessly performed the service. The volleys fired, and taps played. The flag was folded and given to Barbara.

Barbara had no time to grieve. She had four children all under the age of ten who needed her. Barbara had to take care of them and provide stability in their life. She had to be strong, strong for them. Now the total responsibility for the family rested on her shoulders.

David Schultz

As soon as Donna and her family heard that David was dead, her grandmother insisted that they visit David's family. Donna, her mother, and her grandmother drove over to David's mother's house to express their sympathies. There was a pall of sadness hanging over the house. David's grandmother cried the entire time they were there. Donna tried to talk to her in Spanish, but her Spanish wasn't very good, and amid her tears, the old woman probably would not have heard her anyway. Eventually, they quietly left.

The body of eighteen-year-old David finally came home to Harlingen, Texas. It was transported to the funeral home and made ready for the wake. The bronze casket containing the remains sat alone, covered in the American flag, ready to receive those who would mourn the end of David's young life. The family would arrive shortly to begin the visitation. His parents and grandmother would start the sad vigil, greeting all those who came to give their last respects to this fine young man whose life ended so violently.

There would be no viewing of the body. They would have to take the word of the United States Army that he was actually in the casket. There was always that nagging doubt –is he really in there? Is his whole body there? It would have to be taken on faith. Donna thought it was an empty casket.

Donna didn't have any say in any of the arrangements and did not attend the wake. They were betrothed, but no one knew this. To everyone else, she was just a young lady who was David's girlfriend. No one knew the depth of their relationship. Donna was overcome with grief that she had to carry deep inside herself. She carried it for the rest of her life.

The funeral was on Saturday, August 1. It was warm; the temperature would rise to ninety-six degrees. Sunny, no chance of rain. No breeze. The service would begin at the church at 10:00 a.m.; then, he would be buried in Mont Meta Memorial Park in San Benito, Texas.

The family arrived at the church and sat to the side of the alter. Away from everyone, alone in their sadness. Donna sat with her mother, grandmother, and brother at the front of the church. Her grandmother was her savior through this ordeal.

Donna had prayed for David every day he was gone. Now here she was looking at his flag-draped coffin. Her prayers had not helped him in the end. Her tears could not wash away the pain she felt.

When the service ended, Donna's grandmother rushed them out of the church to the car so they would have a good place in the procession to the cemetery. They managed to get in the spot right behind the family limousine. The whole thing was very surreal to Donna. They drove into the cemetery along the winding roads to the open grave—David's final resting place. David was the only person she ever knew who went to Vietnam and never came home.

The procession stopped, and everyone left their cars for the short walk to where the army honor guard awaited. Donna stood under a tree by the grave, watching the ceremony unfold. The sad notes of taps drifted over the cemetery amid the sobs of the mourners. From this day forward, Donna could not handle listening to taps.

The funeral over, everyone lost in their thoughts left. Donna and her family drove home. Donna retreated to her room, crying and trying to process everything that had happened. She went to her mom for consolation but didn't get it. Her mom could be very cruel, and Donna would never forget what she said to her: "I only let you see that boy because I knew he wasn't coming home." Donna was shocked.

Donna went through a lot of emotions after David's death and burial. She resented the war, did not believe in it. Donna decided that she would never marry and have children. She turned away from religion and became an atheist.

Thomas Campbell

Thomas was laid to rest on August 3, 1970. His body was interred at Highland Park Cemetery in Highland Hills, Ohio. The cemetery was part of the cemeteries run by the city of Cleveland.

His military service spanned from 1954 until he died in 1970, just short of sixteen years. During his career, he served two tours in Vietnam as well as a tour in Germany and one in Korea. He was awarded a Silver Star, two Bronze Stars, the Air Medal and now a Purple Heart.

He left behind a wife and two sons.

Robert Oldham

Robert was posthumously promoted to the rank of Sergeant, E5. His only surviving immediate family member was his mother. She elected to have him buried in the Fort Sam Houston National Cemetery in San Antonio, Texas. His mother wasn't notified of his death until July 25.

On August 3 at 10:00 a.m. he was buried with full military honors.

Roy Edward Harris

On July 11, a military army sedan pulled up to the apartment building on Taylor Drive. Two army personnel left the car and rang the bell of Linda Harris. They informed her that her husband, had been in a helicopter crash in Vietnam and was critically burned. They told her that he was going to be moved to the burn center at Camp Zama, Japan, soon, but they did not know precisely when.

They did know he was alive. There was hope. Linda was shocked. His tour was up in six days, on July 17. How could this be?

Linda received a steady stream of telegrams telling her of his condition. None was very positive. One of the soldiers returned on Monday, July 27 and gave her the bad news that her husband had died. He provided her with details about the return of his body. She was also informed about any benefits or insurance to which he may be entitled.

There was a delay pending official notification of his mother and father due to address issues. His mother lived in Bridgeport, Connecticut, and his father lived in Chicago. They were able to work it out and give them the news of their son's demise.

Roy's body arrived in Bridgeport on August 1 and was transported to Morton's Mortuary in Bridgeport. The family met with the staff to conclude the final arrangements. The mortuary was founded by James F. Morton, one of the Tuskegee Airmen of World War II. James's best friend at the time, also a pilot, was killed in a training accident. His remains were not viewable. This experience was the impetus for James to start the mortuary after the war. Now he would have the care of another nonviewable remains from a different war—a war just as deadly on an individual level but on a smaller scale in the world's eye.

Arrangements were made for a service with full military honors. The burial would be on Tuesday, August 4. The city issued an order that all flags at the Bridgeport post offices were to be flown at half-staff on this day.

Following a short prayer at the funeral home, the body was transported to Russell Temple Church for services. The church was a small, white frame, quaint building in a residential neighborhood. The Reverend David Jackson presided, attempting to bring peace to Roy's wife, parents, sister, and grandparents. Following the service, the burial was at Mountain Grove cemetery. Roy was buried with dignity and respect.

Chapter 13

Back to duty

A time to kill and a time to heal,

A time to tear down and a time to build,

A time to love and a time to hate,

A time for war and a time for peace.

-Ecclesiastes 3:3, 8

For many survivors of wounds in Vietnam, their service time was not over. It is hard to understand, but even though many could not perform the duties they were trained to do, they would not be discharged but made to finish their term of service. Be you enlisted or drafted, the army still owned you. It didn't seem to make much sense.

Mike Gandee

His extra seven-day leave finished, Mike once again departed the United States for Vietnam. His duty was done. Now he had to finish his tour. He still had nine months to go.

He arrived back at Cu Chi to take up where he left off. The same job, only now he was the only one left to perform it. Mike Vullo was dead, and Melvin Chase had been evacuated to the States, never to return. The scope of the job hadn't changed in their absence. Out to the field, repair the unit, and get a ride or hop back to Cu Chi. But it would never be quite the same. It was during this period that Mike was promoted from Specialist 4 to Specialist 5.

The 25th Infantry Division stood down four months after Mike's return. Although he had been promoted, he was not one of the fortunate ones to rotate home. He was transferred to the 1st Cavalry Division, northeast of Saigon. Here he was at a small firebase, not the main headquarters. He no longer worked in a central shop; he had his own radar to keep operating. He was on his own, and that suited him just fine.

Mike decided to extend his tour six months to get an early out. He would now DEROS in November 1971. His job would not change for the remainder of his extended tour. When his time was up in Vietnam, it was also up in the army. He would come home and de discharged.

Over the years, he experienced a little guilt over not being the one who was with his friend when the helicopter crashed. He was able to come to grips with that. It wasn't his fault. It was just the way things happened. It was like somebody getting bumped from an airplane, and then the airplane crashed.

Larry Crozier

Larry had seven months left to serve on his tour after the crash of #65-07999. Most of that time was spent on the water in his PBR with his Vietnamese crew. Once in a while, he would get down to the naval base at Nha Be, where hot American chow would be a welcome change from the fish, rice, and other Vietnamese food.

Larry was in Saigon and had to stop in the embassy, where he ran into an old buddy from Panama who was picking up mail. Starewicz was a gunner's mate who was stationed in Saigon. He was living in a BEQ off-base quarters for enlisted men, in comparative luxury. Whenever Larry would get to Nha Be, he would catch a ride to Saigon and spend time with Starewicz. They would grab a steak for ninety-five cents and then have a fun time on Tu Do Street, enjoying a few beers and the company of the local ladies.

February 1971: his tour up, Larry was going home. He would be discharged upon his return to the US. After arriving in San Francisco, he caught a bus to Treasure Island Naval Station. He reported to the out-processing section, and the chief there looked him up and down, noticing the Bronze Star with *V* and Gold Star and Combat Action ribbon. The chief leaned back in his chair and said, "Ah, seen a little shit over there, huh?" Larry replied, "Yeah. Served on a Navy PBR." Usually, sailors being processed for discharge would have to wait for three days at Treasure Island for the paperwork to be completed. The chief said, "I ain't going to get to your paperwork till about two or three days. Come back in three days."

Taking advantage of the time away, Larry hopped a bus into San Francisco where life was completely different compared to the last twelve months in South Vietnam. One of his stops was to have a couple beers. He hooked up with sailors who didn't tell him where they were going. Their destination was a topless bar! They got settled at a table, and the waitress came over, and she said, "Would you like something to drink?" Larry turned around, and there was a pair of bare breasts right in his face. The surprise on his face made his new buddies break out in hysterics! They explained the story to the waitress, who took it in stride. "Yeah. I get a lot of guys who have that same reaction." This was something he certainly wasn't expecting! That was the only welcome home he ever received but for now it was good enough.

Rickey Wittner

Rickey remained in the hospital at Cu Chi for five days. His hands had been pretty badly burned and needed constant care to prevent infection. Once released, he was grounded while he healed. For the next week or two, he had to go to the hospital every day and have his bandages changed. As he healed, the dressings were changed every other day. The healing process was slow but progressed.

During this period, he had absolutely nothing to do. He couldn't shoot pool because he couldn't hold the cue stick. He couldn't even go swimming at the Cu Chi pool. He was bored out of his mind. Finally, he talked the doctor into releasing him as long as he lathered up his hands with medicine and wore his flight gloves. With that, he started flying again. It had been about twenty-one days since the crash, and he was ready, mentally and physically.

Climbing back in a Chinook was an unsettling experience. But he knew it had to be done like getting back on a horse. Rickey was as nervous as a cat when he started flying again. The third day back, they flew into the same location *Love Craft* had, but this time from another direction. It was a scary experience for him. There was no ground fire this time.

In time Rickey got over his apprehension, and soon flying once again became routine. He became a flight engineer and was given his own bird. Dennis Sievers, better known as Tractor Man, became his crew chief, he never had a regular gunner. Tractor Man did not talk much unless you brought up the subject of tractors; that was how he got his nickname. Everyone just called Rickey TEX.

The end of October/beginning of November 1970 brought on significant changes for the 242nd ASHC. The 25th Division at Cu Chi stood down, and the 242nd was moved to Phu Loi in the same general area of operations. Phu Loi would be Rickey's new home until his DEROS in February 1971.

There was no early out for Rickey. He still had ten months to go. Upon his return from Vietnam, he had a leave then reported for duty at Fort Stewart, Georgia. There wasn't a lot to do there. Like so many other returnees, he was warehoused until his discharge. The last two months of his service, the army, in its infinite wisdom, sent him to NCO school. Upon graduation, he was promoted to a hard striper, Sergeant E-5. No raise in pay. Maybe they hoped he would reenlist? That wasn't going to happen.

Edward Whittle

After the crash, while he was recovering from his wounds, Ed was assigned to be the assistant operations officer. It was good in that it kept him busy but he knew that he needed to get back in the air. The healing head wound, and all the stitches prevented him from putting on a helmet. So, he flew a mission with his best friend in the back on a jump seat with just headphones.

It was the night of one of those lengthy missions after sixteen grueling hours that they received a call from operations. They were to fly to the 25th Division pad at Tay Ninh and pick up some bodies and take them to the graves registration collection point at Cu Chi.

Ed was sitting in the back of the aircraft. It was pitch black outside, the aircraft only lit by the interior red lights. They came in to land, and once on the ground, they didn't shut down, just kept the engines running and dropped the ramp. The troops came in with the body bags and lay them like cordwood, right in from of him, all the way down the middle of the aircraft. There he sat, staring at them in the glow of the red light. It was a very eerie experience.

It was typical for aircraft in Vietnam to tune in one of the radios to AFVN (Armed Forced Radio Vietnam) and listen to music while they flew. Today was no exception. As Ed sat there staring at the body bags, Bobby Vinton's "Coming Home Soldier" began to play. For the rest of his life, every time that song played, his mind would be instantly transported to that sight.

He kept going up, going up, and then it finally came time to fly again. Now he had to go through the whole ritual with the IPs of the unit to make sure he still had it. He still had it, but it was hard. "When your bubble's broke, it's pretty broke."

He was continually thinking something was going to happen, so he watched himself. Not long after, he was on the TAC-E mission, which meant loss of life was inevitable. Every Chinook company had one TAC-E aircraft. This aircraft was on standby to be in the air in minutes if needed. They received a desperate call for ammunition to be delivered to LZ Wood, a fire support base north of Tay Ninh near the Cambodian border.

This night the NVA were trying to overrun the base. They needed ammunition, and they needed it now. They flew to Tay Ninh to refuel and load up. Two Cobra gunships were assigned to guide them in with suppressing fire. They took off and were in communication, but the Cobras were lost. With a full belly of fuel and a load of ammo on board, they needed those Cobras.

They jumped up to five-thousand feet, which was higher than the deemed effective range of the enemy's fifty-one-caliber machineguns. Still no Cobras. They turned on every light they had and put the landing lights on rotate so they could be spotted but no luck. In the meantime, the call came from the ground: "Mule Skinner, Mule Skinner, where are you? We really need the ammo. We really need the ammo." They didn't need a map or a direction beacon to find LZ Wood. It was surrounded by a solid ring of fire from green and orange tracers.

Ed looked at that and thought, *I got to fly into that?* Still no Cobras. Five minutes out. He called the Cobras and told them, "Just figure out where you are. Be there for the next guy." Five Chinooks were coming after him. Ed told his crew, "Snap it in. We're going in; we gotta get this ammunition on the ground." There was time to get scared, time to have adrenaline pouring through your body. There was so much light from the tracers that he called to the ground, "OK, no flares. I don't need any illumination; I can see everything." But, while Ed was on short final, one of the troops thought he would help, and he popped off a flare. It floated down right in front of the cockpit, causing the loss of their night vision and whiting out the cockpit. As they descended, green tracers were going by. The fifty-ones look like basketballs, and the other ones looked like baseballs. They dropped their load and got out of there without anyone getting hit. His luck had held.

Robert Henry

Robert was out of commission for about a week after the crash, letting the gash in his knee heal. As soon as the stitches were removed, he was cleared for flying duty.

He finished his tour without incident and came home. He stayed in the army flying Chinooks for twenty years. No more crashes.

Larry Butcher

Larry extended his time in Vietnam to get an early out. He was there one year, one month, and ten days. At that time, the 25th Division returned to Hawaii. The return of the 25th Division delayed his return home. His tour finished he reported for his return flight but there were no many troopers ahead of him. He went to roll call three times a day for six days before his name was finally called. It was November 10, one day before Veterans Day. Fitting.

Finally, it was time to go home. His group loaded on three buses for the ride to the flight home. As the buses started leaving, a GI behind them shouted, waved his hands, and stopped them. Their plane had had engine trouble and was under repair. They were taken off the buses and stood or sat on the dirt behind a chain-link fence for twenty-four hours. Guards were placed around them, and they were given C rations and water. They had no blankets, cots, or chairs.

The repairs finished, they boarded the plane that would take them home. During the entire flight, Larry hoped the mechanics hadn't overlooked anything when fixing the aircraft. They landed in Guam and then in Hawaii to refuel. It was morning when they touched down at Oakland International Airport because Travis Air Force Base was fogged in. When they landed in California, cheers went up, and there wasn't a dry eye on the plane. Even the stewardess had tears. He never forgot that moment.

Of course, Oakland wasn't prepared for them, so they had to wait on the plane several hours before customs officials could check them in. The complement of weary, but happy, soldiers left the aircraft and boarded buses for the short distance to the Oakland Army Base for clearance. That same day at midnight, Larry walked out relieved from active duty. A civilian.

Lowell Ketchum

Lowell returned to the United States in August and was sent directly to Fort Gordon, Georgia. Upon arrival, he was seen by the doctors, headed by a Lieutenant Colonel. The colonel told Lowell that he usually would let the wounded soldiers returning from Vietnam rest for two or three days before examining them as he knew how significant a strain the trip back could be on these soldiers.

He asked Lowell if he was having any problems. He told him how bad his shoulder was hurting and had been since the crash. With that, once again, Lowell was sent to X-ray. Afterward, the Colonel came to visit and laughingly told him, "Hell, no wonder your shoulder hurts—it's broken! You have a broken clavicle." He explained that there was so much blood around the broken collar bone that the X-rays taken in Vietnam didn't pick up the break. By now, the blood had cleared up, and the break was clearly visible.

Lowell asked if it could be fixed. The colonel said, "No. It is healing on its own. We would have to break it again, and I don't want to do that." Lowell wanted to be transferred to the hospital at Fort Benning as his family was there. The doctor replied, "Well, it'll take me a little while. I have to find a doctor at Fort Benning who will accept your case. I will work on that." A week or so later, Lowell was transferred to the hospital at Fort Benning and reunited with his family.

His burns were healing nicely, but a skin graft was required on his left leg. He was discharged from the hospital in October and went back to being a soldier.

Lowell stayed in the army until he retired in 1975. He spent twenty years in service to his country. He spent an additional tour in Germany with the 1st Armored Division and was promoted to First Sergeant, a rank he retired in.

Following his retirement, he moved to Florida and then Georgia, where he sold cars, then insurance. He ended up back at

Fort Benning, working for the government training soldiers of all ranks for the Iraqi war.

Harlen Metzger

Three days after Harlen's family spoke with him in Japan, they were notified that he had been medevacked to Fort Sam Houston's Brooke Medical Center in San Antonio, Texas. Brenda made plans to fly there and see him as quickly as she could. Hank, Harlen's father, wanted his twelve-year-old daughter to fly down with Brenda to see him. Neither one had flown before, so this in and of itself was a momentous occasion.

Brenda was able to speak with Harlen on the phone when he arrived, and he told her to wait at least two days for him to get settled in. Harlen told her that his hair had burned off, and his face and neck had also been burned. Brenda didn't know what to expect when she would see him. They did anxiously wait for those two days to pass and then flew down. They were able to stay in base visitor housing while they were there.

They took a city bus to the hospital to see him. Brenda was terrified of what he might look like as he told her that he had his hair burned off and had burns on his neck, back, arms, stomach, and legs. When they finally saw him, she was so relieved. His hair had only been singed. His face looked more like a bad sunburn rather than anything horrific. The burns were centered on the back of his body, where the fire was. He had a large hoop over his body with his sheet draped over it, and he was naked underneath. He was freezing.

Of course, he had other injuries besides his burns. The whole front of his body had been opened up. The ruptured spleen had been removed. When he was first wounded, they didn't know the extent of his injuries, so exploratory surgery had been done. He was very uncomfortable. He couldn't lay on this back due to his burns, and the front of his body was healing from the surgery.

He told her that the first couple of days were horrible. They would put him in a large stainless-steel tub and scrubbed his burns to keep scabs from forming. Then they put on a cream that felt like he was being burned all over again. He could walk but mainly used a wheelchair. He was lucky not to have needed a skin graft. The soldier in the bed next to him had skin grafts over several areas of his body and was uncovered. The scene in the ward was horrific to Brenda. She observed other soldiers in beds or walking around who had no ears or no nose as they had been burned off. It was indeed a place of healing but also of terror. She knew how lucky Harlen was. It could have been much worse.

Brenda went to a support group when she arrived. The group consisted of the families of the burn victims, and the group leader told her that his improvement over two days since he'd been there was amazing. Psychologically, he was a lot better than most of the patients. His attitude had changed entirely, just by his family being there.

Hank drove the rest of the family in from Indiana. Harlen's brother, Mike, was in the navy and stationed at Virginia Beach, Virginia. He flew in with his wife to visit. Brenda remembers standing behind him while he was in the wheelchair and lightly scratching or rubbing his back because he was itching so bad with the healing of his skin. Harlen said this was what he remembered the most from that time.

He told her that the doctor told him he had to eat and drink a lot for the burns to heal. They said this to the wrong person because Harlen had always been heavy. He weighed about 185 pounds while in the hospital but was able to gain back all the weight he had lost in short order.

Harlen was in the hospital for about thirty days then he received orders to report to Fort Polk, Louisiana. He came home for a thirty-day leave first. When they came back to Indiana, Brenda and Harlen had their church wedding. Although they were already married by a justice of the peace, they had a formal Catholic wedding. People said they hardly recognized Harlen because he was so skinny.

Richard Green

When soldiers were discharged from the burn center at Fort Sam Houston, they were allowed to choose their next duty station. It was the least the army could do after the horrible burns suffered by the soldiers who were evacuated from Vietnam. But sometimes, the army had other ideas. They would not medically discharge Richard and did not offer him his choice of assignments. At the time, a medical discharge would have entitled him to VA disability benefits for the rest of his life. That was not in the cards for Richard. He was given orders for Fort Benning, Georgia.

He reported in and was assigned as a cadre in a training brigade. The brigade was located about thirty miles away from the main post. Rangers were trained there, and at times, they would bring in officer candidates or people from the different military academies to get up to speed on what infantry people do. They supported all the field cadre with tanks and armored personnel carriers and riding in helicopters.

Richard had been through a lot and had a little bit of gumption back then. He was assigned to one of the old wooden WWII barracks that were so common in the '60s and '70s. When he walked into the barracks, he took his duffel bag and just threw it into the sergeant's room because nobody was in there and no one said a damn thing to him. He put his lock on the door and stayed there for another five or six months.

The problem was that he wasn't making much money at the time. Soldiering was not a highly paid profession, not even those who were sergeants. It didn't help to be so far away from the main post. It was an hour bus ride to the main post, then another thirty minutes winding through the streets and the large establishment to the PX, movies, or whatever. Richard hardly ever made it into town as he didn't have a car.

His physical condition was such that he was extremely limited in what he could do. His burns were still raw and far from healed. In actuality, he wasn't able to do just about anything.

The first thing they wanted him to do was to stand on the interstate or the highway and be a road guard. He would literally start bleeding if he stood for too long. His whole leg had almost been lost to the fire, and standing for a prolonged time caused it to start to bleed again. His regrowing skin was still just a thin membrane holding him together. So when he was told to be a road guard, he whipped out his medical profile that was two pages long. The first sergeant looked up at him and asked, "Well, Jesus. What can you do?" Obviously, he wasn't used to getting people like Richard sent there. Richard looked at him and said, "You know what? If I try real hard, I can make it to the chow hall," and he left it at that.

He didn't have to make morning formation or anything because they couldn't make him stand up for more than just a few moments. In his medical profile, he was pretty much exempt from starching his clothes or wearing boots. He was stopped by a general for looking sloppy like Sad Sack, and he whipped out that profile, and showed it to him. The general just gave it back to him and drove off.

When it came time to be discharged, they ran him through the VA so fast, his head was spinning. They didn't even catch half the things that the burns had caused, not to mention his other wounds. They needed to do better.

Tim Petersen

Tim finished his service at the Presidio and was discharged on June 3, 1971. With army life behind him, he returned to his wife and civilian life. He served during the Vietnam crisis stateside and was grateful for that experience. Now, he was happy to put it behind him and move on.

Chapter 14

Living with Loss

I would say to those who mourn… look upon each day that comes as

a challenge, as a test of courage. The pain will come in waves, some

days worse than others, for no apparent reason.

Accept the pain. Do not suppress it. Never attempt to hide grief.

-Daphne du Maurier

By September 1970, all of the dead had been buried and the wounded were either in the hospital recovering or returned to duty. By mid-October, those remaining wounded had returned to duty to finish their service obligation. None were granted medical discharges due to their wounds. I guess that the army needed them to fill the ranks, although it almost seemed like they would rather warehouse them than let them go home. Maybe this was the army's way of reacclimating them to civilian life? I doubt it.

In a televised speech on October 7, President Nixon proposed a cease-fire in South Vietnam. Previously the US had demanded the withdrawal of all North Vietnamese forces from South Vietnam. North Vietnam rejected Nixon's proposal as it required an eventual withdrawal by North Vietnam, which claimed that it had the right to maintain forces in South Vietnam as South and North were a single country. The war dragged on.

The 25th Infantry Division departed Vietnam for Schofield Barracks, Hawaii, on December 8, 1970. This did not mean everyone left in the division went home. Many men rotated to other units within Vietnam, and many from other units close to coming home were assigned to the 25th for the trip home. The 2nd Brigade of the 25th stayed and became a separate brigade under II Field Forces control. The 2nd Brigade operated at color guard strength in the Long Binh and Xuan Loc areas east of Saigon until its departure for Schofield Barracks on April 30, 1971. There was always a way of manipulating the numbers to create the illusion of gradual withdrawal. However, the withdrawal of American troops was real. The numbers were dropping. On January 1, 1970, there were 475,200 troops in Vietnam. By the end of the year, there were 334,600. All wanted to go home. None wanted to become a final statistic.

In 1971 the Vietnamization program continued to progress, and the American military turned to more defensive operations and continued airstrikes on military targets. American battle deaths spiraled down. There were sixty-six American deaths in July 1971, the lowest monthly loss since May 1967. It is easy to throw that number out there happily at the decreased amount of casualties. It has to be kept in perspective. The families of the sixty-six felt the loss as deeply as they would have if there had been as many as a thousand or as few as one.

Over the last few years of the war, the politicians would argue about the shape of the negotiation table and would try and out-leverage each other. Meanwhile, more Americans would die and be wounded. Families would continue to mourn. Protests against the war would continue. Some returning GIs would be mistreated and made to feel that somehow they were solely responsible for the war. It would take a long time for the country to heal. General Ronald R. Fogleman USAF retired said: "The road from peace to war is often too short, and the road from war to the fruits of peace is often too long."

Denny Martin

Denny's widow, Sue, struggled for normalcy like most war widows of the time. She experienced her high and low moments and didn't give in to bitterness about the war. She didn't think about it much, one way or another. She had lost her husband, and she struggled to deal with that. She just didn't think about it. She was indifferent about it. She was so young that she didn't dwell on it. She just tried to move on.

She had a teaching degree and taught second grade at Madison School. That saved her. She didn't know what she would have done without it. It gave her a way to support herself and keep busy. Being with the children was a saving grace that helped her deal with the tremendous loss she felt.

Sue kept the fact that she was a widow mostly to herself. She just didn't feel a need to tell people that her husband was killed in Vietnam. Over the years, there were only a handful of people that she shared this part of her life with. When she did share, they were totally shocked. It was hard for her to talk about. She didn't want pity or for people to feel sorry for her. It was a very private grief she kept within over the years. It is only in the last five years or so that she has talked to people about losing her husband in Vietnam.

In January 1972, her life took a turn. She went on a blind date with John Sundberg. A high school friend of Sue's was married to a fraternity brother of John's. They clicked. John knew about Denny from his friend. John was recently discharged from the army. He had known he would be drafted, so he enlisted instead. He received training as a stock control and accounting specialist, MOS 76P. After training at Fort Lee, he was sent to Korea, a much-preferred duty station than Vietnam. Because of his military service he didn't have a problem talking to Sue about the loss of her husband.

They were married in September of that year. John began working for the government doing defense work, and the couple eventually moved to New Jersey. New Jersey became too expensive for them, so they moved to Alabama, and John worked at Redstone Arsenal.

Sue and John decided that they needed to visit the Wall. It was an extremely emotional time for Sue. It was also for John as he had several friends he went to high school with on the Wall. John was very supportive of Sue throughout their visit. He understood her pain.

Sue and John went to Hawaii in 1997. Sue loves to travel but was reluctant to go to Hawaii, understandably so. She initially had no desire to go there, but she eventually had a change of heart. The memory of getting ready to go there to meet Denny on R & R was still raw. But she did go and enjoyed it. It wasn't as difficult as she thought it would be. Maybe it was the timing, or perhaps she was just able to begin to find peace with that chapter of her life.

Sue's healing continued. She had a wonderful, loving, and understanding husband, children, and grandchildren. Life was good.

Over the years, Denny's parents never talked about their feelings, ever. They never spoke about his death. The family hardly ever mentioned his name for over twenty years. When someone would say Denny's name, his mother would just freeze. She just couldn't talk about it. She held all her grief inside.

His dad never talked about his feelings relating to Denny's death either. Denny's sister Barbara is sure that he felt a profound loss and sorrow, but he never showed it. Like his wife, he kept the grief buried inside. They did not cry at his funeral. They may have cried behind closed doors but never in public.

Barbara and her dad were polar opposites, politically. Of course, this caused friction before Denny's death but never afterward. They argued about many things but never argued about the war after that. Barbara decided never to bring it up. She felt that if her parents received some comfort from the thought that Denny died a patriotic death, then she would never take that away.

Barbara is a musician. She had been a social worker in Virginia. She took a job as an adult protective service worker working with a lot of older people. In her downtime the meantime, she was performing in restaurants with another woman.

In her job she met with many older people during a lot of nursing home placements and listened to their life stories. So many expressed their regrets in life: "I wish I would have done this," or, "I wish I would have tried this before the end of my life," and it worked on her. Finally, she thought, *You know, I don't want to be at the end of my life, thinking, "I wish I would have tried to be a professional musician."*

Despite having a good job, she decided to leave it and try to make a career in music. She took a part-time job, and things just started happening. She became a bass player in a country band, and then she was playing solo in restaurants. She honestly thought, *Well, I'll do this for a couple of years, but it probably won't work*, but it just kept working!

Denny's parents relocated to New Jersey for Robert's job. Barbara visited them there in 1994 and was shocked when her mother came up to her and handed her a wooden box. She told Barbara that it contained Denny's letters. She had saved them all these years. Barbara took the box up to her room and began to read the words, emotions, hopes, and dreams that Denny had put on paper. As she read them, she cried and cried.

All this time, she didn't think they knew how unhappy and angry he was while in Vietnam. She felt they didn't know, but now she understood that they did. Her parents had been distraught with her for demonstrating against the war, and she was, in turn, angry with them. She had thought, *You don't know what he felt about the war. You don't know that he was not into the war at all, that he hated it.* But then when she read the letters, she realized he had told them even more than he had told her about how he felt. It was tragic that for all those years, she didn't know that.

Things changed after that. Now, for the first time, her mother could talk about him.

Afterward, Barbara was performing at the Kennedy Center; her parents and brother were there for the concert. She told them that she wanted them to come with her to see the Wall and see Denny's name. Her younger brother was fine with it, but her parents were resistant. Finally, her mother agreed, but her father didn't want to go, which was a surprise. In the end, they all decided to go. They went as a family. There was his name, *Dennis K Martin,* on panel 08W, line 8. His parents and brother were stoic, so there weren't a lot of tears shed that day. Tears or not, it was an extremely emotional day for everyone.

Robert Martin died in 2003, and Gladys Martin died a little over a year later. Finally, they were reunited with their son, Denny.

Harlen Metzger

Following their wedding, the not-so-newlyweds traveled south to Louisiana and "beautiful" Fort Polk to complete Harlen's service commitment. He was still suffering the effects of his burns, but in its infinite wisdom, the army saw fit to keep him rather than grant him an early discharge. Even though Harlen was very limited in what he could do, the army found ways to keep him busy.

His assignment was a general posting that could entail just about any job that needed him to do. He was a big man and cut an excellent soldierly figure when he checked in, standing tall in his dress green uniform, sporting his Combat Infantry Badge and the Bronze Star, Purple Heart, and Army Commendation ribbons. He was a combat veteran.

He was assigned to light indoor duty because he couldn't be in the sun. He also couldn't stand long periods. So, they sent him to the Judge Advocates Office to work with court-martials. He was promoted to Specialist 5 and worked the slot customarily assigned to an E-7. He would take notes at the trials he monitored and then type a report for each.

He was one of the few men back in that day who could type. Of course, he brought the typewriter home, and a lot of the times, Brenda typed the reports for him. This should have been a happy time, but Harlen had changed. He was negative and started saying mean-spirited things to Brenda. It was almost as if he was trying to distance himself from the ones he loved. Brenda did not know or understand this. Combat soldiers did not get attached to many while in the field. It was too hard to lose them. Unfortunately, avoiding close attachments followed many soldiers' home.

Harlen had never acted like this before Vietnam. He was very nice until it seemed he was back in the military environment. He became abrupt, coarse, and negative. The overall experience of war and his burns had taken its toll on him. Trauma changes people. It changed Harlen.

About two weeks after reporting to Fort Polk, he broke out with large weeping blisters. They were mostly located on his face and scalp. They went to the ER on base, but the doctors had no idea what it was or what was causing it. The blisters kept recurring, and each time they went to the ER, it was the same response –no one knew what was causing them. Other doctors, including dermatologists, were called in, but it remained a mystery.

The blisters would usually clear up after one to three weeks, and he would sometimes go months between breakouts. There was severe itching involved, and occasionally they would get infected. Sometimes his face was so swollen he looked like he was deformed and he wouldn't go out in public.

Harlen finally received an early out in April of 1971. He would not have to serve until July when his obligation of service was supposed to be complete. The couple packed their belongings and returned home to Indiana.

Harlen went to work for his father at Metzger Construction Co. He excelled. He was an excellent businessman and had a great reputation in the community. Brenda worked at an insurance agency and was also making a good salary. Even so, they had their ups and downs. She loved him, and he was kind about 50 percent of the time, and then he would be nasty. He was occasionally mean but never physically abusive.

They tried to have children, but Brenda suffered a miscarriage in the first two years. It was at this point that they decided to adopt. They made an appointment with Saint Elizabeth's Home in Indianapolis, and as luck would have it that same week, Brenda found out that she was pregnant with their first child. Because they had tried for about six years, they didn't even think about birth control. Right after the first child was born, she became pregnant right away with her second. They were only eleven months apart.

Their family continued to grow, three children Heath, Tim, and Amy. The business grew too. Harlen and Brenda loved their children and never fought in front of them. Harlen didn't talk about Vietnam much, but the whole experience affected him. PTSD was not something that was even a subject back then, but it seems evident that Harlen was suffering the effects of it. Anger outbursts and bad dreams indicated this. He talked in his sleep a lot, arguing, fighting, and mumbling. Depression plagued him the throughout his life. Physical ailments were constant. Harlen never expressed any bitterness about the war. Like so many veterans, he just seemed to bury it. Despite dealing with these problems, Harlen was a wonderful father who adored his children.

One thing Harlen wouldn't do was go camping. He always said he would never go camping because he had slept out in the jungle one too many times. Out on patrol, he would sit out in the rain and swear he would never do this again. He did finally relent, but he would take his dad's camper. He would only stay where there was electric service, and he brought a fan, television, and other luxuries. He would never sleep on the ground—ever. He had to have a comfortable environment to go to. It would take him two days to get ready. He would bring a lot of food, most of which they didn't eat and brought back home. To Harlen, this was roughing it. As primitive as he was going to get. After being in the field in Vietnam, who was to blame him.

After their second child, Harlen and Brenda decided on marriage counseling. They went together for about three months; then Harlen went alone for another year. Things improved during this period. Harlen started treating Branda better, and the marriage improved. The daily stress lessened.

Everyone liked Harlen. Brenda would often hear, "Harlen, you're a good man." He helped so many people financially and in other ways. He had a lot of friends, and the company donated money to schools over the years, not to mention the little league teams they sponsored. He also donated labor costs to the local Warrick County Schools PTOs and PTAs. When anyone ever spoke of Harlen, the same compliment was inevitably repeated: "He is a good man."

Harlen inherited a strong work ethic from his father. Even though he was depressed most of his life and had varying degrees of health issues he never missed a day of work.

Harlen became obsessed with weapons. Every weekend for years he and a friend would travel to different gun shows. He amassed an arsenal of over eight hundred guns, swords, bayonets and thousands of rounds of ammunition. He never fired them. He once told Brenda that he had a dream where he was defending their home and he never have enough guns to get the job done. All his weapons were sold at auction after his death.

Harlen continued to deal with the physical issues that were caused by the burns and immersion in the Saigon River immediately after. He broke out every time he was exposed to the sun. He had to wear a hat all the time when outdoors. Whenever he was sick or running a fever, he would break out.

For years Harlen came home from work, sat in his chair and fell asleep. Brenda felt that if she was going to lonely, she might as well be by herself. They divorced in 2001. They remained friends and actually only lived apart for ten months. Their youngest child was moving to his own place and Harlen had a fear of being left alone so he asked Brenda to move back in with him. She did. In total they were together for forty-six years. They did everything together, just never legally remarried.

In the early 2000s, they went back and forth to the VA Hospital in Marion, Illinois. The doctor there was duly impressed and interested as he hadn't seen anything like it before. He sent biopsies off, and the results came back as pemphigus vulgaris. A local dermatologist also did a biopsy and came back with the same results.

There are two forms of pemphigus. They told him, "You're lucky. Some people get it in their mouths, and they can't eat, and they die."

Pemphigus vulgaris is a rare, severe autoimmune disease in which blisters of varying sizes break out on the skin and sometimes the lining of the mouth and other mucous membranes. Pemphigus vulgaris occurs when the immune system mistakenly attacks proteins in the upper layers of the skin. This is considered rarer than the so-called "orphan" diseases as it is estimated that only one in one million people worldwide has this condition.

The more Brenda looked into it, the more she was sure that he did not have pemphigus vulgaris but rather pemphigus foliaceus. His symptoms matched the latter to a T. One of the leading causes of a breakout is exposure to the sun. Pemphigus foliaceus is also a rare autoimmune disease that causes painful itching and blistering. The immune system mistakenly attacks your healthy tissue.

It makes one wonder if, after he was burned, he could have been exposed to an agent that brought on this disease? Could he have been bitten by something in the jungles of Vietnam or Cambodia, or was his exposure to Agent Orange a contributing factor? Could some of the medicines he was put on and antibiotics he received after the helicopter crash or even something he was exposed to in the polluted river the soldiers went into after the crash been the trigger? Was it the removal of his spleen? It took over forty years to get a diagnosis with no answers and no clear-cut method of treatment. Take steroids and stay out of the sun, he was told.

It was around 2010 that he had a breakout that never cleared up—continuous blistering and severe itching. The only thing the local doctor knew to do was put him on long term steroids. (There are other treatments available including chemotherapy, blood transfusions, etc. that may have helped, but since this condition is so rare, there are only a handful of doctors in the world who know how to treat it).

Harlen developed A-fib, and his blood sugar was extremely high. His diabetes spun out of control since steroids play havoc with blood sugar numbers. He grew weaker with age. He got to the point that he sometimes fell trying to get into and out of his pickup truck. He started getting huge boils and would have to take antibiotics which led to a cycle of severe diarrhea and urinary tract infections; of course, that led to hospitalizations and even more antibiotics. Every time he was hospitalized, the first thing they did was to lower or quit the steroids; then he would immediately break out in the blisters and severe itching, and they would have to increase the dosage again. With all the medicines he was taking, he would start to have kidney or liver failure, so they kept stopping one medication and trying another. It became hard to know what he was supposed to be taking or not as different doctors kept changing different medicines. Steroids also mess with your brain chemistry, and he often had what is known as "steroid rage."

The last five years of his life were physically miserable for him. It only got worse after he went into the hospital for a urinary tract infection. After four days, the doctors decided to release him. Harlen told the doctor that he could walk to the bathroom fine when he came in but could barely make it to the bathroom from his hospital bed. His lower abdomen and groin area were bright red, which was something new. The doctors ignored these symptoms and sent him home. This was in November of 2013.

Little did they know that this was the beginning of the end for him. After Harlen got home, he sat in his recliner and could not get up. He was forced to use a urinal. He refused to go back to the hospital. After he was home for two days, he agreed to let Brenda call an ambulance. Their boys came over and lifted him out of the chair so she could clean him before the ambulance arrived. She felt a boil deep in his groin and knew he had an infection. When he got to the hospital, she told everyone who came into the room that he had an infection in his groin area. The next day they did a cat scan and said he didn't have an infection.

Harlen lay in the bed for two more days when a nurse said he had to have a doctor look at him because she could see a significant infection. The surgeon came in and took a look at Harlen's groin, and he was livid. He looked at the CT scan and said it clearly showed an infection and that it was a crying shame that the other doctor ignored it because it was a Friday evening, and he didn't want to be bothered with it. The surgeon went out into the hallway, yelling and talking to Harlen's brother. The nurse did her best to try calming him down. The doctor said it was an emergency, and within twenty minutes, Harlen was in an operating room. The boil got infected and turned to gangrene basically, and they had to cut out a massive portion of his groin.

He ended up hospitalized for ten months, then back and forth into rehab centers. He almost died. He was even medevacked to the University of Louisville Medical Center. He only walked about twenty steps after his surgery and was completely bedridden after that. He missed a Thanksgiving, Christmas, his birthday, Easter, and Memorial Day. He finally came back home on Labor Day of 2014.

It took Brenda six weeks to set up a hospital room at home. The VA helped with widening some of the doorways in the house and provided them with a hospital bed. Harlen had to get a special kind because of his skin condition. They also received an electronic lift, a wide wheelchair with a custom cushion, a VA-supplied ramp, a triangle bar above his bed, and most of his supplies. He had to have special bandages for his legs as they had to be kept wrapped because of the excessive swelling and oozing. The steroids for his A-fib made his skin super thin, and sometimes just bumping against something could cause him to bleed. He had to use a catheter as he had become incontinent. He also had to use diapers and lots of pillows because his legs had to be kept elevated.

He couldn't even move his legs at this point or turn over in bed. He could help a little by using the triangle bar above his head, but he weighed around three hundred pounds. Brenda needed help to get him into the wheelchair because she was not strong enough to do it on her own. They had two grandchildren living with them at the time, so the older, who was eleven would help if the caregivers they hired weren't there.

Harlen had numerous trips back and forth to the ER, and several more hospital stays, mainly from urinary tract infections. At the end of February 2015, he was very sick again and running a fever but kept refusing to go to the hospital. Finally, he agreed to go for a chest X-ray. The doctor came in and told Harlen that he was being admitted, but he refused. The doctor explained that he had double pneumonia and was in kidney and liver failure. Harlen still refused and asked the doctor for antibiotics and to go back home. Brenda called hospice, and they started taking over his care and got him oxygen and morphine for pain. He had been going through hell the last two years of his life. He went from being an independent man who was always on the go to being bedridden and wearing diapers.

Monday, April 6 Harlen called Brenda in the middle of the night, saying that he needed something. He was having a hard time breathing, so she increased his oxygen a little and gave him some morphine. She had been told not to increase it too much because that made it harder to breathe. He needed his legs redone. She was in there for about forty-five minutes taking care of him.

Brenda went into his room every night and took care of him. He would be in pain, and she would assure him that she would never do that on purpose. "I'm doing everything I can to take care of you." He would say, "Well, it's OK because if I need you again, I'll call you again." "No," she'd answer, "don't call me till six o'clock in the morning." It was about midnight, and she had to get their two grandchildren up for school.

On April 8, 2015, at 6:00 a.m. Brenda got the boys up to get ready for school. All the way across the living room, she could hear the gurgling sound coming from his room, even with the door closed. She could tell this was the end. Brenda went into the room, and Harlen was unresponsive except for the gurgling in his lungs. She felt like she had to do something even though he had signed a DNR. She told their older grandson to call his mother, her two sons, and 911, which he did. Their older son arrived first and then the ambulance. The sounds from Harlen's chest had quit by this time. They didn't have the EMTs try any lifesaving efforts. Harlen's battle was over.

Despite all the challenges Harlen faced, he lived a full life. He lived long enough to meet his youngest and sixth grandchild, Simon Metzger.

On Thursday evening, April 10, 2015, there was a visitation at Bradley's funeral home. On Friday, April 11, 2015, his funeral was held at St. Clements Catholic Church in Boonville. The burial followed at Center Cemetery, which is located across from his family's home and Metzger Construction Co. He received a military salute at the cemetery and a very poignant message from the military commander. Brenda had them give the flag to their older son, Heath.

Everybody has their confrontations in life. Harlen was another casualty of the Vietnam War. The crash of #65-07999 began a downward spiral for Harlen from which he would never recover. The removal of his spleen and submersion in the dirty Saigon River with open wounds greatly affected his immune system.

The horrific crash he survived, as well as the daily stresses of combat, took its toll. He was never officially diagnosed with PTSD, but I believe it is evident that he suffered from it. He was fortunate to have had a loving family to support him throughout his struggles.

David Schultz

A couple of months after David's funeral, Donna met with David's mother and grandmother. Donna tried to introduce herself to the grandmother, but the grandmother could not stop crying long enough to understand who she was. She cried the entire time, wrapped in her grief. Donna doesn't know if she ever recovered, but it is doubtful. David's death may have taken her to the grave.

The ranch started working on its addition, thanks to David's insurance money. Of course it was dedicated to David. David's mother gave his medals and award certificates to the ranch, and they hang there still to this day. David was frequently mentioned at services, but Donna didn't think that they treated it as the tragedy that it was. David had gone on to glory. His suffering was over, and his worries were finished. Easy to say unless you loved him.

Donna became very bitter toward the ranch and Wally Morillo. She felt their attitude was "Thank you, David, for giving your life for your country, and thank you for leaving us all of your money" but no real sadness. She thought it was very insensitive. It seemed that the only time they ever mentioned David's name was when they were passing the plate to try to generate more money.

Her resentment toward Morillo culminated in a physical altercation between the two. Morillo was giving her a hard time about something, yelling at her, and she had had enough. She slapped him, and he hit her back. It ended there, but the hard feelings only intensified. Today the outcome of that exchange would probably have ended differently. Her riff with Wally Morillo was never repaired.

Donna was consumed with a lot of anger and pain. She doesn't think she would have survived her childhood if it hadn't been for her grandmother. Her grandmother was her best friend. She grounded her and made her life tolerable. Her life at home was miserable, and she started making plans to get out and be on her own.

She left home and stayed with a friend from school at that friend's parents' house for a couple of weeks while looking for an apartment. She had a part-time job and remained in school, but things weren't going too smoothly. One day the attendance officer called her in, telling her that they were going to have to take out guardianship for her to stay in school. Donna said, "No you don't. I am eighteen years old, and I can stay in school and have my place and be on my own." They went back and forth—"Well, no, you can't." "Yes, I can." "No, you can't."—until out of frustration, he called the central office. What he didn't realize was that she had already called central office and knew the rules.

Donna rebelled in high school. She had a lot of home issues she was dealing with, and then there was the loss of David. He would have been her savior. Either sadness would have been challenging enough to deal with, but the combination was a recipe for disaster. She moved around a lot and succumbed to depression and despair. At the age of twenty-three, she decided on one last-ditch effort. She would give school a shot, and if that didn't work out, she would end it all. End the pain and suffering by committing suicide. Her mind was made up. She had done all she could. She would go peacefully.

While in school, two things happened that would change her life. She met her future daughter's father, and things with her mother reached a crisis point.

So, Donna struggled on. Her life was a mess. The grief over David was always hanging over her. She didn't always attribute her problems to that because she had so much else going on. She was confused, resentful, and unhappy. She made a lot of bad choices— bad choices made by a good person with a good heart.

After David died, she was asked for a photo of him for the display at the ranch. She had none. They found someone to do a pencil drawing of him from his high school yearbook photo, and they hung it by his medals. She still has not found a photograph of David.

Donna wasn't the only one to feel David's loss. Besides his parents, his siblings did too. Every family has one person who is the glue, holding it all together. Young David was that person in the Schultz family. After his death, the family seemed to fall apart.

Many years later, Donna wanted to visit David's grave on his birthday. She hadn't been there since he was eighteen. She called the ranch to see if anybody had any contact information with the family. Finally, they came up with a phone number for Jimmy, the second oldest. He was informed that someone was reaching out and trying to find him. They spoke, and Donna asked, "Do you remember me?" He replied, "Oh yeah, you were my brother's girlfriend." They arranged a time to meet and visit David's grave.

They met on October 3, which would have been David's birthday. The cemetery had changed; the trees that used to be there had been cut down. They had changed the headstones from upright stones to flat ones.

When Donna was eighteen, her grandmother taught her how to bead. At that time, beaded flower necklaces were trendy. She beaded one for David and left it draped over his headstone. She hadn't expected it to still be there still twenty-five to thirty years later, of course the necklace was gone along with his original headstone.

Larry Butcher

Larry lived in Modesto, California, at the time of his discharge, which is about a two-hour drive east of Oakland. Friends brought his mother over to pick him up the night of his release from the army. On the drive home, he was sitting on the passenger side in the back seat and could see the speedometer. His friend was driving south on I-5 at one hundred miles an hour. Larry thought, *Damn... I lived thru my tour in Vietnam, and I'm going to die a few miles from home!*

Before he left Vietnam, Larry had his mother prepare a place for him to live. He didn't want to stay at his mother's house. Many nights Larry would wake up and be afraid to move or open his eyes. Smells and sounds weren't familiar, and he didn't know where he was. He would be completely disoriented, heart pounding, breathing rapidly. For several months after returning home, he left a light on in the room while he was sleeping.

Like most returning vets, Larry felt lost and totally out of touch. Friends were talking about events he didn't know anything about, things like Apollo 12. More often than not, he would sit quietly while friends and family spoke about current events because he couldn't contribute anything to the conversation. They weren't interested in Vietnam, and he didn't want to talk about Vietnam anyway. He felt distant, numb, and very alone. During his tour, "the World" had changed, so had he. He was quite upset that he had "lost" a year of his life. No one wanted to know anything about his experiences in Vietnam. So he clammed up and buried it, just trying to go back to "normal" and deal with it on his own.

Larry worked at several jobs and attended school, using up his GI bill. He finally found himself as an optician trainee, leading to a career he would thrive in for the rest of his life.

He moved to Merced, California in 1976 and bought a new house on a cul-de-sac. Castle Air Force Base just north of Merced and was a B-52 training base before and during the Vietnam war. There were three Vietnam veteran B-52 pilots and a forward air controller pilot living on the same street. The forward air controller had flown light aircraft slow and low to maintain constant aerial surveillance. They would often be a target for Charlie.

The pilots had many block parties, and as a Vietnam veteran, Larry was always invited. Having been a combat medic with the infantry pulling ambush patrols, going on search-and-destroy operations and pounding the ground for seven months, Larry was a little detached from this group. He found it very interesting to listen to their stories and how at risk they felt they were flying their high-altitude bombing missions. But in the beginning, he had a difficult time relating. The forward air controller pilot and Larry talked about it. His missions were always hazardous, and he had difficulty relating too. After living there many years, Larry came away understanding that we had all been at risk. We all needed each other to do our part to come home alive.

Like most, Larry's wartime experiences changed him. He was concerned when he was on the Freedom Bird returning home at the end of his tour, worried he had lost his ability to "feel" emotions. A WWII veteran who had been a POW in Germany later told him... "It will always seem like yesterday; it will never go away." At the time, he thought the memories would fade and be forgotten, but that old vet was right. They never went away.

Everyone who served in Vietnam changed in some way. Each had different experiences, and each dealt with them in different ways.

For Larry, it was not possible to stay the innocent, carefree person he used to be after watching other human beings shot, maimed, and killed. Treating his combat-wounded friends and buddies changed him. There are thirteen names on the Vietnam Veterans Memorial Wall of people he went out on ambush patrols, search-and-destroy missions, and air assaults with. He thought about this with a heavy heart and a bit of guilt. He felt he should have been better trained, better prepared, and done more for the grunts he was responsible for.

For forty-five years, he considered his four divorces, occasional panic attacks, and waking four and five times every night as "normal" and not at all associated with his time as a combat medic with the infantry in Vietnam. But eventually he attended meetings with his VA counselor and realized many things he has always thought were "normal" were not. In Vietnam, his duty was first to keep his platoon healthy and second, alive when they were wounded. To this day, Larry feels he came up short treating the buddies who lost their lives in the boonies. He still relives, second-guesses, and questions himself wondering if he could have, should have done more to save them.

Larry went to see a VA psychologist on August 18, 2015 and was pleased with the process. The psychologist was very experienced with people living with PTSD. She herself had been deployed several times with different units and branches of the military. She was part of their chain of command, stayed with them, and returned with them. Today's military returning experience is very different from the typical Vietnam veteran's experience.

Starting out, the psychologist carefully explained the process, the questions she would ask, and the reasons they were necessary. She then asked him what he wanted to tell her.

He told her about things that happened in Vietnam while out with the infantry that he never told anyone, things he would never talk about outside the field. Things that, after forty-five years, still haunted him and simply wouldn't go away.

As he was standing ready to leave, she commented, "You definitely have PTSD. There is no question about it."

Larry walked out, feeling he had just taken one of the hardest examinations he had ever sat for …. but he was only telling it like it was. There were no wrong answers, nothing to lose, no penalties, no peer pressure, no grade to strive for. No reason to be stressed out.

Carey Pratt

Carey was gone, but those left behind were forced to carry on. Theresa had to raise their daughter Shannon by herself. Despite all the help from family and friends, there was no substitute for a father. Theresa was able to get by for a while without working and devoted her time to raising Shannon. The demands of taking care of a newborn forced her to bury her sorrow and carry on.

Carey's parents focused on their other children and grandchildren. Every family member and close acquaintance of Carey lost some of the innocence of the era. And still, the war continued, played out on the evening news—a constant reminder of their loss.

Carey's mother went on, as women and especially mothers can, the pain and hurt bottled up inside. She never discussed his death after the funeral.

Carey's dad coped with his son's death with anger. His anger didn't seem directed at anyone or thing in particular. He was just angry and probably remained so until his death. The second thing Carey's dad said after his son Thomas informed him that Carey had died, after "What a hell of a way to go," was "Goddamnit, I knew I should have made him go to Canada." Perhaps he was angry with himself. Hopefully, he knew deep in his heart that there was no way he could make Carey do anything. Carey was very much his own man.

The American flag that raised on Christmas Day in front of Carey's parents' house still flew. His father had sworn that it wouldn't be lowered until Carey returned home safely from Vietnam. Carey had returned home, but not safely. Now the tattered flag rippled in the wind, a somber reminder of dreams lost forever.

Theresa tried to keep Shannon away from knowing how her father died. She just didn't talk about it much, focusing on other things. Theresa held her emotions inside, which was harder on her later in life. As time went on, Shannon was told the story of the flag in front of her grandparents' house. But when she was a toddler, all she knew was that flag flew for her dad, so every time she saw a flag flying anywhere, she would say, "There's Daddy's flag!" She thought all the flags were his.

Carey's grandmother, Grace Lyons, used to stay overnight often with Theresa and Shannon. The morning of February 11, 1977, started as a typical day. Theresa got six-year-old Shannon ready for school and made everyone breakfast. Grandma Lyons just wanted orange juice, which was strange. As Shannon was leaving for school, her grandma said, "I can't breathe. Can you get me a sack?" She had had this issue before, so they brought her a paper bag to breathe into. As she hyperventilated into the bag, she fell forward. Theresa started giving her mouth-to-mouth, trying to do CPR chest compressions. Theresa had Shannon call Carey's mom, and she was the one to call the ambulance. Shannon, unfazed by what was happening, said, "Bye, Mom. I'm going on to school." Theresa stopped her lifesaving efforts when the ambulance arrived. They knew that she was gone and nothing further could be done to save her. This affected Theresa a lot. Some of Cary's family started coming over, but she was somewhere else, in a daze once again. Grandma Lyons was eighty-six years old. It was another tragedy added to the life of the Pratt family.

In 1981 Theresa took a job at the Kokomo AC Delco plant, the same plant where Carey and his parents had worked. It was a bittersweet time to be working in the same building, but it was a good job that paid well. It was also a time of significant changes in other ways. Teresa married Paul Jacques, and the next year they had a child, a son named Jeremiah.

The family lived a normal life in central Indiana, but for Shannon, something was missing. Her father. Paul was her stepfather, but she always felt an emptiness, a hole in her heart where her father should be. Her mother tried to move on and made every effort to raise Shannon the best way she could, but this part of her life was always missing. Shannon needed to have a father who loved her. She deeply missed his presence, especially on holidays and her birthday. She also felt it whenever she saw a flag flying, like the one still flying at her grandparents' house.

In 1986, Shannon was sixteen years old; a country song came out titled "Daddy's Hands," sung by Holly Dunn. The song received two Grammy nominations, Best Female Country Vocal Performance and Best Country Song. The song was about a father's love. Shannon was able to get that song on a cassette tape, and when she got home, she brought her mom up to her room so they could be alone, and she played the song. The lyrics for the first verse. Though she had never seen her own daddy's hands folded in prayer, felt them comforting her after a nightmare, or holding a book for her at bedtime, as the song described, she felt connected to Carey by those lyrics.

Within a year after the release of "Daddy's Hands," Shannon received a phone call from a man claiming to be Carey—her father was alive! Shannon clung to the hope that it may be him. Theresa tried to convince her that it couldn't be him. It was just a cruel trick someone was pulling on her. Shannon never was quite sure what to believe. When she was in her late thirties, she talked to her mother about that phone call so long ago. She could never quite rid herself of the idea that maybe, just maybe, he was still alive somewhere.

Life took a wrong turn for Shannon. She started doing drugs. Was it because she lost her father in Vietnam shortly before she was born? Theresa tried to avoid talking to her about the loss of her dad, trying to make her feel as normal as possible. Later she told her mom that she wished she had talked to her more about her dad. This was always hard on Theresa, knowing she might have failed her daughter. We all have things in our lives we wish we could have done differently. There is no turning back the clock. We do the best we can at the time. Feeling guilty or sad won't change it.

Shannon married Vincent Hale in 1988. She was eighteen; Vincent was twenty-three. He had a son, Joshua, who was born in 1984. Shannon adopted Josh. The couple had a child of their own, a daughter named Vinessa. Unfortunately, the marriage didn't last, and the couple divorced in 1991.

Shannon continued to struggle with drugs, wrestling with her demons. She married again in 1994 to Richard Brock, but that marriage didn't last long either. The drug issues continued, and Theresa did her best to get Shannon into rehab. Shannon insisted that she could beat this on her own.

Theresa dealt with a lot of other mixed emotions at this time. She harbored a resentment toward all Vietnamese which eventually eased. Now she can go to a nail salon run by Vietnamese without feeling anger. It took years for her to be able to do even that.

Theresa met Don Tapscott in 1999. He is a musician, and they would go out and have a good time. They made a lot of new friends and were married in 2005. Since then, they have made a good life. Theresa is now at peace or at least as much as she can be. She still carries the grief of losing Carey deep in her heart.

Theresa told me, "No one close to them will ever have a normal day again. Mostly you have a lot of good days; you are doing stuff that you like. I'm getting ready to go on a cruise. I'll be with two of my brothers, my sister-in-laws, my husband, and I'll be able to get my mind off it for a while. But it will always drift back to that day. It never goes away. I still get mad about not having that young family experience. I am in my late sixties now, and I don't think it ever will go away."

Theresa holds no blame for anyone involved in that crash. It was a war. Just war. She blames the people in Washington who kept sending troops over for a war they knew they were not winning.

Carey's loss was also deeply felt by his siblings. His brother Thomas divorced three years after Carey died. He had been married for twenty years. Later, his former wife told him that he changed after his brother's death. He would not attribute the end of his marriage to Carey's death, but he did agree with her that he was not the same after it.

Thomas moved away from Indiana, settling in California. But he did visit his parents often. Thomas recalled that as the years passed, the flag in his parents' front yard slowly disintegrated. Each time he visited, it was a sad reminder of those happy days, so filled with hope and joy. For his last visit there, as he came over the hill, the flag slowly came into view. The shiny brass eagle was now a dull green, and the flag, the consecrated flag, was in shreds. Until his death in 1984, his father steadfastly refused to allow it lowered. Over the years, Thomas tried to honor his brother at every opportunity:

Veterans Day, Memorial Day, Carey's birthday, visits to the Wall in DC and when its mobile counterpart traveled to several cities.

On October 9, 1985, the traveling Wall came to Santa Barbara, California. Thomas went to see it and visit his brother's name. It was his first experience visiting the Wall.

He arrived very early to where the Wall had been erected next to the beach. It was a beautiful day, white clouds out over the ocean, peaceful and serene. He parked the car and made his way toward the information tent. A very solemn air prevailed. He gave Carey's name and was provided a piece of paper with the panel and a line number. Slowly, he walked to the Wall, not knowing what to expect, and began looking for the right panel. He passed row upon row of the names inscribed there. Each name was representing a fallen service member, male and female.

Out of the corner of his eye, he noticed a veteran nearby. He wore fatigues and staff sergeant stripes. Soon he approached Thomas. "Sir," he said, "did you lose someone in Vietnam?" "Yes," Thomas responded, "my brother." The soldier suddenly wore a very pained expression. Then he slowly approached Thomas, put his arms around him, and began to cry. Thomas was shocked. He had not expected that. Recovering his composure, he took the piece of paper and drew him to Carey's name. Several times after that morning, Thomas saw the man around town, and they always waved. Many times over the years, Thomas encountered similar experiences with other veterans. It was as if veterans needed to reach out on behalf of their fallen brethren.

Thomas attended the Memorial Day Parade in Santa Barbara in 1990. As he walked along the parade route, he passed veterans of different units forming up to march together. He found a bunch of Vietnam veterans grouped on the side of the street. Some wore fatigues; some wore jeans; others a combination. As he watched these veterans, one beckoned him. After some hesitation, Thomas crossed the street, and as he neared him, the man asked, "Are you a Vietnam vet?" Thomas immediately answered, "No, but my brother died in combat there." The vet studied Thomas for a moment and then said, "You have to march for him." Shocked, he shook his head and said, "Oh no, I couldn't do that. I wasn't there." Looking him in the eye, the man said, "Your brother was there, and he can't march. You have to march for him." "I'm not a veteran," Thomas continued. "I could never dream of marching for those who had served." But that year, he did.

As the parade formed and began to march, a man in the crowd lining the street shouted, "Bunch of losers!" The Vietnam veteran marching next to Thomas muttered, "Just ignore him." He did so for a moment, and then, overcome with anger at the injustice, he broke out of the march and ran back to the man. Getting in his face, Thomas told the man, "My brother died in combat in Vietnam. He was not a loser." Startled, the man leaned back and in a weak voice said, "Well, I landed at Iwo Jima." That exchange prompted Thomas to write a letter to the newspaper. His words stuck in Thomas's mind. He couldn't shake the anger. This man, a veteran himself, disparaging Vietnam veterans. This was an all-too-familiar attitude toward Vietnam veterans back then. They weren't respected, even by some fellow veterans of previous wars.

Thomas wrote a letter to the editor of the *Santa Barbara News Press*. The story was picked up by the *Kokomo Tribune* with a huge headline across the front page: "Gone but Not Forgotten," by Mark Fletcher.

On September 20, 2014, the first Howard County Vietnam Veterans Reunion was held. It is an annual tradition now. On Highway 26, eight miles east of Kokomo, there is what was once was a small airport; it's now a memorial to the fallen warriors of Howard County. Each year in the fall, veterans of the Vietnam War meet to connect over their shared fate. They come from near and far: Illinois, Michigan, Kentucky, Ohio, Missouri, California, New York, and others. Distance and time have no bearing. They are there to honor those lost and to renew friendships with other aging veterans, especially those made when they were young, in that distant place, a place where they shared the bizarre and unique burden of war. Among the corn and bean fields, these veterans and their loved ones eat, drink, laugh, and remember. It is an uncommonly sacred place; however, not one of them can ever forget the comrades they lost in Vietnam. None can ever discard the haunting question in their minds, "Why them, not me?" Their numbers are dwindling. But those who can, once again, gather to revisit the memories and friendships they've made over the years. More importantly, it is a place where those lost in that faraway place and all those many years ago can be honored and remembered once again. The veterans have given it a hopeful name, the Healing Field.

Living in California, Thomas lost touch with Shannon. His wife Lynn would send her a birthday card, but that was the only contact they had. Thomas had received an invitation to participate in the opening ceremonies of the Howard County Vietnam Veterans Reunion by reading his story about that incident years ago in Santa Barbara. Thomas wanted Shannon to be a part of the ceremony, so he phoned her. She recognized his voice immediately.

"Oh, oh my God, you can't know how good it is to hear your voice." There was a note of anxiety there, and Thomas felt a pang of guilt because he had not reached out to her more over the years. He briefly explained the plans for the reading and asked if she would like to join him. She began sobbing and said, "Oh yes, yes, I would love to. Oh, Uncle Tom. It is so good to hear from you."

When Thomas arrived the next morning, she wanted to show him her home. In the corner of her living room, she proudly displayed a little shrine of mementos she had made to honor her dad.

When they arrived at the reunion, he and Shannon joined a multitude of people who grasped the edges of a huge American flag. The song "When You Are a Soldier, I'll Be Your Shield," by Steven Curtis Chapman, played loudly, a strong backdrop to the emotional procession of the flag.

Holding the flag with his left hand as Shannon held his right, Thomas processed slowly started toward the memorial plaza. Strangers reached out and touched them. Glancing down at Shannon, he saw the tears were streaming down her cheeks, and yet, through the tears, she wore the most beautiful smile. She was paying tribute to her dad. Thomas unashamedly sobbed every step of the way.

When the procession reached the memorial garden, it paused; the flag was attached to the halyard. A ten-men color guard from American Legion Post 317 Greentown, Indiana, resplendent in their white-gloved formal military attire, awaited.

As the flag slowly began its ascent, flapped in the autumn Indiana breeze. Commander Brad Flook ordered, "Ten-Hut," followed by, "Present arms." The seven men with rifles saluted by holding on straight in front of them; the others gave the hand salute. On Flook's command, the seven riflemen fired three volleys into the morning's brilliant white clouds. Slowly, slowly, the flag was raised. When it reached the top of the flagpole, a distant trumpet slowly, mournfully issued forth with taps.

Later that morning, they were welcomed on stage to address a swelling crowd of veterans and loved ones, including many of their own family. Thomas's daughter Cindy stood at his left and Shannon his right. Thomas had the great honor of reading his story "Marching for my Brother." He dedicated the story to Shannon.

"I don't know your name and it doesn't matter. What does matter is that my brother, Butch, was drafted, went to war in Vietnam, performed his duties as required by his country. Doing so, he died there. You, one of the lucky ones, a survivor of Iwo Jima, you, of all people, should appreciate his sacrifice. Butch was not a loser. He was a warm, loving young man of twenty-one. His comrades-in-arms were just like him, someone's husband, someone's dad, someone's son, someone's grandson, someone's brother. Not losers, heroes." Thomas continued, "I can understand your frustration when you see military pride you respect demeaned, but to our country's great shame, it did not honor the Vietnam veterans upon their return, as it did you and your comrades. The Vietnam veterans deserve no less. Thank you for your service in World War II."

The *Kokomo Tribune* wrote the next morning; "Staff Sergeant Carey Jay Pratt was being remembered nearly 45 years after his death. In front of childhood, grade school, high school, Delco friends, including most of his extended family and every reader of the Sunday edition of the *Kokomo Tribune.*"

Elroy Simmons

Elroy's brother, Dwight, received his draft notice in July 1970, around the time the family was notified that Elroy had been wounded. Dwight did not go to summer school in 1970 because he had just gotten married. That was when the draft grabbed him.

Obviously, it was a very difficult time for the Simmons family. They had heard stories that two brothers were not supposed to be in Vietnam at the same time, but that did not seem to be the case. Elroy's brother Lacy was in Vietnam at the same time and stationed only about five miles away. Another brother was also in the service, and now Dwight was drafted.

With the death and burial of Elroy so close, the army held off on activating Dwight until September. Basic training was at Fort Leonard Wood in Missouri. It was no surprise to find out he was slated to go into the infantry. Dwight already had a couple of years of college under his belt, so he decided on the option of enlisting and serving an extra year, but in a field he could choose. He chose preventative medicine. After basic, he was sent to Fort Sam Houston, Texas, for medical training. At the time, he was told he wouldn't be sent to Southeast Asia. They tried to send him anyway, but he never got closer to Vietnam than Okinawa.

Elroy's death was extremely hard on his parents. They had to deal with the lost son as well as the uncertainty of three other sons in the military, one already in Vietnam. They were tough people and struggled through this horrible time in their life.

Barbara struggled to deal with the death of her husband as well as the task of raising four children. Shortly after Elroy passed away, she received a box from the army containing his personal effects. Opening it, she was surprised to find someone else's belongings. Someone somewhere along the line had made a mistake and sent her the wrong package. She was shocked and distraught, expecting to see Elroy's personal belongings only to see items she did not recognize. She had to pack it back up and send it all back to the army so they could straighten it out and find the correct package. They were able to correct the mistake but it took a while.

That fall, Barbara was contacted by the army and told that Elroy had been awarded the Bronze Star posthumously, and they wanted to present it to her. There would be a formal presentation at Fort Sheridan, which was very close to where she was living in Waukegan. She gathered up her children, and they drove to Fort Sheridan, where they presented her the Bronze Star.

Dwight was assigned to Okinawa as a medic. The army command there decided that they wanted to start a football program. They didn't have enough men to get it off the ground. The coach was from Japan, so Dwight and one other soldier were sent to Camp Zama to play football. Because Dwight was a medic, he was allowed to stay in one of the hospital rooms. The room he stayed in was the exact one that his brother Elroy had stayed in when he died. Dwight remained in that room for a week. He felt comforted being there. No eerie feelings, just a sense of peace, that someone was watching over him. The unusual thing was when he was in high school, he had a premonition that he was going to be in Japan and in a hospital.

Barbara stayed in the Waukegan area after Elroy's death so she could be near the hospital and commissary. She knew the military life and was comfortable there. In 1974 Barbara met Jacob "Jake" Wallace through some friends. Jake was a career navy man. He had been in the navy since 1952. He had served on six ships and completed two tours in Vietnam's waters. They bonded and became soul mates, marrying in November 1974. They lived a good life.

Jake retired in 1982 as a Master Chief Petty Officer. Where Elroy left off, Jake picked up. He was a real father to Barbara's children, Sherry, Michael, Terry, and Michele. He was a good husband to her.

Elroy's parents lived long lives. His father passed away in 2004 at the age of eighty-five. His mother passed in 2006 at the age of eighty-six. The sorrow they felt about the loss of their son in Vietnam was over.

Barbara and Jake raised the four children with love and instilled in them the confidence that they could succeed at anything they desired. Michael became a lawyer; the younger son, Terry, became an administrator at Gateway College. The older daughter,

Sherry, became a social worker and served ten years in the reserves. And the youngest daughter, Michele, served twenty-two years in the military.

When there were graduations, marriages, and birthdays, Barbara would look up to the heavens and say, "Elroy, this is your family."

Barbara had more tragedy in her life. Her eldest son, Michael, died of colon cancer in 2006, and her wonderful husband, Jake, died in 2010. He was seventy-five years old. He was laid to rest with full military honors at Warren Cemetery in Gurnee, Illinois.

Ross Bedient

Ross's parents took his death hard. His mom internalized it. His dad was visibly heartbroken over the death of his youngest son. Brother Zane helped out as much as he could but then had to report back to the navy. Zane and his dad never did get along well. The rift between them continued after the death of Ross.

Ross's buddy SP4 Jim Calabrese left the 242nd ASHC for home on July 12, 1970. Two days after the crash. He received an early out from active duty and was discharged in Oakland, California, on July 15. He returned to upstate New York to begin his life as a civilian. He worked construction, married the love of his life, Mary Anne Campbell, and raised two sons. Ross was always in the back of his mind.

Jim and his family lived in Geneva, New York, which was only a thirty-minute drive from Dundee, where Ross had lived. Jim's son was in the high school band, and they were in a competition called Pageant of the Bands, where they competed with the other local high schools for trophies. As they read the names of the competing seniors over the microphone, Jim heard the name Bedient, and right away he perked up. He found the student after the competition and inquired if he was related to Ross, who had died in Vietnam. The student replied, "Yes, I think he is my third cousin." Jim asked him to please give Ross's parents his address. About two weeks later, the doorbell rang, and Jim opened the door to find two older people standing on the front porch.

Francis, who was going by the nickname Pete, looked at Jim, hat in hand, slightly unsure of himself, and said, "I'm Pete Bedient. I am Ross Bedient's father." Jim and Mary Anne welcomed them in. This meeting began a friendship that lasted until the Bedients passed.

Jim showed Pete and Maddie his photos of the company area, helicopters, and personnel. He also showed them the yearbook a local Vietnamese printer had put together. Jim had two and gave them one. Occasionally they had dinner at each other's houses and even spent a few Thanksgivings together. Jim and Mary Anne met Ross's brothers, Jerry and Zane.

Maddie was always quiet and never said a word when Ross was discussed, but Pete would break down and sob. Jim occasionally accompanied them to the cemetery and put flowers on Ross's grave.

Pete had done some investigating on his own and found Rickey Wittner in Texas. The Bedients were driving to Texas, and they made arrangements to meet with Rickey.

The day before they were supposed to meet, Rickey was driving home from work and saw someone in the road trying to stop him. He noticed the New York plates and right away knew who it was. Pete was trying to make sure of his directions before driving to Rickey's house the next day when they happened upon each other.

Pete didn't realize who he was talking to when he asked for help finding Rickey's address. Rickey just said, "Mr. Bedient," and he jumped out of the truck, and they hugged right there in the middle of the road. The Bedients spent the weekend with the Wittners, even going to church with them.

Pete later wrote and told Rickey of a fellow his niece had met in upstate New York by the name of Jim Calabrese. He gave him Jim's address and phone number. Rickey did meet the Bedients several more times. In the Easter of 1997, the Wittners drove to Georgia to see their daughter and her family. They then ventured down to Florida, where Pete and Maddie were visiting their son Jerry.

In June 1997, the Wittners went to New York and visited with Pete and Maddie, this time where Ross was raised. They were able to see the farm he grew up on and were he was buried. Maddie died in 2006, and the still deeply saddened Pete died in 2013. They are buried beside Ross in Hillside Cemetery, Dundee New York.

Pete Bedient also looked up Ed Whittle. He called him years ago. How he tracked Ed down is a mystery, but he did. The first thing he said was "I just really want to find out what happened, what you saw. How did my son do?" After that, he had many questions about that fateful day. Ed couldn't tell him. There was no way he was going to answer him and have his last memories of his son be of that crash. As they spoke some more, Pete went into his hatred of the

Vietnamese, all of them. Ed just listened to him. He understood. But they were doing their job; we were doing ours. Pete tried to call Ed back several times, but he would never take the call. He knew he wanted to hear about his son, and there was no way Ed was going to tell him.

Pete's anger was overwhelming. Ed felt that he couldn't see the commonality there. We killed plenty of their kids. They had mothers and fathers and brothers and sisters and wives and children, and their hatred for us was probably there too.

There was a psychic in Geneva who had been in the area for a long time. Jim and Mary Anne went to her two or three times. On one occasion, the psychic asked, "Is there anybody you want to talk to?" Jim replied, "Yeah, I want to talk to Ross Bedient." The psychic said, "Ross says he saw a big flash, and then it was hot. 'Hot, awful hot.'" The hair stood up on the back of Jim's head.

Mike Vullo

With the funeral over, it was time to get back to normal. Whatever that was. Kathi didn't remember much about the first weeks after the funeral. She continued working at the horse ranch. There was always a lot to be done, and that kept her mind off the husband she had lost.

There was a posthumous awards ceremony held in San Pedro, in the fall of 1970 for some of the families of Vietnam casualties. The Army planned a full parade with all the pomp and circumstance for the remembrance of the fallen. Unfortunately, it poured that day and they held a makeshift ceremony indoors. It was more than disappointing for all those who attended.

Kathi became involved in a start-up in the '70s that built a lot of portable barns and corrals. She was a part-owner but then decided to move on. She had had enough. She drove a long-haul eighteen-wheeler for a couple of years. She liked being paid to see the country.

Kathi's father worked for Rockwell International in California as a subcontract administrator. He worked on the space program, from Mercury to the shuttle. In 1980 Kathi decided she wanted to do something different, so her father got her an interview. She was offered a job also as a subcontract administrator in support of the space shuttle program. She took it.

In the fall of 1992 it was time for another new start. Kathi moved to Huntsville, Alabama.

Kathi was still receiving survivor's benefits after Mike's death. It wasn't much, initially only eighty-six dollars a month, but it helped. Because she was an unmarried widow, she had all the benefits that a retired veteran had. She was able to utilize the PX and commissary as well as free medical care at any base. So all along, Michael was providing for her or helping anyway.

Ed Whittle

Ed was twenty when that crash occurred. He still thinks about it, and the people involved, every day. Many days he gets tears in his eyes, thinking about the people for whom he had responsibility, the passengers, the flight engineer, and his gunner.

But hindsight is twenty-twenty. If he had refused the mission, who knows what would have happened. In the army, you don't refuse missions. One thing is for sure the Viet Cong were waiting for a helicopter to come in. They knew it would come. It was fate. Inexplicable, unchangeable fate. It was going to happen, and there was nothing anyone could do to change it. It was meant to be. Some things happen that are out of your control. You can second-guess yourself until you are blue in the face, but it still will not change the results. That aircraft was going to be shot down, and people were going to die. Fact.

Anyone who has been shot down knows what a horrible event it is. To lose people in a crash remains with you forever. All such incidents are horrific. They eat at your soul. It is hard to get past it.

Despite this, Ed always had a little hope. He was sure that, after a while, the United States would have a relationship with Vietnam. He felt they were nice people, very industrious. We would put the war behind us, and so would they.

Now, Ed is the vice president of a large company employing five hundred people. He attributes a lot of his success to the discipline that he learned in the army. He also feels a responsibility for every one of the employees he has. He feels responsible not just for the employees but also the families they support. He is sure that this came from the responsibility he felt for the crew and passengers that were on that aircraft.

When President Bush died, Ed was glued to the broadcast of his funeral. President Bush had cleared up a lot of things for him, in his mind. At one point, President Bush talked about the day he was shot down. He said they got hit, and they continued on their mission, dropping their bombs. He knew he was in trouble because the left wing was on fire. So, he turned back around; he knew he had to get out of there. He told his two crewmen, "Hit the silk." He wanted them to go out first. He finally bailed out and looked for the parachutes of his crew. He saw one way west. That was it. There was only one chute. The second guy never got out of the airplane, and he said to that day, he didn't know if he was shot, hit, hurt, or what happened. But he never got out of the airplane; the future president watched the aircraft go down, and to his knowledge, that man rode the plane into the water.

He said he thought about it every day. They were his responsibility. And he said, "I failed them." Bush said that he thought that those feelings helped him in his life, and as a president—thinking of that responsibility.

Ricky Wittner

Rickey was discharged from the army in March of 1972. He returned home to Texas and resumed his relationship with Kathie Hicks. They married in May after she graduated from high school. They are still happily married today.

Rickey decided to become an EMT. He obtained his license and started on the job. Everything was going fine until the first time he went to a wreck where someone was burned up. The smell of burnt flesh brought him back to July 10, 1970. It took him about three months to get over that. He knew that he didn't want to be exposed to that again, so he quit and surrendered his license.

Rickey is a volunteer fireman and works a lot of accidents. He is always able to do his job and do it well. Everyone he works with knows what happened to him, and they watch out for him. If there are enough people there, he will do traffic control. He tries to stay away from the accidents as much as possible because it brings back a flood of memories that linger. He eventually became the chief of the volunteer fire department.

Rickey also operates his own consulting business, guiding other companies with documentation of their assets for tax purposes. He is an active member of his local church and can always be counted on when there is a need for help. He knows or has dealt with more people in his county than anyone would expect. He and his wife are a great asset to the community.

In February 1999, Rickey talked with Ed Whittle on the phone. It had been almost twenty-nine years. What surprised Rickey was that Ed was younger than he was. Another surprise was that he never knew his name was Ed. Ed also lived in Texas, and a month later, Rickey drove to see him. They had a great day together.

After the crash, Ed recommended Rickey for the Medal of Honor. The army decided to downgrade the award to a Soldiers Medal. The criteria for the Soldiers Medal is for heroism not involving armed conflict with an enemy. It would seem that this action involved an armed conflict. After all, he did receive a Purple Heart. Rickey felt this was a joke. If he wasn't involved in an armed conflict, then how did they get hit with three rockets?

Robert Henry

Robert was twenty-two at the time of the crash in 1970. He continued to fly with the 242nd and finished his tour in April 1971. He was able to get right back in the saddle and fly without any aftereffects.

He elected to stay in the army and make a career of it. He continued to fly Chinooks for twenty years. He retired as a CWO4.

Chapter 15

Carrying On

Let everything happen to you

Beauty and terror

Just keep going.

No feeling is final

-Rainer Maria Rilke

Larry Butcher

Larry's life took a significant turn when he married Duangjai. He feels that he couldn't have gotten luckier. It was better than winning the lottery. Life was good until he was thirteen, and then it all changed. Finally, life was good again.

Larry didn't want anything to do with the military after he was discharged. Slowly, after forty years, he started to reconnect with a couple of old friends. He met with his old friend Lieutenant Robert Klee three or four times. Then he met with Gary Trapman, who had been a medic back at the aid station. The meeting with Gary was an extremely emotional one for both men. When they reached out and shook hands, Larry's wife immediately saw the emotion there and snapped a photo.

Larry tried to find the family of John Robinson, his mentor and first casualty. Jim's mother had married John Hill, and at the time of John's death, they were living in Washington, DC. Finding her was almost impossible. Was she still alive? Did Robinson have siblings? These were unknowns that prevented Larry from finding any relatives he might have. The commonality of the name made it even harder. So, Larry found another way to reconnect.

The Wall That Heals is a half-size replica of the Vietnam Memorial. Unveiled in Washington, DC, on Veterans Day, 1996, it has since toured all over the country, visiting over 600 communities. In 2015 it visited Lolita, California, a small town just south of Eureka. It provided a perfect opportunity for Larry to pay his respects.

The emotions Larry felt that day were beyond words. He visited each name of the men who had served with him in Delta Company, 2/14th Infantry, 25th Infantry Division. As he kneeled and looked at their names, he saw his reflection in the shiny black granite Wall, and he thought that a part of him was with them still. Vietnam is a part of all who served there. A part of who we are.

Several years later, he looked at the photo his wife took of him at the Wall. He began to cry softly. While he was looking at the picture, his wife asked, "What's wrong?" He pointed to his reflection on the Wall. There were three on the Wall he had cared for in the woods. One died instantly, and two who survived for the urgent Dust-off later succumbed to their injuries. He was haunted by the memories and wondering if he could have done something differently. "I am myself, along with many others," he said, "still in the process of coming home."

Ross Bedient

Ross is buried in a quiet country cemetery just west of the small town of Dundee, New York. The peaceful rolling hills are a stark contradiction to the way he died.

Ross's father carried the loss for forty-three years after that day in 1970. He passed away in 2013. Ross's brother Gerry died two months before his father. It is hoped that Ross is now reunited with them.

Zane finished his career with the navy and retired in 1981 as an E-6. He has visited the Wall and has a rubbing he did of his brother's name. Zane had told Ross not to go into the army. He felt it was a political war and had no value, whether we won or lost.

David Schultz

After David's funeral, his younger brother, Raymond, would come over to Donna's house, and they would hang out. They would sit outside and talk about David. He was the only one Donna could speak with about David. When the evening was upon them, and the light was just starting to change, everything looked surreal. Still daylight, darker and longer shadows. Raymond would tell Donna that this was David's favorite time of day. Donna still thinks about that. When she is outside at that time, she feels closer to David. He is there.

When Raymond would come over, they would talk about how they didn't believe that he was dead, they thought that he was probably a POW. Even at the funeral, Donna thought the closed casket was empty.

Donna was never able to go to Washington, DC, and see the Wall. But she did see the traveling Wall when it came to Houston. It was the early '90s, and Donna was close to thirty-eight years old and still in denial that David was dead. She just couldn't accept the fact that he was gone.

Donna made plans to go to the traveling Wall with her young daughter. When the time came, she was an emotional wreck. One of the veteran guides there offered to help her. He inquired when he died and directed her to the correct place. Panel 08W, line 9. He took her over to the panel and helped her find his name. David was about halfway to the top.

He stayed by her, and they talked. She told him that she never was able to accept the fact that he was gone. She said to him that he was in a helicopter crash and died, but she just couldn't accept it. He looked at her and said, "Ma'am, you really would prefer what happened to him compared to what would have happened if he'd survived. He would have been a prisoner of war. And that is not something you would wish on anybody."

They talked more, and finally, Donna was convinced that David was dead. She had been starting her life as a young adult and carried the doubt of death her whole life. Now her daughter knew about David. She'd seen the panel. She'd seen his name. She was too young to relate to it, but she knew who he was.

Donna stayed there for over an hour. It wasn't very crowded when she was there. She couldn't stay longer with a young child in tow and a long drive home through heavy traffic. It was the closest she had been to David in a long, long time.

She went through an awful lot that day, just having to face the reality of everything that she had buried so deeply. After all these years, even though she accepted his death, even as recently as a few years ago, she wondered if somebody would knock on her door and she would answer it and if it might be David. Would she even recognize him? He would be an old man, gray hair, a few extra pounds.

This is something that will follow her for the rest of her life. She tries to cope with it as best she can. Facebook has helped her a lot because she can support veteran causes. And every year on his birthday, Veterans Day, and Memorial Day, she posts a memorial to him. People who didn't know about him at the time know about him now.

The Wall comes to Houston on occasion, but Donna can't bring herself to go anymore.

When Donna was watching the John McCain memorial, toward the end, there was a reading from 2 Timothy that jarred her memory. It was a dedication that David sent her, and in retrospect, it epitomizes the kind of young man that he was. The type of faith that he had that led his life. She had to find a Bible and then look it up: "I thank God whom I serve from my forefathers with pure conscience that without ceasing I have remembrance of thee in my prayers night and day; Greatly desiring to see thee, being mindful of thy tears, that I may be filled with joy."

Donna and David were young and idealistic. That was the kind of man he was and the kind of woman she was.

Because of the writing of this story, I was able to put Donna in touch with Rickey Wittner, David's crew chief. Rickey told her that David used to talk about her and that he knew he was going to get married to her and that he was excited about it. It was a validation that she had never really had before.

Elroy Simmons

Elroy's brother Dwight has been to the Vietnam Memorial, the Wall, in Washington, DC, several times with his wife. He has a rubbing of Elroy's name. "It's a good place where we can finally mourn our dead. You know, there was such controversy with Vietnam that so many people buried a lot of their grief because it was just… It's just the country was a mess at that time, as you know."

Dwight graduated from high school in January 1968. He had a really good buddy he grew up with and who graduated at the same time. In February, he went into the military; he volunteered. "I think it was three or four days after he was sent to Vietnam, he was killed," Dwight said

They brought his body back for burial. At his funeral, Dwight was one of his pallbearers. The reality of it hit him, and he knew that either he went to school or into the military. He ended up doing both.

That wasn't the plan, but sometimes the plan just doesn't work. Even though Dwight was married, he was drafted. A break in your school was all it took for Uncle Sam to call him up.

Elroy's widow, Barbara, visited the Wall a couple of years ago with a tour group. They were in Washington, DC, for about seven days. She thought that it was a remarkable monument. Seeing it brought back a flood of memories. All those names. All those men and women who died to preserve our country. It was a good thing they did, building that monument. It says something for those soldiers.

She walked the Wall and found Elroy's name. It was a touching moment. A flashback. What could have been. It was a compelling moment of remembrance.

Dwight feels like Elroy walks with him every day. They were very close, and he feels his presence with him.

He feels that Elroy was probably purposefully taken instead of him. Dwight was the younger brother and was more gung-ho than anybody. After college, he was going to join the marines or become a Navy Seal. That was his dream. And then, when Elroy was killed, it all changed. After the military, he became an educator and administrator, dealing with boys and girls, trying to teach them the right way to live their lives.

Barbara looks back at the war without bitterness or blame. She just feels that it was a war that wasn't supported the way that it should have been. There were so many deaths. It's been a long time, and it seems the people were more against it than they were for it, and the military men that came home didn't come back with flags flying and people greeting them as they had in other wars.

Rickey Wittner

Rickey still has recurring dreams of that day in July many years ago. Discussing his story has not made it easy for him to get a good night's sleep. He had a rough night every time we talked. His wife always wants to know when I will call so she can be prepared. But it isn't just me he talks to. He tells people about what happened. It is a part of his life, and he needs to share it.

He teaches a class at the local school once a year, a history class on Vietnam. And he has a hell for a week before and about a week afterward. But it's part of history; it's his history, it's made him who he is and what he is.

He can laugh about a lot of it. Some of it makes him tear up. Some of it bothers him for a while. After our last conversation, it took him probably a week to get over it. He doesn't mind telling me that. His wife told him that maybe he shouldn't talk to me anymore, and he said, "No, I'm not going to do that. I'm just not going to do that. I think if he thinks there's a story, then he needs to put it in writing."

He told me once, "One thing about it, I don't actually remember the noise. I remember the smell more than the noise. OK? The smell of burning flesh just eats me alive. But I don't remember the noise. I don't even remember what all I was doing. I just knew that when I hit the ground, and I got up, that I had to find Ross. That was the only thing on my mind, was finding Ross. And don't ask me why I didn't have it in my mind that I had to find David. But in my mind, all I could think about was 'I got to find Ross.' But the smell's still there. The smell of burning magnesium and fuel and bodies."

He continued, "Yeah, and you know, I realize that Mr. Whittle feels guilt over this, and it just tears me up to know that he's carrying that burden with him so much. Because, in actuality, he couldn't do anything about that. No, there is nothing that he couldn't have done differently. It wouldn't have made any difference. No, no. They told him to go over there, and he did it, you know?"

He said, "It's a crying shame, but I know a lot of guys that have that guilt because 'If I'd have walked a little faster. If I'd have walked a little slower." You know? And so, it's just one of those things you can't get over. It's destiny. It's what it is. And there's not much you can do about it, you know? You just can't feel that way, but I understand when people do."

Harlen Metzger

Harlen's son Tim remembers that his dad never wore a veteran's hat or had a veteran's license plate. As far as PTSD, he kept that pretty much to himself. You had to kind of work it out of him, any little details you could. He just didn't come out and talk about the war voluntarily too much. When he did, you just kind of listened because you didn't want to push the issue too much. He teared up about it a few times, but he never got outwardly emotional.

He never said it, but he had a distrust for the government and wars, in general, but he was still a patriotic person. Harlen always said, "You fought for the man next to you. You didn't know why the hell you were there, what you were doing, the political motivations." He said, "You were just trying not to get killed, and you're fighting for your buddy next to you."

Harlen saw all the soldiers coming home from war; some were treated like heroes. He was OK with that. But at the same time, he said, "Not everybody's a hero, and we were spit on when we came back."

Tim went to the Wall in Washington, DC, and called his dad from there. He asked him if there was anyone he should look up. Harlen was sick at the time but told him to find Carey Pratt's name. Tim found him on panel 08W, line 13.

Harlen always felt guilty about his friend Carey Pratt. If Carey didn't have Harlen's belongings maybe he could have been able to get out of the helicopter sooner.

In Harlen's last months, he talked more about the crash that caused him so much trouble throughout his life. He told Tim how he jumped out the open hatch in the floor and burned over 40 percent of his body. He talked of jumping in the river and returning fire.

Tim is positive that the war had a profound effect on his dad's life. He knows the war tormented him, but he seemed to have made peace with those demons, or they would have destroyed him. He died early by most modern standards. Tim is positive that his experience, wounds, and exposure in Vietnam played a large part in his early death.

Carey Pratt

Shannon was always restless, and drug use plagued her throughout her life. Her father's wartime death overshadowed her. Her health began to fail. She was forty-five years old and admitted to the hospital, trying to correct some of her health problems. She was in the hospital for over a week. She wanted to go home. A week after her release, on Monday, September 21, 2015, she was gone. The official cause of death was listed as a drug overdose.

That afternoon Thomas's sister Pat called him with the news. It saddened him but was not unexpected. Thomas wrote the following letter to the *Kokomo Tribune* one week before Veterans Day, 2015, in tribute to Shannon.

My 45-year-old niece, Shannon Rae Brock, née Pratt, died recently, another casualty of the Vietnam War. "How can that be?" One might ask.

"She would not yet have been born, or, at least, she would have been only a baby when it ended." In fact, she was born one month after her dad, Staff Sergeant Carey Jay Pratt, died in combat there. Those who have not been touched by the horror of war cannot really appreciate what it is like to lose a loved one in that manner. Not only are the family, relatives, friends overwhelmed with grief, but such loss can and does severely alter survivors' lives. Many will carry the pain the remainder of their days. Even future generations are not exempt. Shannon Rae is evidence. She never met her dad, but he lived in her heart as a huge presence, ingrained there by her great-grandmother, her grandmother, her grandfather, and countless other family members. She knew her dad as soon as she was old enough to understand. Shannon lived her entire life in the aura of the dad she

never met. She was fiercely proud of him, and rightfully so. Her dad was a hero in every sense of the word, and she held onto that all her life.

Shannon was laid to rest where her father is buried in Knox Family Chapel in Port Isabel, Indiana. The internment was on September 25. At last, she is close to her father.

Mike Vullo

While vacationing in Florida in 1994, Kathi met David Lee. David was a career air force NCO who, at the time, was stationed at Eglin Air Force Base. David had been drafted in 1969, the same year as Mike. David's father was in the air force, also a career man. He had served during World War II, toward the end, in Germany. David's father said, "No, you're not going in the army." He did not like the fact that David was going to be drafted in the army, so with his guidance, he and David went down to the recruiter, and he joined the air force.

David served all over the world. He was sent to Europe and was spared a tour in Vietnam. He served a total of twenty-six years in the air force, retiring in July 1995 as a Senior Master Sergeant, E-8. His father also retired after twenty-six years, as a Chief Master Sergeant, E-9.

Kathi moved to Cocoa Beach, Florida in the spring of 1998 where she worked at the Kennedy Space Center. She worked on the space shuttle program for a total of twenty-six years from before the first launch of the *Columbia* shuttle in 1981 until three years after the

Columbia loss in 2003. She enjoyed this job but wasn't too crazy about Florida.

David's son, Paul, also served in the air force. He had taken ROTC in college and graduated as second lieutenant. He was stationed at the Pentagon in 2003 when he was promoted to Captain. They had a formal ceremony, including his father and grandfather in their uniforms. Three generations of airmen. It was quite a sight.

Kathi didn't want to retire in Florida, so in 2006 she managed to get a job at the Boeing facility in Huntsville, Alabama. She and David moved there even though David's parents and two sisters lived in Florida. David and Kathi married in Huntsville in 2009. David tells everybody that they didn't get married right away because he had to wait until she was old enough.

Because Kathi was getting the military survivor's benefit from Michael's death, she had to be fifty-seven years old before she could remarry and not lose that benefit. They researched that thoroughly, even going it to the judge advocate general's office at the Redstone Arsenal, where they verified the fact that she had to be fifty-seven to remarry and not lose that benefit. Kathi's birthday was in October. They married the following May.

The diamond engagement ring Kathi received from Mike after his funeral remains a special part of her life. David used the diamond when he designed her *"Past, Present and Future"* wedding band.

Denny Martin

Sue and John discussed taking a trip to Asia. At first, she thought the idea of going to Vietnam was just plain crazy. But the idea grew on her. Denny had sent her many photos of Vietnam while he was there. Beautiful pictures of the countryside and people. She told herself, "This is just crazy to go." But she could not fathom a good reason not to, so they made plans.

In 2016 she and John embarked on the trip and an attempt at closure. It was a cruise out of Hong Kong and included stops in Vietnam. She wanted to see for herself some of what Denny had experienced, where he had been, and where he had died. Not for the sadness, but just to get a glimpse of what he had experienced.

They first visited Hai Phong, and from there, it was a short trip to beautiful Ha Long Bay. They went to Da Nang and drove by China Beach, the famed in-country R & R center.

The only upsetting part of the trip was their visit to the War Remnants Museum in Ho Chi Minh City (Saigon). The museum is, of course, operated by the Vietnamese government. An earlier version of this museum opened on September 4, 1975, as the Exhibition House for U.S. and Puppet Crimes. It was located in the former United States Information Agency building. The exhibition was not the first of its kind for the North Vietnamese side but instead followed a tradition of such exhibitions exposing supposed war crimes, first those of the French and then those of the Americans.

In 1990, the name was changed to Exhibition House for Crimes of War and Aggression, dropping both "U.S." and "Puppet." In 1995, following the normalization of diplomatic relations with the United States, including the end of the US embargo a year before, the references to "War Crimes" and "Aggression" were dropped from the museum's title as well; it became the War Remnants Museum. But the typical Vietnamese Communist slant is still there. Of course, no mention was ever made about crimes perpetrated by the Viet Cong or North Vietnamese.

From Vietnam, they sailed to Bangkok and ended their trip in Singapore. It turned out that it was just what Sue needed, and she thoroughly enjoyed it. John paid close attention to her, making sure she was OK the whole time. She was. It was sad, at times upsetting, but a good experience. She loves to travel and likes to be places where something has happened, good or bad. To feel that emotion while you're there can make life more meaningful in other ways.

Barbara, Denny's sister, has continued to perform. She appeared in many venues across the United States and even in Ireland.

Barbara would occasionally get out Denny's letters and reread them. Every time she did, she would cry. Then she thought that she must do something with the letters to preserve Denny's words. She met Holley Watts, a former Donut Dollie from Vietnam who invited Barbara to Washington, DC, to meet some people from various veteran organizations who were planning for the fiftieth anniversary of the Vietnam War. Through Holley, she met Monica Mohindra, who was head of program coordination and communication of the Veterans History Project through the Library of Congress.

Barbara and Monica hit it off right away. Monica read Denny's letters and was very impressed. She said, "These are so important. We don't have many letters that are like this because people don't want to bring them in because they're angry." And she added, "They're so well written." When Monica was contacted by researchers from the Ken Burns documentary series "The Vietnam War," she gave them Barbara's information, and they approached her. She spoke with them about Denny and the letters. His story never made it into the series, but his voice is no longer silent.

Barbara donated Denny's letters to the Veterans History Project. She was invited to sing at the Vietnam Wall by the Sons and Daughters In Touch at their ceremony on Father's Day. Sons and Daughters In Touch is an all-volunteer national support organization committed to uniting the Gold Star sons and daughters of American service members who were killed or who remain missing as a result of the Vietnam War. Membership also includes other family members as well as those who served and those who lost their lives there.

Barbara decided to write a song about Denny from the letters he sent home. "But I didn't write an honest song because I was afraid to sing the honest song, so I wrote a different song—a sanitized version. And then I came back, and I thought, *I have to write the real song*. And so I rewrote the song, 'I Won't Forget.'" It is a deeply emotional song that reflects the loss she still feels at losing her brother in Vietnam. She has written another song for Denny called "Ashes."

Barbara thought there might be a lot of negative comments on "I Won't Forget." There never was. Vets have come up to her saying they loved the song. No name-calling or comments that she was unpatriotic.

Sue kept all of Denny's letters but hasn't read any of them since the day she received them except the very last one he wrote, dated July 1, 1970:

It is difficult to believe it is already the 1st of July. For a long time I didn't think I would ever see that day arrive just like now I find it hard to believe the 13th will ever come around. However with only 12 left I guess I am going to make it. Wish me luck and keep looking forward to Hawaii.
Love Denny

Richard Green

Richard experienced some anxiety after his discharge. Car backfires would make him hit the dirt or run for cover. He suffered a couple of panic attacks about being out at night without a gun. Weird things you wouldn't expect but that were happening nonetheless. He indeed had some post-traumatic stress issues.

He thought about the crash a lot. He didn't wake up screaming about it. He was pretty calm about it. He was just kind of surprised after the copter crashed that he was still alive. At that time, he thought, *Oh, this is it. This is how it's going to all end.* Since he was seated right where the hook was, he could see the ground coming up, and he thought, *Oh, shit. This is not good.* He kind of came to, saw a hole, saw daylight, and ran to it.

"That's a long time ago for me, so I don't hold any bad feelings to anybody," he said. "It was an interesting part of my life. I can't say that I like being all scarred up. At least my face didn't get scarred up, and most of my body looked pretty decent after a while. I can't say that it mentally screwed me up too bad."

Richard went on to have a very successful electrical contracting business. Not the typical GI Vietnam veteran's story that you hear propagated on the television all the time. Richard has thought about that a lot.

Chapter 16

The Visit

Occasionally we must disconnect to reconnect later on.

-Dominic Riccitello

Larry Butcher and Carey Pratt's Family

In the 1990s, internet sites started popping up about the Vietnam War and the men and women who served there, especially those who died there. Sites listing all the Vietnam casualties began to appear, some allowing family, friends, and fellow veterans to leave comments, remembrances, and tributes about those who were lost.

Larry's first casualty was John Robinson. John's death was a tragedy, especially so because he was wounded by friendly fire. The official report said, "Individual died as a result of wounds received while on a combat operation when he was mistaken for a hostile force by a friendly force and fired upon. He was admitted to a military medical facility and later expired." It meant a tragedy for his family and a life of guilt for the man who mistakenly shot him. On May 11, 2014, Larry left a remembrance on the Vietnam Memorial website with his email address.

He was never contacted by any of John's family or friends. There were no comments left by anyone who claimed to be a relative of his.

"I will never forget my twenty-first birthday. July 10, 1970," Larry has said. He lost his good friend, Carey Pratt, that day. On April 30, 2014, Larry posted a remembrance on the Wall of Faces website. He left his email address, never thinking that he may be contacted. Carey's death, like all of those in Vietnam, was also a tragedy. A death lost in the fog of war.

Not long after Larry posted that remembrance, Thomas Pratt returned home from his Indiana trip and retired early for an evening of reading in bed. His thoughts were consumed with the veterans' reunion he had just come from—thoughts of the veterans and how nicely they welcomed him and his family. Finding nothing of interest on his bookshelf, he reached for his phone and started browsing the internet. He typed in his brother's name, *Carey Jay Pratt*. He had done this dozens of times in the past, and all the usual websites came up. Then he found one he hadn't seen before. Most of the comments were just versions of "thank you for your service." But there was one from Larry "Doc" Butcher. That person had noted that he had served alongside Carey in Vietnam.

Thomas was surprised and shocked. Over the more than forty-four years since Carey's death, Thomas and other family members had wanted to communicate with someone who knew Carey in Vietnam. Larry went on to ask that anyone knowing Carey please leave his contact information. Thomas did so, saying that Carey was his brother, and pleaded with Larry to contact him, leaving his email address. The next morning there was an email from Larry giving his phone number.

Thomas called it immediately, and Larry answered right away. Thomas noted that he had a pleasant, mild-mannered voice that reminded him of Carey's. Their conversation at first was somewhat awkward, both of them tentative, not sure where to begin, what to say. Soon, though, they settled into a comfortable back-and-forth conversation. Larry told Thomas that he had tried for years to make contact with Carey's family, without success. He explained that their friendship was one of mutual respect, that they both took their duty seriously. He told Thomas that he wanted Carey's family to know that the Carey he knew in Vietnam was "a courageous, fearless infantryman," his exact words. He said that he had the highest possible respect for Carey as a man, a leader, and a soldier. They both broke down and cried.

Larry explained that he had been the medic for Carey's company. He'd been pulled off the line a few months before Carey's death. He went on to say that as a medic, he had seen a lot of blood, a lot of pain, and too much death. He said that when he received word of Carey's death on his twenty-first birthday, he was devastated.

He told Thomas that he and his wife lived in Eureka, California, and were planning a trip down the California coast, returning on Thanksgiving Day. They arranged to meet at Thomas and Carey's sister Kathy's home in San Luis Obispo, California.

Already there visiting from Indiana were another sister, Pat, and her husband, Bob. Thomas and his wife, Lynn, drove up to join them.

They met and had an extremely emotional evening together. They sat on Kathy's patio, sipping wine, and Larry told them all about Carey's time in Vietnam. Larry gave the family all the original photos he had of Carey. He also brought other images and maps he projected to their widescreen TV. Larry's wife quietly listened and took pictures of the meeting.

Thomas called Carey's daughter, Shannon, and Larry was able to talk to her on the phone. He told her that her dad was a wonderful person and a great soldier; she would be very proud of him. He told her that he would love to talk to her more, that she could call him anytime. Shannon never called him. We will never know why.

The visit way extremely cathartic for everyone there. So may years had passed, but now this was a true time of healing.

Their trip ended, the Butchers drove home to Eureka. He soon received an email from Kathy. She said, *So glad you could come to SLO for a visit this weekend. It was a bittersweet time to share with family. I cannot emphasize enough what a remarkable experience it was for all of us to meet Larry Butcher. On a personal level, it was wonderful to see our Butch through your eyes. I could picture him joking and joshing with the guys and then assuming a leadership role when they had to do their duty in the field. On a different level, it was fascinating to see first-hand the effect of serving in Vietnam on a man who has spent 67% percent more of his life off the battlefield and yet is haunted every day by those experiences. Fascinating.*

After all these years, Vietnam veterans now seem willing, almost anxious, to talk about their experiences. The families of those who were lost are also opening up, maybe for the first time, to talk about their grief and loss.

They must never be forgotten.

Final Thoughts

The war has been over for many years. All of us who lived during those tumultuous times are approaching the end of our life. We have laughed, loved, cried, and for many, watched our children and grandchildren grow. This was denied to so many of our peers. We now have the time to reflect on our life and those events that shaped us into who we are now.

As we have aged, many events have faded into the deepest recesses of our mind and all but disappeared. Some events never left and never will. The memories of a friend or loved one who was lost in that war so far away - lost to violent suffering and eventually death from wounds either physical or psychological. Our thoughts of a young life left at home and spent without a husband, father, or friend. The holes in young hearts that sometimes mended and other times did not.

Happiness comes from within, but what if a wounded heart won't heal? I pray that everyone whose stories I have told has found peace in their life. Telling this story has helped me find it for myself. Vietnam is now part of my past. An important part? Yes, but only a part. I will never forget those I knew who died in that war. I cannot now and never will be able to find a reason that justifies their deaths. I just pray that when the youth of today are asked to pick up a rifle and go to war that is for a damn good reason.

My friend Larry Butcher said, "I realized at one point, I would be just as happy or unhappy as I chose to be… I choose to be happy. It is a conscious choice!" I have made the same choice.

The End

Crew and Passengers of #65-07999

Aircrew

Whittle, Edward (CWO2)

242nd Assault Support Helicopter Co.

Aircraft Commander

Army Aviator Badge, Purple Heart, Air Medal (remaining awards unknown)

Henry, Robert F. (WO1, Retired CWO4)

242nd Assault Support Helicopter Company

Pilot

Army Aviator Badge, Bronze Star, Purple Heart, Air Medal (Numeral 12)

Passed away October 25, 2020

Bedient, Ross (SP4)

242nd Assault Support Helicopter Company

Flight Engineer

Died of wounds

Aircraft Crewman Badge, Purple Heart, Air Medal (Numeral 5), Army Commendation Medal

Wittner, Rickey (SP5)

242nd Assault Support Helicopter Company

Crew Chief

Aircraft Crewman Badge, Soldiers Medal, Purple Heart, Air Medal

Schultz, David P. (SP4)
242nd Assault Support Helicopter Company
Door Gunner
Killed in action
Aircraft Crewman Badge, Purple Heart, Air Medal, Army
Commendation Medal

Passengers
Ivey, Robert (MSG, Retired CSM)
HHC, 2nd Bn., 12th Infantry, 25th Infantry Division
Combat Infantry Badge, Bronze Star Medal (4OLC), Purple Heart,
Air Medal (Numeral 4), Army Commendation Medal (V & 4OLC),
Vietnamese Staff Service Honor Medal, Vietnamese Civil Action
Medal (2nd Class)
Passed away December 31, 2009

Ketchum, Lowell (1SGT)
Co. E, 2nd Bn., 12th Infantry, 25th Infantry Division
Bronze Star Medal, Purple Heart, Army Commendation Medal (V)

Campbell, Thomas (SFC)
Co. B, 2nd Bn., 12th Infantry, 25th Infantry Division
Killed in action
Combat Infantry Badge, Silver Star, Bronze Star (OLC), Purple
Heart, Air Medal

Simmons, Elroy (SFC)

HHB, 3rd Bn., 13th Arty, 25th Infantry Division

Died of wounds

Bronze Star, Purple Heart, Army Commendation Medal (V)

Pratt, Carey (SSG)

Co. D, 2nd Bn. 14th Infantry, 25th Infantry Division

Died of wounds

Bronze Star Medal (V), Purple Heart, Air Medal, Army
Commendation Medal (V & OLC)

Green, Richard G. (SGT)

Co. D, 2nd Bn., 12th Infantry, 25th Infantry Division

Combat Infantry Badge, Bronze Star Medal (V & OLC), Purple
Heart (OLC), Air Medal, Army Commendation Medal (V & 2OLC)

Martin, Dennis (SGT)

Co. D, 2nd Bn., 14th Infantry, 25th Infantry Division

Killed in action

Combat Infantry Badge, Bronze Star Medal (V & OLC), Purple
Heart, Air Medal, Vietnamese Military Merit Medal

Oldham, Robert (SGT)

Co. B, 2nd Bn., 12th Infantry, 25th Infantry Division

Killed in action

Combat Infantry Badge, Bronze Star Medal, Purple Heart, Army
Commendation Medal (OLC)

Chase, Melvin C. (SP5)
Co. D, 725th Maintenance Bn., 25th Infantry Division
Purple Heart, Army Commendation Medal (V)

Metzger, Harlen (SP5)
Co. D, 2nd Bn., 14th Infantry, 25th Infantry Division
Combat Infantry Badge, Bronze Star Medal, Purple Heart, Army
Commendation Medal (V & OLC)

Coleman, James (SP4)
Co. B, 2nd Bn., 12th Infantry, 25th Infantry Division
Combat Infantry Badge, Bronze Star Medal, Purple Heart, Air
Medal,
Army Commendation Medal (V & OLC)

Harris, Roy (SP4)
HHC, 2nd Bn., 12th Infantry, 25th Infantry Division
Died of wounds
Purple Heart, Army Commendation Medal (V & OLC)

Schwab, David (SP4)
Co. D, 3rd Bn., 12th Infantry, 25th Infantry Division
Purple Heart, Army Commendation Medal (V)

Thompson, Bruce (SP4)

Co. D, 2nd Bn., 12th Infantry, 25th Infantry Division

Combat Infantry Badge, Purple Heart, Army Commendation Medal (V & 2OLC)

(Possible award of Soldiers Medal: Tropic Lightning News, August 17, 1970, https://www.25thida.org/TLN/tln5-31.htm)

Vullo, Michael (SP4)

HHC, 725th Maintenance Bn., 25th Infantry Division

Died of wounds

Bronze Star Medal, Purple Heart, Army Commendation Medal (V)

Notes:

(V) means an award was given for Valor

(OLC) means Oak Leaf Cluster. Each Oak Leaf Cluster indicates an additional award.

Sources

Interviews: Forty-nine hours of recorded interviews

National Personnel Records Center: Military Service Records

Golden Arrow Research: Mortuary Files

Tropic Lightning News

Vietnam Helicopter Pilots Association

Vietnam Helicopter Crewmembers Association

The Wall website

The Virtual Wall website

Vietnam Veterans Memorial Fund: The Wall of Faces

Army Air Crews: Aviation casualties website

Veterans History Project

Vietnam Center and Archive, Texas Tech University

The Gamewardens Association

Kubler-Ross grief model

Vietnam Veterans of America

Air Force Historical Research Agency

6994th Security Squadron website

Mobile Riverine Force Association

25th Division Association

Stars and Stripes Newspaper

PsychCentral: On grief

Thomas Pratt interview: Conejo Valley Chapter of the Daughters of the American Revolution

Interviews

Al Coppa

High School friend of SP4 Mike Vullo

Amanda Banda

Niece of SP4 David Schultz

Zane Bedient

Brother of SP4 Ross Bedient

Bill Bullock

Veteran, Co. D, 2nd Bn., 14th Infantry, 25th Infantry Division

Served with SGT Dennis Martin

Larry "Doc" Butcher

Veteran, HHC, 2nd Bn., 14th Infantry, 25th Infantry Division

Served with SSG Carey Pratt and SP5 Harlen Metzger

Jim Calabrese

Veteran, 242nd Assault Support Helicopter Co.

Served with SP4 Ross Bedient and SP4 David Schultz

Passed away on June 19, 2019

Marshall Croy

USMC Casualty Notification Officer, Vietnam

Larry Crozier

Veteran, River Patrol Group 52, US Navy

Richard Frysinger

High School friend of SP4 David Schultz

Mike Gandee

Veteran, 725th Maintenance Bn., 25th Infantry Division

Served with SP4 Mike Vullo

Richard Green

Veteran, Co. D, 2nd Bn., 12th Infantry, 25th Infantry Division

Robert Henry

Veteran, 242nd Assault Support Helicopter Co.

Donna Herrin

Fiancée of SP4 David Schultz

Thomas Hutchings

Veteran, 6994 Security Squadron, USAF

Lowell Ketchum

Veteran, Co. E, 2nd Bn., 12th Infantry, 25th Infantry Division

Dan Krehbiel

Veteran, Co. D, 2nd Bn., 14th Infantry, 25th Infantry Division

Served with SSG Carey Pratt, SP5 Harlen Metzger and SP5 Larry Butcher

Kathi Lee
Widow of SP4 Mike Vullo

Barbara Martin
Sister of SGT Dennis Martin

Harold Martin
Veteran, Co. D, 2nd Bn., 14th Infantry, 25th Infantry Division
Served with SSG Carey Pratt and SP5 Harlen Metzger

Martin Matelan
Army Casualty Notification Officer, Vietnam

Brenda Metzger
Widow of SP5 Harlen Metzger

Tim Metzger
Son of SP5 Harlen Metzger

Glen Murdock
Veteran, 76th Military Airlift Squadron, USAF

Dennis Neely
US Army Nurse, An Khe

Dean Nelson

Veteran, 242nd Assault Support Helicopter Co.

Grace Oberholtzer

Veteran, Nurse 93rd Evacuation Hospital

Tim Petersen

Veteran

Friend of SGT Dennis Martin

Thomas Pratt

Brother of SSG Carey Pratt

Gary Redlinski

Veteran, US Army Mortuary, Tan Son Nhut

Frank Rodriguez

Veteran, 725th Maintenance Bn., 25th Infantry Division

Served with SP4 Mike Vullo

Dwight Simmons Sr.

Brother of SFC Elroy Simmons

Larry Spence

Veteran, 242nd Assault Support Helicopter Co.

Susan "Sue" Sundberg

Widow of SGT Dennis Martin

Theresa Tapscott

Widow of SSG Carey Pratt

Barbara Wallace

Widow of SFC Elroy Simmons

Edward "Ed" Whittle

Veteran, 242nd Assault Support Helicopter Co.

Rickey Wittner

Veteran, 242nd Assault Support Helicopter Co.

Glossary

AIT: Advanced Individual Training, Advanced Infantry Training

AO: Area of Operations

ARVN: Army of the Republic of Vietnam (South Vietnamese soldiers)

ASH: Assault Support Helicopter

AWOL: Away Without Official Leave

BOQ: Bachelor Officer Quarters, buildings for quartering commissioned officers

C & C: Command and Control Helicopter, the commander of a military operation who is orbiting above troop insertions or combat operations.

Charlie: Viet Cong

Chicken plate: Armored chest plate worn by flight crews

Civies: Civilian clothes

CO: Commanding Officer

CONUS: Continental United States

DD214: Certificate of release or discharge from active duty; given to all military personnel upon discharge from active service

DEROS: The date you catch the Freedom Bird and fly home.

Drop: Early end of a tour in Vietnam or release from active duty.

Dust-off: Medivac helicopter

Early out: Being released from active duty prior to your original discharge date.

EOD: Explosive Ordnance Disposal

Escharotomy: A surgical procedure used to treat third-degree burns

ETS: Expiration, Term of Service, date of discharge

FNG: Fucking New Guy; a newly arrived trooper.

Free Fire Zone: An area considered enemy held; shoot anything that moved in there

Freedom Bird: Any aircraft (usually a commercial chartered airliner) that takes you out of Vietnam

FSB: Fire Support Base

HE: High explosive artillery or M-79 grenades

H & I Fire: Harassment and Interdiction Fire. Artillery fire directed at possible enemy targets

JP-4: Aviation fuel

KP: Kitchen police

Lifer: A career soldier

LZ: Landing Zone

MAC: Military Airlift Command

MACV: Military Assistance Command, Vietnam

Medevacked: Evacuated from combat when wounded or injured

MOS: Military Occupation Specialty, your job designation

MP: Military police

MR III: The area around Saigon from the South China Sea to Cambodia

MR IV: Farthest south of the four areas of operation in South Vietnam

MSG: Master Sergeant

NCO: Noncommissioned officer

Nomex: Flame-resistant flight suites

NVA: North Vietnamese Army

OCS: Officer Candidate School

OSS: Office of Strategic Services; precursor to the CIA

PBR: Patrol Boat River. Navy patrol boats

PRC25: Backpack radio used by the infantry as their main source of communication; commonly called "Prick 25"

Permanent Party: Cadre assigned to a duty station on a permanent basis, not troops who rotated in and out on a temporary basis.

POL: Petroleum, Oil, Lubricants. An Army acronym to refer to gas, diesel, and other types of fuel.

POL Point: Where helicopters refueled.

PZ: Pickup Zone

R & R: Rest and Recreation leave. Normally seven days.

RPG: Rocket propelled grenade.

RRG: Radio Research Group

RRU: Radio Research Unit

RTO: Radio/Telephone Operator

Ruck: Rucksack

RVN: Republic of Vietnam

SAC: Strategic Air Command

Sea-Tac: Seattle–Tacoma Airport

SFC: Sergeant First Class

Short: Anyone whose tour is approaching an end; usually less than thirty days

Short timer calendar: A drawing with 365 segments which are filled in every day as a tour progresses.

Single digit midget: A trooper with less than ten days to go on their tour

slick: Troop-carrying helicopter

SNAFU: Situation normal, all fucked up

SP: Shore patrol

Spec 4: Army rank with the pay grade of E-4.

Spec 5: Army rank with the pay grade of E-5; equivalent to a buck sergeant but without the responsibility

Spider hole: A one-man fighting hole used by VC and NVA troops to ambush the enemy

TAD: Temporary Additional Duty

TDY: Temporary duty assignment

The Sad Sack: A movie set in the United States Army in World War II, it depicted an otherwise unnamed, lowly private experiencing some of the absurdities and humiliations of military life; "sad sack" became slang for an inept, blundering person

T O & E: Table of Organization and Equipment

Tube: Artillery piece

USAID: United States Agency for International Development

USARV: United States Army Republic of Vietnam

VC: Viet Cong

Viet Minh: Communists who fought the French. Precursor of the Viet Cong. Literally means **Viet Minh**: Communists who fought the French; precursor to the Viet Cong; literally means League for Vietnamese Independence

WESTPAC: Western Pacific

Xin Loi: Vietnamese term meaning "excuse me" or "pardon me" but commonly used by American military personnel to say "sorry about that," "too damn bad," or "tough shit"

THOSE LEFT BEHIND

ABOUT THE AUTHOR

Jack McCabe was born and raised in Chicago, Illinois. He graduated from high school in 1969 at the age of 17 and two days after he turned 18 he joined the Army. He was sent to Vietnam less than a year later in October of 1970. He finally came home at the end of May 1972.

After his return from Vietnam, he pursued his education using the G.I. Bill, receiving an associate degree in electronics engineering and a bachelor's degree in management in 1981.

He had a deep passion for helping veterans, especially fellow Vietnam veterans. After his retirement in 2016 he devoted his time volunteering his services helping veterans with PTSD, financial crises, substance abuse, homelessness, and obtaining veteran benefits.

He published *When We Came Home, How the Vietnam War changed those who served* in 2017, which shared the stories of Vietnam veterans when they returned home. He interviewed many male and female veterans as well as veterans from Australia and Donut Dollies.

THOSE LEFT BEHIND

Made in the USA
Middletown, DE
05 October 2021